汉英双语版

教育的目的
The Aims of Education

[英] 阿尔弗雷德·诺斯·怀特海　著
靳玉乐　刘富利　译

中国轻工业出版社

图书在版编目(CIP)数据

教育的目的:汉英双语版／(英)怀特海(Whitehead, A. N.)著;靳玉乐,刘富利译. —北京:中国轻工业出版社,2016.10(2025.1重印)
ISBN 978-7-5184-0937-2

Ⅰ.①教… Ⅱ.①怀… ②靳… ③刘… Ⅲ.①教育-文集-汉、英 Ⅳ.①G4-53

中国版本图书馆CIP数据核字(2016)第103694号

保留所有权利。非经中国轻工业出版社"万千教育"书面授权,任何人不得以任何方式(包括但不限于电子、机械、手工或其他尚未被发明或应用的技术手段)复印、拍照、扫描、录音、朗读、存储、发表本书中任何部分或本书全部内容,以及其他附带的所有资料(包括但不限于光盘、音频、视频等)。中国轻工业出版社"万千教育"未授权任何机构提供源自本书内容的电子文件阅览、收听或下载服务。如有此类非法行为,查实必究。

责任编辑:吴 红　　责任终审:张乃柬
策划编辑:吴 红　　责任校对:刘志颖　　责任监印:吴维斌

出版发行:中国轻工业出版社(北京鲁谷东街5号,邮编:100040)
印　　刷:三河市鑫金马印装有限公司
经　　销:各地新华书店
版　　次:2025年1月第1版第7次印刷
开　　本:710×1000　1/16　印张:16
字　　数:205千字
书　　号:ISBN 978-7-5184-0937-2　定价:48.00元
读者热线:010-65181109
发行电话:010-85119832　　010-85119912
网　　址:http://www.chlip.com.cn　http://www.wqedu.com
电子信箱:1012305542@qq.com
版权所有　侵权必究
如发现图书残缺请拨打读者热线联系调换
242366Y1C107ZYW

译者导读

怀特海（Alfred North Whitehead，1861—1947）是英国数学家、哲学家和教育家。他曾任教于剑桥大学、伦敦大学、帝国理工学院和哈佛大学，从事数学、物理学和哲学等学科的教育工作，同时也从事高校的一些教育管理工作。跨越大西洋，从英国到美国，从剑桥到哈佛，怀特海以其学术成就影响了各个学科的历史发展，并以其教育思想指导着各个层级的教育实践。

怀特海一生著述甚多，在诸多领域都有着重大的影响。他与学生罗素（Bertrand Russell，1872—1970）合著的三卷本《数学原理》（*Principia Mathematica*）是关于哲学、数学和数理逻辑的重要著作，是数理逻辑发展史上的一个重要里程碑。他的哲学著作《过程与实在》（*Process and Reality*）是过程哲学的奠基之作，其中的重要思想对哲学、物理学、生物学、生态学、心理学、经济学、教育学等学科的发展起着重要的指导作用。而《教育的目的》（*The Aims of Education*）则集中体现了怀特海在教育哲理上的系列思考。

在本书中，怀特海的论述涵盖了教育实践中的多个方面。既有语言、文学、历史、艺术这样的人文教育，也有数学、物理、化学、生物这样的科学教育；既有一般学术教育，也有职业技术教育。另外，怀特海基于其严密的逻辑思维和深刻的哲学素养批判了教育理论中的多个问题。既有对基础教育的观察，也有对高等教育的反思；既有对学校内部的课程与教学的批判，也有对国家层面的文化与体制的建议。

第一章"教育的目的"、第二章"教育的节奏"、第三章"自由与规训的节奏"探讨的是教育的基本理念问题。我们为什么要进行教育活动，教育的终极目的是什么，我们该如何恰切地把握教育的进程，教育的有效方法是什么，诸如此类的根本问题都需要进行深入的研究。怀特海从哲学的高度一一进行了详细解答，告诉我们教育的本质、主题、起点、逻辑、方法、过程等基本的概念和范畴。在此基础之上，后面的四章分别就不同的专题展开了深入探讨。在第四章"技术教育及其与科学和文学的关系"中，怀特海直言不讳地指出世界上各个民族之间的最终竞争是在工厂里而非战场上，那么在技术教育之中如何融合科学教育和人文教育就是一个非常现实的问题。第五章"教育中的古典文化"针对的是传统文化与现代文化之间的衔接与连贯问题，虽然怀特海讲的是关于欧洲的古希腊、古罗马的古典文化，但是对于我们中国的传统文化教育依然可资借鉴。第六章"数学课程"具体分析了数学教育的核心要素，以及数学教育对于哲学素养提升的重要价值。第七章"大学及其功用"从文化传承的历史视野告诉我们何谓大学、何谓科研、何谓教学，大学对于我们的国家和民族、人类的现在和未来都有着什么样的本质意义。

本书的论述主要是针对英美两国的教育问题，特别是英国的情境。英美两国的教育问题有所不同，但是两者具有一定的通约性。我们发现，本书中的基本原理也基本上是适用于中国教育的，可以作为参考来研究我们本土的教育问题。

怀特海是一位卓越的思想家，在本书中以其严密的逻辑和深刻的哲学剖析了教育的一些关键问题。读之思之，相信我们能够从中得到启发，并且促使我们思考教育中的理论问题和实践问题。

译者导读

第一章"教育的目的"要点

在第一章"教育的目的"中,怀特海开门见山地指出:"在训练学生的思想活动的时候,我们必须特别注意我所说的'惰性思维'——只是通过大脑去接收某些观点,而不去应用、验证或与其他新事物有机地融合起来。"这是贯穿整本书的一个核心观点,是怀特海论述教育问题的一个逻辑起点。依此看来,如果要避免思维的呆滞,就要对知识进行应用、验证和实践,这就是教育保持其鲜活生命力的应用之义。因此,如何看待知识和运用知识就是一个摆在我们面前的现实问题:

"教育就是让学生去深刻体会知识的伟大力量、知识的迷人魅力、知识的基本条理,以及让学生掌握某种专业知识,并让学生将其应用到自己的生活之中。"

"我所极力倡导的解决途径就是消除各学科知识之间致命的孤立状态,这种孤立状态扼杀了我们当代课程应有的活力。教育只有一个主题,那就是丰富多彩的生活本身。"

这是怀特海对教育中的知识观的批判和指引,知识观的指向决定着教育的思想和方法,也最终决定着教育的走向和成败。教育的思想和方法要落实到教育对象的心智发展上,人的发展是教育活动的最终目标。"教育面向的是国家的年轻一代,无论从历史的长度来看还是从现实的广度来看,它都是非常重要的。漫不经心地对待教育,从而导致生灵涂炭、希望破灭、国家危亡,肯定就会成为千夫所指。在现代生活条件下有一条规律是牢不可破的,即一个不注重智力教育的民族是注定要灭亡的。"

教育的意义如此重大,因其面对的是"活生生的人的思想"。教育的技艺难以掌握,因为这是"教人们掌握怎样运用知识的艺术"。在教育的具体过程之中,如何才能掌握这门艺术呢?怀特海指出:"最好的教育就是要让学生利用最简单的工具获得最丰富的信息。"回到这一章的题目上来,教育的目的究竟是什么?怀特海概括为:"在教育中我们所要实现的目的,就是要让学生的思维既能更为具体,又能更为抽象。"只有学生的思维变得更为具体也更为抽象,学生的自我发展才真正得以被激发和引导。

第二章"教育的节奏"要点

在第二章中,怀特海把一个人的心智发展过程从整体上加以思考,从儿童期、青春期一直到大学时期,针对每一个时期都做出了详细的阐释。每一个时期的心智特点不同,那么相应的每一个时期的教育侧重点就有所区分。结合黑格尔的辩证法思想,怀特海把每一个智力发展的周期又划分为三个阶段:浪漫阶段、精确阶段和综合阶段。需要注意的是,这里所说的"浪漫"、"精确"和"综合"指向的智力发展的内涵特征,并非其字面意义上的感情问题或者操作问题。在不同的时期或者不同的阶段,一个学生倾向于想象还是记忆,倾向于语言还是科学,倾向于归纳还是演绎,这些都是需要我们认真思考的。只有这样才能符合学生的心智需求,从而才能真正促进学生的心智成熟。概括来讲,"我们应该努力在学生的头脑中编织出一幅知识的和谐图景,协调教育中的各个因素达成各个周期,使得每个周期对学生的当下学习都有内在价值。"

例如,在青春期,"一个人的品性基本上固化形成。一个人的青春期是怎么度过的,胸怀什么样的抱负,拥有什么样的梦想,将会决定这个年轻人后面一生的道路。"再例如,中学生和大学生的学习应有本质的不同:"形象地说,中学生一直在伏案学习,而大学生就要站起身来,并环顾四周";"一个中学生在中学阶段逐渐学会从特殊到一般的抽象概括,而一个大学生在大学阶段就要尝试从一般到特殊的具体应用"。

人的心智发展有其内在的规律,我们就要实事求是地思考其间的种种问题,我们所采用的教育的内容和方法就要符合教育的节奏性特点。就课程而言,"课程的主要问题不在于诸多科目如何排列组织,而在于这些科目如何从根本上启发心智。真正需要排列组织的,是教育中的各个程序应该达成的相应素质。"总而言之,"所谓教育的节奏,就是在学生心智发展的不同阶段,寻找合适的时机,采用恰当的方法,实施相应的课程。"教育的节奏贯穿在教育的整个过程中,周而复始,有常有序,怀特海以一种类似自然科学的严谨方式为我们刻画了这个根本性问题。

第三章"自由与规训的节奏"要点

第三章开篇即讲"知识"和"智慧"的相互关系:

"如果说我们人类的努力遭遇了什么挫败,让人感到悲哀的莫过于理想的消逝。回望过去,我们的先贤在学校里倾心传递智慧;再看现在,我们在大学里的目的变得如此卑微,仅仅是教授一些知识。"

"没有知识的基础,一个人是不可能有智慧的;一个人虽然可以轻易地获得知识,但可能仍然没有智慧。""智慧关系着知识的运用、问题的解决、经验的升华,智慧是对知识的掌控,是我们所能获得的最本质的自由。"

从"知识"和"智慧"的逻辑关系出发,怀特海把我们引向了"自由"和"规训"的逻辑辩证:

"通往智慧的唯一道路是对知识的自由把握,通往知识的唯一道

路是对学习的不断规训。"

"学生的心智是一个不断发展的有机体，不是像一个空匣子那样可以随随便便地收纳什么新知识。但同时必须按部就班地学习新知识，这样才能给心智的发展提供足够的营养。在理想的教育之中，'规训'应该是学生的一个主动选择；在此基础之上，'自由'才能有所作为，才能促进学生的心智发展。"

"从教育的节奏来看自由与规训的主题，我认为在教育的初始阶段和终结阶段，我们应以自由为基调；而在教育的中间阶段，我们应以规训为基调，辅以自由作为搭配。"

"教育的要旨就在于在实践中发现自由与规训之间的精确平衡，从而以最快的速度让学生学习知识。"

如果在教育实践中没有遵循客观规律，就会导致一些严重的后果：

"积极而富有创新精神的思维习惯只会在比较自由的氛围中产生，而胡乱的规训只会让学生的头脑更加混沌。"

"真正有效的规训是一种自我约束，而学生能不能做到自我约束取决于学生的心智是不是真的自由。"

"学生学习的主动性与训练都是必要的，但是训练往往会扼杀主动性。"

在"知识"和"智慧"之间、"自由"和"规训"之间，如何才能通盘考虑，从而使对立的两极并行不悖、协调发展，这是一个两难问题。对这个两难问题的考量，自然就会让我们去思考教育的有关形式与内容、思想与方法，也就会让我们去研究教育的有关现象与问题、理论与实践。

第四章"技术教育及其与科学和文学的关系"要点

第四章的主题针对的是技术教育问题，而技术教育问题又与科学教育和人文教育密不可分。怀特海从其间存在的关系入手，辩证地看待技术教育的必然支撑和应然走向。其实，在怀特海看来，教育的关联性无处不在，不只是技术教育中存在着如此复杂的关系，"每一种教育形式都应传递给学生一种技能、一种理论、一种常识、一种审美，而诸多要素之间是相互依托、共生共长的。"

怀特海认为现代的人文与科学教育可以溯源到柏拉图的思想，认为"这种柏拉图式的教育理想对欧洲文明的发展做出了不可磨灭的贡献：促进了艺术的发展，培养了作为科学之源的中立客观的求知精神，保持了精神自由在物质条件面前的尊严。"同时他又尖锐地批评了其中的缺陷：

"柏拉图的文化发展理论中强调了认知的客观中立，这就是一个心理学上的错误。"

"所谓客观中立的科学精神其实是一种科学热情，这种热情期盼在复杂关联的事物之间寻找到一个井然有序的理论构架。"

"一个科学家并不是为了认识而去探索，而是为了探索而去认识。"

"柏拉图式的人文教育传统中的这个缺陷有其背后的根本原因，即自身体系中存在的两个错误的对立：心智和身体之间的对立，思想和行动之间的对立。"

在怀特海看来，解决"心智和身体之间的对立"、"思想和行动之间的对立"这两个问题，就要把技术教育、科学理论教育、文学艺术教育三者结合起来，在融合之中达到"相互依托"和"共生共长"。具体来说，"只有动手去创造，并且通过所创造之物才能获得生动而深刻的认识。如果想要有所理解，那就必躬必亲，这是一条牢不可破的定律。只有在具体的实践中，也只有在现实的拘囿中，我们的潜能才会得以发挥，我们的思维才会跃然欲动，我们的知识才会有所增益。"通过这样的对立与统一，技术教育才能完成其自身的使命，也才能实现其负载的价值。

第五章"教育中的古典文化"要点

这本书中所讲到的"古典文化"，有其特殊的内涵，指的是古希腊和古罗马时期的文化，包括哲学、历史、语言、文学、法律、艺术等方面，这个时期的诸多文化遗产促进了欧洲的文明发展，也奠定了几乎整个西方世界的文化基础。怀特海就此指出：

"古罗马文明对欧洲文化发展具有极其重要的影响，核心就在于古罗马留给欧洲的两个文化遗产。古罗马文明吸收了希伯来的宗教思想，又融合了古希腊文明，这两个文化要素一起深深地影响了欧洲的历史发展。"

"美索不达米亚和埃及依赖水利灌溉成就了他们的古代文明，而罗马帝国的辉煌依赖出色地运用各种技术。"

"罗马帝国的历史本身就是一出动人的戏剧，而启迪后世的哲学思想更是引人入胜。"

"我们在教育中所要注重的是漫漫历史长河中不断变化的观念和思想，纷繁复杂的审美意识和种族冲突，正是这些要素决定了、影响了我们人类的发展历程。例如，我们可以通过罗马帝国的兴衰史来看过去与现在之间的联系。我们可以把罗马帝国看作历史的一个瓶颈，这样历史就会从这个瓶颈缓缓倒出陈年佳酿。"

怀特海从历史的纵向维度论述了古今之间的辩证关系，并把这个古今、新旧之间的联系腾挪到教育之中的现在与过去的辩证关系上。过去与现在之间存在着有机的衔接和连贯，现在与未来之间同理亦然。那么，在教育中如何让学生学习拉丁文、阅读拉丁文献，从而体悟人类文明的历史进程，进而有可能直接或间接地推动人类文明的历史发展，这就成了一个具有重要历史意义和现实价值的问题。

很明显，怀特海在这里所论述的是关于西方文化的历史传承问题。那么，回看我们中国的文化继承与发展问题，我们依然可以从怀特海的论述中找到思考的切入点。

第六章"数学课程"要点

怀特海是一个数学家、哲学家和教育家，就其本行的数学进行教育上的论述，是再合适不过了。"局外人往往会抱怨数学课程深奥艰涩，对此我们最好予以承认，在一般人的观念中数学的确让人感到高深莫测。但是我觉得深奥艰涩并不意味着数学课程有多难，只是说数学课程的应用有着较大的局限性，与人们的思想意识较少发生直接联系。"对于这个问题，怀特海给出了简单的回答："我认为在教育中一定要祛除数学课程的深奥艰涩，'祛除深奥艰涩'是我对这个问题的简单概括。"

回头来看，在教育中人们为什么感觉数学是深奥艰涩的呢？"在教育过程中，我们应该有条不紊地传授一系列具有重要意义的知识，坚决避免一些看似花里胡哨实则离题千里的教学活动。数学教育的根本目的是为了让学生熟悉抽象的思维方式、懂得理论的实际应用、掌握方法的恰当使用。如果不是为了这个根本目的，在数学教材中盲目罗列各种各样的数学公理，强迫学生死记硬背，还要这样那样地考试，那真是糟糕透顶了。"怀特海对此现象提出了严肃的批评，并且从具体的代数和几何中的数、量、空间关系进行了阐释，指明了数学教育的一般规律。

另外,学习数学也并不只是停留在学习数、量、空间关系上,应该上升到哲学素养的高度。"数学教育不应该是盲目地教给学生一个又一个数学公理。而应该让学生认识到,他们以前所学习的各种知识其实都是与数、量、空间有关系的,这才是数学教育的要义所在。从特殊到一般,这种教育方式是形成所有哲学思想的根本基础。实际上,任何一个人只要恰当地掌握了数学的基础知识,他都能具备哲学思想的基本素养。"

第七章"大学及其功用"要点

一般来说,大学是实施教育、开展科研、服务社会的机构。但是该如何实现这些职能呢?怀特海给出了一个关键词——"想象"。"想象"一词贯穿在本章的整个论述之中:

"大学存在的理由在于紧密联系年轻人和老年人,发挥想象,为学为道,搭建知识生长与生命热望之间的桥梁。"

"只有展开想象的翅膀上下求索,方能激发灵感、求得新知。如此一来,所见事实就不再是简单的事实,而能从中发现无限的可能。所学知识也不再是记忆的负担,而是鲜活灵动、蓬勃欲发,犹如诗人一样吟诵我们的内心梦想,犹如建筑师一般勾画我们的人生蓝图。"

"通过自由想象,发现一般规律,检验于既存客观事实,应用于未知的新的疆域。有赖于如此这般的想象,我们才得以用知识去构筑一个新的世界,才得以用智慧去追寻人的生生不息。"

"如果要求年轻人的想象一定要有条有理、切实可行,那么无偏见的思维习惯就无法养成,从一般规律到具体演绎之间的种种可能就会被遮蔽。"

>　"大学存在的根本意义就在于大学的教师队伍，他们的为学问道都应被想象的火炬熊熊点燃，这是大学教育的重中之重。"

>　"大学教师的卓越之处就在于能够充分认识和熟练掌握想象力与学问的结合，而正是基于这一点，大学的育人功能和科研功能才会有机地融合在一起。"

>　"如果离开了想象，大学将无一是处，或将百无一用。"

　　如果进一步思考，我们自然就会追问："想象"的方向何在？怀特海又给出了一个关键词——"新"。"所谓教育，其实就是引导人们探索生活；所谓研究，其实就是思想的历险；所谓大学，其实就是年轻人和老年人一起迈向未来的场所。教育的成败在很大程度上取决于有关知识是否新颖，知识的新颖可以体现在知识自身的更新换代上，也可以体现在知识应用的与时俱进上。鱼儿一刻也离不开水，知识一日也离不开'新'。"在此目标之下，大学前进的方向被想象的火炬照亮，大学存在的意义也才得以彰显。《大学》中论及"苟日新，日日新，又日新"，这也正是作为教育、科研、服务机构的大学的重要功用，也正是我们的文明和文化向前发展所能获得的源源不竭的推动力。

译　者
2015年11月于西南大学

目　录

译者导读·· I
第一章　教育的目的·· 1
第二章　教育的节奏·· 19
第三章　自由与规训的节奏······································ 35
第四章　技术教育及其与科学和文学的关系······················ 51
第五章　教育中的古典文化······································ 73
第六章　数学课程·· 95
第七章　大学及其功用·· 109
译者后记·· 121
怀特海生平简介·· 125
怀特海主要著述目录·· 127

CONTENTS

Chapter 1　The Aims of Education·································· 131
Chapter 2　The Rhythm of Education································ 147
Chapter 3　The Rhythmic Claims of Freedom and Discipline·········· 161
Chapter 4　Technical Education and Its Relation to Science
　　　　　　and Literature······································· 175

Chapter 5	The Place of Classics in Education	193
Chapter 6	The Mathematical Curriculum	209
Chapter 7	Universities and Their Function	223

第一章　教育的目的

文化指的是思想活动、审美感受、情感共鸣,而支离破碎的信息与文化毫无关系。一个人仅仅见多识广,那么他不过是普天之下最无用的人。我们旨在培养既有文化修养,又在某个特殊方面具有专业知识的人。专业知识将会奠定他们的个人发展基础,而文化修养将会引领他们达到哲学思维的深度和艺术境界的高度。我们必须谨记:最有价值的智力发展应该是自我发展,一般发生在16岁至30岁之间。对这种自我发展最重要的训导应该由母亲在孩子12岁之前给予。坦普尔大主教[1]的一句名言说明了我的观点。一个男孩在拉格比公学[2]表现得并不出众,而长大后却成就斐然,人们往往对此感到惊奇。坦普尔解释道:"人们在18岁的时候表现如何并不重要,重要的是18岁以后他们会怎么发展。"

---

[1] 坦普尔大主教(Archbishop Temple,1821—1902),英国坎特伯雷大主教,学者,教师,教育改革家。1842年任牛津大学讲师,讲授数学和逻辑学。1858—1869年担任拉格比公学校长,强化古典文化教育,同时创建实验室开始自然科学的教育工作。1896年起任坎特伯雷大主教,成为英国圣公会的精神领袖。——译者注

[2] 拉格比公学(Rugby School),英国著名的私立学校,创建于1567年。位于英国沃里克郡(Warwickshire)的拉格比市(Rugby),是英式橄榄球的发源地。请注意,本书中所谈到的一些英国"公学"(public school),指的是英国的一些顶尖私立学校,它们培养了大批精英人士,在英国教育体系中占有重要地位。——译者注

在训练学生的思想活动的时候，我们必须特别注意我所说的"惰性思维"[1]——只是通过大脑去接收某些观点，而不去应用、验证或与其他新事物有机地融合起来。

在教育史上有这样一个非常引人注目的现象：有的学校在某个时期充满活力，极其善于培养教育人才，而在随后的时期却愚迂有加、墨守成规。其原因就在于它们已为惰性思维所拘囿。拘囿于惰性思维的教育是无用的，甚至是有害的。古谚有云，"最恶者乃由最善者堕落而来"[2]。教育史上的个别时期的确有着思想解放的灿烂光辉，但更多的时候是被惰性思维深深影响。这就解释了为什么那些聪慧的妇女虽未受过什么教育，但阅历丰富、涵养深厚，步入中年以后成为社会中最有文化修养的群体——原因就在于她们摆脱了惰性思维的枷锁。历史上每一次引导人们走向伟大与崇高的知识革命，都是对惰性思维的强烈批判与抵制。然而令人遗憾的是，某些教育方式完全无视人们的心理特点，不断地用某种貌似精致的惰性思维去蒙蔽人们。

现在让我们来看看，在我们的教育体系中应如何避免这种精神和思想上的僵化陈腐。我们倡导两个教育原则：第一，不可教授过多科目；第二，教授知识务必精细透彻。

在众多的科目中选择一小部分来进行教授，其结果是学生被动地接受不连贯的知识，难以引发他们的活力，无法激发他们的思想。因此，引入教育的主要知识要少而精，它们要能形成各种可能的组合。学生应内化这些知识并在他当下的真实生活情境中理解知识的应用，这样学生在他早期的教育中就能够体验到发现的快乐。学生在学习中

---

[1] "惰性思维"的对应原文是"inert ideas"。——译者注

[2] "最恶者乃由最善者堕落而来"的对应拉丁文原文是"Corruptio optimi, pessima"，也可直译为"最坏的事物是最好的事物败坏的结果"。作者怀特海用这个谚语来辨析教育中的"善"与"恶"，即促进人们思想发展的教育是善的，而束缚人们思想发展的教育是恶的。——译者注

的诸多发现可以帮助他理解生命中涌现出的一连串事件。我所说的"理解"不只是逻辑上的分析,尽管逻辑上的分析的确很重要。这里所说的"理解"的意义来自法国谚语"理解即宽容"[1]。迂腐的学究也许会嘲笑这种实用性的教育。但是,如果教育无用,又如何成其为教育呢?难道教育的目的就是教导人们藏而不用吗?当然,无论你有什么样的生活目的,教育都应该是有用的。教育对于圣·奥古斯丁[2]是有用的,对于拿破仑[3]也是有用的。教育之所以是有用的,是因为理解是有用的。

我不打算去探讨教育中的文学层面所蕴含的理解,也不想去评判某个古典课程或者某个现代课程的价值,我所关注的理解是对持续的当下的理解。过去的知识唯一的用处就是武装我们以应对现在。没有什么会比轻视现在能给年轻人的智力造成更致命的伤害了。现在包含着所有的一切,是我们的"圣地",因为它既包含着过去,又孕育着未来。同时,我们必须注意到,一个两千年前的时代并不比一个两百年前的时代离我们更久远。我们不要被形式上的日期或者年代蒙蔽。莎士比亚[4]和莫里

---

[1] "理解即宽容"的对应原文是"To understand all, is to forgive all",也可直译为"理解一切即宽容一切"。怀特海的意思是教育的目的应服务于学生在生活中的体验、发现和应用,而不是与生活相脱离。这里的理解与宽容具有西方宗教文化的意味,即运用上帝所赋予的智慧,完成上帝所给予的使命,去除人们的苦痛,消除人们的怨念,从而达到救赎的目的。——译者注

[2] 圣·奥古斯丁(Saint Augustine,354—430),罗马帝国后期的天主教神学家,公元391年开始在希波(Hippo,今阿尔及利亚安纳巴)担任神父和主教,因此他又被称为"St. Augustine of Hippo"。他留下了大量宗教著作,对欧洲中世纪的天主教思想产生了深远的影响。——译者注

[3] 拿破仑(Napoléon Bonaparte,1769—1821),法国军事家和政治家,1804—1814年任法兰西第一帝国皇帝,1815年复辟后兵败滑铁卢,1821年病逝于圣赫勒拿岛。他颁布《拿破仑法典》,确立了资本主义社会的立法规范,多次率军对外扩张,对欧洲的政治和历史产生了重要影响。——译者注

[4] 莎士比亚(William Shakespeare,1564—1616),英国文艺复兴时期的诗人和剧作家。代表作有:悲剧《哈姆雷特》、《奥赛罗》、《李尔王》、《麦克白》等,喜剧《第十二夜》、《仲夏夜之梦》、《威尼斯商人》、《皆大欢喜》等,历史剧《亨利四世》、《理查二世》等。——译者注

哀[1]的时代是过去的，索福克勒斯[2]和维吉尔[3]的时代也是过去的，后者并不比前者更久远。正如"圣徒相通"[4]，它是一个伟大而壮观的集会，但是集会的殿堂只可能有一个，那就是"现在"。任何一个特定的圣徒团体都必须穿越时光隧道到达"现在"这个殿堂，因此表面的时光的流逝其实并没有太大的意义。

再来看教育中的科学层面和逻辑层面所蕴含的理解，我们必须注意到，不加应用的知识是非常有害的。所谓知识的应用，是指把知识与生活事件联系起来，这关联着我们的感觉、知觉、希望、欲望和能调节思想的精神活动，这些事件构成了我们的生活。我可以想象出有这样一批人，他们被动地一遍又一遍地死记一些互不关联的知识，可能想要以此来强化他们的灵魂。但是，人的心性可不是这样形成的——当然，或许某些报纸的编辑应当除外[5]。

在科学训练中，学习某个概念时首要的事情就是要去证明它。这里所说的"证明"指的是要去证明这个概念的价值所在。只有当包含某个概念的命题是正确的时候，这个概念才有价值。一个概念的核心证明就是证明包含它的命题的正确性，或者是通过实验验证，或者是通过逻辑分析。但是，对命题的正确性的证明不能作为第一次采用这

---

[1] 莫里哀（Molière，1622—1673），本名为让·巴蒂斯特·波克兰（Jean Baptiste Poquelin），莫里哀为其艺名，法国17世纪古典主义文学时期的喜剧作家。——译者注

[2] 索福克勒斯（Sophocles，公元前496—公元前406），古希腊三个悲剧作家之一。——译者注

[3] 维吉尔（Virgil，公元前70—公元前19），古罗马诗人，著作有《牧歌集》（*Eclogues*）、《农事诗》（*Georgics*）、《埃涅阿斯纪》（*Aeneid*），对欧洲文艺复兴和古典主义文学产生了巨大影响。——译者注

[4] "圣徒相通"的英文原文为"The Communion of Saints"。在基督教传统中，"圣徒相通"的教义是一个给人安慰的提示，意指生命并未终结而只是发生了变化，死去的亲人与他（或她）的家人之间仍具有某种精神上的联系。——译者注

[5] 怀特海以此批判一些人的机械学习，但是又承认了编辑的工作特点。——译者注

个概念的必要条件。毕竟，某些受人尊敬的教师做出的权威断言，是开始讨论这个概念的充分依据。因此，当我们最初接触到某些命题的时候，总是会先去评价其重要性，这也是大家在学习中都会经历的事情。我们都没有从严格意义上去进行证实或者证伪，除非是某些概念的确非常重要而需要我们去下功夫。对于一个概念来说，其狭义的证明和正确的评价这两个过程在时间上并不需要严格分隔开来，其实它们往往是同时进行的。但是，如果一定要给这两个过程分出先后，那就优先考虑应用中的评价过程。

此外，我们不应该独立地应用命题。我的意思肯定不是说要通过设计精巧的一系列实验来解释命题1，然后证明命题1，再通过设计精巧的一系列实验来解释命题2，然后证明命题2，依次类推，直到一本书的末尾。这样做实在是无聊至极。相互关联的知识要从总体上加以应用，各种命题可以按照不同的顺序反复使用。在理论科目中要选择一些重要的应用领域，同时要用系统的理论来进行深入研究。理论研究成果的形式要小而精，要尽可能地做到严格精确；如果太过冗长，就会导致人们不容易理解其完整性和准确性。不求甚解、泛泛而谈的理论知识是很糟糕的。另外，理论与实践之间的界限也应该清晰可见。对于理论的证明和理论的应用之间的分野，任何学生都应该了然于胸，不致混淆。我的观点是：经过证明的知识应该被应用，而被应用的知识也应该——只要可行——是经过证明的。我绝不会认为，证明和应用是同一回事。

讲到这里，我可以非常直接地表达我的观点，虽然表面上看起来似乎有些离题。我们现在已经认识到，教育的艺术和科学需要具备一定的天赋，也需要对它们进行研究。这种天赋和研究绝不只是关于某门科学或文学的空洞的知识。上一代人对这个道理有部分的认识，而一些中小学校长未经深思熟虑，就要求学校教师学习用左手打保龄球或者培养对足球的爱好，以此来取代对文化知识的学习。然而，文化素养不只是玩板球，不只是踢足球，也不只是掌握知识的多少。

教育是教人们掌握怎样运用知识的艺术。当然，这是一种非常难以掌握的艺术。无论何时，当一本具有真正教育价值的教科书问世时，你就肯定会发现，有评论家站出来说这本教科书难以教授。它当然难教；如果容易教的话，它就应该被焚毁了，因为它不可能具有教育价值。在教育领域里就和在其他领域里一样，平坦且舒适的道路只会引向危险之地。在学校教育中，这条有害的道路就是指唆使学生死记硬背的一本教材或者一系列演讲，学生通过死记硬背或许能回答校外考试[1]中的所有问题。我顺便在这里说一下，一个学生在任何考试中需要直接回答的任何问题，若不是由该学科的任课教师事先进行设计或者修改，那么这种教育制度就很可能会失败。校外评价人员可以对该课程或学生的学业表现做出报告，却无论如何都不可以向学生提问一个未经他们的任课教师认真教授过的问题，这个问题最起码得是教师经过与学生的长时间讨论引发而来。当然也会有少数例外的情况，但是由于它们是例外，所以在总的规则下是容易被接受的。

现在让我们重新回到我之前提到的观点：在学生所学习的课程中，理论知识必须永远具有重要的应用价值。这不是一个容易实施的原则，而是很难做到的。它本身涉及使知识充满活力的问题，以及防止知识变得僵化的问题，而这是所有教育活动的核心问题。

最理想的教育取决于若干不可忽视的因素，例如教师的才能、学生的智力类型、学生的人生理想、学校周边环境提供的教育机会，及

---

[1] 校外考试（external examination），英国的一项考试制度，由校外机构提出评价标准，拟定评价方案，由学校教师组织测试，用以进行校际之间的审查和督导。与之相对应的就是校本考试（school-based examination），即由学校自主进行的测试。——译者注

其他诸如此类的因素。这就是统一的校外考试如此有害的原因。我们不会因为自己思想怪异或喜欢对既定事实吹毛求疵，而公开指责校外考试，我们不会如此幼稚。当然，校外考试在检测学生的学习惰性方面确有其作用。我们不喜欢校外考试的原因是非常具体且现实的，因其抹杀了文化的精髓。当你根据经验来分析教育的核心任务时就会发现，成功完成这一任务取决于对许多可变因素的微妙调整。其原因在于教育应对的是人的思想，而不是没有生命的客观物质。因此，如何激发学生的好奇心，如何提升学生的判断力，如何提高学生驾驭复杂环境的能力，如何帮助学生运用理论知识对重要事件做出预判，所有这些能力都不是靠体现在考试科目表中的既定规则可以培养的。

在此我提请诸位有实践经验的教师注意，通过良好的训练，教师可能会不断地向学生灌输一定量的僵化知识。比如，你选择一本教科书让学生照着学，按说这样也不是不可以。然后，学生就学会怎么解二次方程了。但是仔细想想，我们教学生学会解二次方程的意义何在呢？对于这个问题，人们通常的回答是：人的大脑就像一件工具，"工欲善其事，必先利其器"；让学生习得解二次方程的能力就是磨砺其大脑的一部分过程。这个回答的确相当有道理，因而代代相传。尽管该观点有一定的道理，但是它包含着一个根本性的错误，可能会扼杀现实世界中的天才。我不知道是谁最先把人的大脑比喻为一件无生命的工具。据我所知，也许是古希腊的七位先贤之一，或许这一观点是他们共同的看法。虽不知最初提出这个比喻的人是谁，但是由于那些名流贤士的赞同与附和，这个比喻就有了不容置疑的权威性。但是，不管这个比喻有多大的权威性，也不管有多少名流贤士予以赞同与附和，我都会毫不犹豫地抨击这一观点，并认为它是教育理论中最致命、最错误、最危险的观点之一。人的大脑从来都不是被动的，它对外界刺激的反应是精细敏锐的，而且这种刺激—反应活动是永无休止的。你不可能先去磨砺大脑，然后再去使用它。不管你想激发学生对知识产生什么样的兴趣，这种兴趣都必须在此时此刻予以发展；不管你想训练学生什么样的能力，这种能力都必须在此时此刻予以锻炼；不管你想赋予学生什么样的思想，这种思想都必须在此时此刻予以展现。这就是教育的金科玉律，也是一条难以遵循的规律。

上述困难在于：学生对一般概念的理解、思维的习惯、思考的乐趣，都不是任何形式的文字所能引发的，无论文字表达多么准确无误。所有富有实践经验的教师都知道，教育是一个需要在细节把握上极具耐心的过程，经年累月，反复如是。学习无捷径，不可能通过书本上的那些条条框框得以实现。谚语说"见树不见林"，表达了思想认识上的一个困难所在。而我们教育中的困难所在就是我要强调的一个问题，即要让学生通过个别树木的存在而看到整个森林的所在。

因此，我所极力倡导的解决途径就是消除各学科知识之间致命的孤立状态，这种孤立状态扼杀了我们当代课程应有的活力。教育只有一个主题，那就是丰富多彩的生活本身。而在教育中我们总是偏离了这个独一无二的主题：教给学生代数、几何、科学、历史，结果学生什么都没有学会；教给学生一两门语言，结果学生什么都没有掌握；最后，最让人失望的是文学，教给学生莎士比亚的一两个戏剧，甚至都事先配上了语言方面的注释、对剧情和人物特点的简要分析，然后就等着学生死记硬背了。这样的教学活动能代表丰富多彩的生活本身吗？充其量，这就是造物主在创造这个世界的时候胡思乱想出来的一个目录表，而那时造物主还没有决定如何将这些东西真正融为一体。

回头再看二次方程教学的这个例子，我们还是没有得到答案。为什么要教给学生二次方程的解法呢？除非二次方程被纳入一个有机联系的课程体系之中，否则就没有理由去教与其相关的任何知识。另外，由于数学在一个发达文化中应用广泛，所以我有点怀疑，对于不同类型的学生而言，是否要学习二次方程的代数解法可能并不取决于数学学科的专业性。在此我请你们注意，我在这里并没有论述什么教育心理学或者学科专业知识，而这二者是理想教育的必要组成部分。如果论述教育心理学或者数学专业知识，就相当于回避了我们的实际问题，我提及这两点只是为了避免我的回答被误解。

二次方程是代数的一部分，而代数是人们创造出来的一种智力工具，用来清晰地表达对这个世界的度量。我们不可能脱离度量而存在，这个世界无处不为数量所影响。我们的语言表达也是需要度量的。说一个国家很大是没用的——它到底有多大？说镭是稀有的也是没意义的——它到底有多稀有？你不可能回避量的概念。你可以转向诗歌和音乐领域，而在你的节奏和音阶方面，你仍会遇到量和数的问题。有些学者貌似高雅，蔑视有关数量的理论，他们其实算不上成熟的学者。与其指责他们，不如同情他们，因为他们小时候在学校学到的零碎的莫明其妙的代数知识是有问题的，是会遭到轻视的。

无论从表面上看还是从事实上看，学校教育中的代数都退化成了无意义的知识碎片，这是一个可悲的例子。这个例子告诫我们，如果我们不明了自己想要在学生活跃的头脑里面施加的教育的根本属性，那么任何教育改革的计划表都是无用的。几年前有人呼吁要改革学校的代数课程，但是其结果就是大家一致认为，在代数课程中利用图表教学能消除所有弊端。于是其他代数教学方式被清除出课堂，图表教学方式大行其道。在我看来，这样的代数课程已经没有什么教育原理可言了，除了图表还是图表。现在每一次考试的试卷中总会有一两道关于图表的题目。就我个人而言，我是图表教学方式的积极拥护者，但是我怀疑采取图表教学方式是否很奏效。如果不展示出教育与学生的智力发展、情感认知的紧密联系，那么就无法把生活融入一般教育的活动计划之中。这个道理比较难懂，但是千真万确，而我也不知道怎么表达才能使其更通俗易懂。当你进行一点教育上的改革时，总是会被事实的真相击败。正如你与一个很有技巧的老练的对手搏击，对方总是能够稳操胜券。

教育改革必须从另一头做起。首先，你必须确定一些足够简单的、要纳入一般教育体系的关于现实世界的数量知识；其次，要拟订一个代数课程计划，并且保证代数课程中有例子来阐明数量知识在现实世界中的应用。我们不必担心自己喜爱的图表教学，只要我们把代数作为度量现实世界的一个重要手段，图表就肯定会大量存在。关于社会的一些最简单的研究中会用一些简单的图表予以描述。描述历史的一些曲线图比那些干巴巴的人名和日期的目录更生动直观，而学习那些干巴巴的人名和日期的目录，在枯燥乏味的学校教育中占了很大一部分。学习那些鲜为人知的国王和王后的人名列表到底要达到什么目的？汤姆、迪克或者哈利，他们都已经不在世了。过去的不可能复活，未来的还没有出现，而影响现代社会的各种因素的变动是可以通过数量做出简单勾画的。而在另一方面，代数中的一些知识可以单独进行抽象的科学研究，例如变量、函数、变化速率、方程式及其解法、消元。当然，我在这里提及这些并不是为了卖弄什么，目的还是强调可用于教学的一些简单的、特别的案例。

如果照此进行分析，从乔叟[1]到黑死病[2]，再从黑死病到现代劳工

---

[1] 乔叟（Geoffrey Chaucer，1343—1400），英国诗人和作家，被誉为"英国诗歌之父"。代表作品为《坎特伯雷故事集》（*The Canterbury Tales*），收集了29位朝圣者在前往坎特伯雷朝拜的旅途中讲述的故事。朝圣者的身份各异，有骑士、僧侣、学者、律师、商人、手工业者、自耕农、磨坊主等各个阶层的人士。该作品展示了英国资本主义萌芽时期广阔的社会画面。——译者注

[2] 黑死病（the Black Death），14世纪蔓延欧洲和亚洲的鼠疫，导致欧洲约2500万人死亡，又被称为"大灭绝"(the Great Dying)或者"大瘟疫"(the Great Pestilence)。——译者注

问题，中世纪朝圣者的故事与抽象的代数就联系起来了。朝圣者的故事与抽象的代数都反映了同一个主题的不同方面，这个主题就是生活本身。我知道很多人就这个问题是怎么思考的。我所勾勒出来的路线与你们所可能选择的不同，甚至你们也不清楚到底是怎么回事。对此我非常理解，而且我也不是说自己一定会这么做，但是大家的不接受态度恰恰说明了统一的校外考试制度对教育是有害的。展示知识应用的过程若要获得成功，基本上取决于学生的禀赋和教师的才智。当然，在这里我并没有论及大家都熟悉的最简单的知识应用，我指的是涉及数量的科学，例如力学和物理学。

　　用同样的方法，我们可以绘制统计图表来研究与时间维度相应的社会现象的数量关系。我们可以在类似的两种社会现象之间去除时间变量，也许就能发现它们在多大程度上存在着因果联系，或者在多大程度上只是时间上的一致关系。我们要注意，我们可以按照时间维度研究一个国家的一组统计数据，然后研究另一个国家的另一组统计数据。通过对研究主题的适当选择，就可以得到一些有关偶然联系的统计图表，同时也会得到一些带有明显因果联系的统计图表。如果我们想继续研究如何在各个变量之间进行关联分析，那么就可以用这种方法不断进行下去。

　　对于这样的代数知识应用，我必须请你们记住我上面所坚持的观点。首先，某一种思维方式并不适合所有的学生。比如说，我认为擅长手工的学生面对客观事物时可能比我想象的更为实际、更为敏捷。也许我的看法是错误的，但它是我不得不做出的猜测。其次，我不认为上好一节课就能一下子带好整个班级，教育的步骤绝不可能是这个样子的。在学习期间，学生要不断地努力答题、画图表、做实验，直至他们充分地掌握整个课程的内容。我在此提出了相关解释，也指出了学生的思维需要引导的方向。在教育中学生应该感觉到自己在学习某些东西，而不是像随小步舞曲[1]翩翩起舞一样，教育不是智力上的哗众取宠的炫耀。

最后，如果教学就是为了应付某种大型测试，那么如何进行有效的教学也是个非常复杂的问题。大家有没有注意到诺曼式拱门[2]上的那些锯齿形折叠花纹？古典建筑是那么的精致迷人，而现代建筑却是如此的粗鄙不堪。这是因为现代建筑是根据精确尺寸堆砌出来的，而古典建筑是根据工匠的个人风格雕刻出来的。现代建筑因此而局促，古典建筑因此而疏朗。而现在，应试教育的本质就是在教学活动中采取整齐划一的度量方式。但是人各有不同，一个人可能会从全局来俯瞰，另一个人可能会从局部来细查。当然，在一个广博的文化体系中设计一个统一的课程体系，同时又允许个别的、特殊的教学活动存在，这看起来似乎是个矛盾问题。不过话说回来，这个世界如果没有矛盾问题，可能会变得更简单，也可能会变得更单调乏味。可以肯定地说，如果在教育中排除了个别与特殊，就等于毁灭了生活本身。

现在再来看普通数学教育中的另一个重要分支，即几何课程，上述同样的原则对于它也是适用的。关于几何的理论部分应该清晰明了、简单扼要。如果一个几何命题体现不出知识点之间的关联，就要把这个几何命题从课程中删掉。一些重要的几何基础知识必须保留下来，例如"相似"与"比例"。我们必须记住，在图形的视觉形式的帮助之下，

---

[1] 小步舞曲（minuet），源于法国民间的三拍子舞曲，17和18世纪流行于法国宫廷，节奏轻快，风格典雅，往往描绘社交礼仪姿态，后常用于奏鸣曲第三乐章，发展到贝多芬的交响乐中的小步舞曲演化成了谐谑曲的戏剧风格。——译者注

[2] 诺曼式拱门（Norman arch），源于法国11和12世纪的建筑风格。法国诺曼底公爵威廉于1066年渡海入侵英国成为英国国王，建立了诺曼王朝，留下了大量城堡形建筑，例如厚实的石墙、窄小的窗口、粗圆的立柱、方形的塔楼，给人以厚实感和庄严感。"诺曼式拱门"是圆拱形，刻有大量的几何装饰形状，经常被称为"锯齿形角线"（zig-zag）。——译者注

几何可以有效地锻炼学生的推理演绎能力，还可以有效地锻炼学生的手眼协调能力。

而像代数课程一样，几何课程和几何绘图教学都应该超越几何知识本身的范畴。几何学可以在实践中应用到一个工业园区，应用到机器上、车间中。例如，伦敦技工学校[1]通过这种方式取得了显著的成功。对于中等学校来说，我建议在教学中采用测量与绘图的方法，尤其是平板仪测量能让学生对几何原理的实际应用产生形象直观的理解。简单的绘图工具，比如说测量人员常用的测链或者罗盘仪，就能帮助学生从勘测和丈量一块地开始，进而绘制出一个街区的地图。最好的教育就是要让学生利用最简单的工具获得最丰富的信息。因此，我们坚决反对给学生提供先进的仪器。通过简单的工具，让学生绘制一个街区的地图，并且掌握这个街区的道路、地形、地质、气候、与其他街区的关联、对当地居民地位的影响，这样的几何课程将会教给学生丰富的历史、地理知识。学生通过这种教育方式学到的历史、地理知识，远比关于珀金·沃贝克[2]的历史知识或者关于贝伦海峡的地理知识更为鲜活。我不想继续展开，不想泛泛而谈，我只是以此为例来论述一个重要的道理，即在教育中我们可以利用精密的理论知识来认识客观的现实世界。因此，理想的数学教育应该是这样的程序：测量一个地方，按照某个比例绘制这个地方的地图，然后掌握这个地方的特点。通过这种很好的方式，学生就能先学会一些必要的几何知识，

---

[1] 伦敦技工学校（London Polytechnics），创建于 19 世纪，它是英国威斯敏斯特大学（University of Westminster）的前身。——译者注
[2] 珀金·沃贝克（Perkin Warbeck，1474—1499），英国历史上一个被认为是意图夺取王位的骗子。1485 年亨利七世建立了都铎王朝（the Tudor Dynasty 或 the House of Tudor），之前的约克王朝（the House of York）的残余分子仍心存不满。珀金·沃贝克，一个船夫的儿子，冒充约克公爵，骗取了一些人的支持，并且对亨利七世展开军事进攻，最后被俘虏并处以绞刑。

即便学生还没有进行详细的证明。而在测量活动进行的同时，学生也能学会证明这些几何知识。

幸运的是，专业领域知识的教育要比一般文化知识的教育简单一些。这有多个方面的原因。首先，二者之间的诸多原理、步骤相差无几，在此不予赘述。其次，专业领域知识的教育往往是发生在——而且应该发生在——学生学习的较高阶段，此时会有比较容易的材料供学生学习和使用。最后，也是最重要的一个原因就在于专业领域知识的教育满足了学生的兴趣爱好，学生学习某个专门领域的知识是因为他们往往想掌握这门知识。这样就产生了一个本质性的区别：一般文化知识是为了培养思维活动，而专业领域知识则运用思维活动。当然，我们也不能过分强调二者之间的简单对立。在教育实践中我们往往能发现，在一般文化知识的教育中，学生会形成对某些知识内容的特殊兴趣；而在专业化的学习中，学生的思想也会驰骋于该专业领域之外的、与其具有联系的广阔空间。

再回头看二者之间的联系，在教育中不可能用一门课程去传授一般文化知识，然后再用另一门课程去传授专业领域知识。为一般文化知识的教育而设计的学习科目，都是需要学生专门学习的专业领域的科目；同时，发展学生的一般文化知识素养的途径也应该体现在学生掌握某种专业领域知识的过程中。二者之间的教育活动是浑然一体的，是不可分割的。教育就是让学生去深刻体会知识的伟大力量、知识的迷人魅力、知识的基本条理，以及让学生掌握某种专业知识，并让学生将其应用到自己的生活之中。

学生在学习掌握某门专业知识的过程中，会逐渐领悟知识的结构，由此而形成一定的文化素养。这种文化素养能让学生具备俯瞰全局的眼光，以及由此及彼、触类旁通的思维。因此，只有在学习掌握某门专业知识的过程中，学生才会达到对一般文化知识的深刻理解，例如文化知识内在的相互联系、外在的广泛应用。在教育中我们所要实现的目的，就是要让学生的思维既能更为具体，又能更为抽象。也就是说，要让学生不但能够分析客观的事实，而且能够理解抽象的思想。

最后一点，在教育中应该培育出一种最为本真的思想素养，即风格意识。所谓风格意识是一种审美意识，是对所遇事物的精彩之处的不由自主的、发自内心的欣赏。艺术的风格、文学的风格、科学的风格、逻辑的风格、实践的风格，它们在根本上都有着共同的美学特质，即外显与内敛的共为一体。风格源自对事物本身的热爱和对风格本身的专注，不可能源自浮光掠影式的浑然不觉。

现在我们回到本次论述的起点，即教育的用途。从最为核心的意义上来讲，风格是教育素养中最重要的一部分，也是最有用的一部分。它渗透到了我们存在的方方面面：如果一个管理者具备一定的风格，那么他就会憎恶浪费；如果一个工程师具备一定的风格，那么他就会节约材料；如果一个工匠具备一定的风格，那么他就会工艺精湛。风格是思想的最佳德性。

但是，超越风格之上，超越知识之上，还有一个冥冥之中能决定希腊众神命运的上帝之力。所谓风格，就是力量的塑造、力量的控制。而归根结底，有助于实现预期目标的力量才是最根本的。首要的事情就是要去实现你的目标，暂时不要考虑你的风格，而要去解决自己的问题。要为上帝给人们做出的安排[1]而辩护，做好自己的本职工作，做好任何你该做的事情。

风格何用？在一定的风格的指引下，你可以专心致志、心无旁骛，直至实现你的既定目标。在一定的风格的指引下，你可以深思熟虑、谨言慎行，从而实现你的远见卓识。在一定的风格的指引下，你可以心

---

[1] "上帝给人们做出的安排"来自宗教中的宿命论观点。——译者注

有所驻、身体力行，直至达到你的最终目的。只有专家才有一定的风格可言，业余画家、业余诗人有什么风格可言？风格永远属于某一专门领域的学问，风格是专业领域知识对一般文化知识的一个独特贡献。

英国现今的教育缺乏一个明确的目的，深受外部社会体系所害，因而教育的活力被扼杀殆尽。在本次演讲中，我自始至终都在反思对教育起决定性作用的一些目的。英国的教育目的到底是培养专门型人才，还是培养业余型人才？我们似乎对此犹豫不决。19世纪以来世界上发生的深刻变革告诉我们，知识的增长赋予了我们预见未来的能力。业余型人才有一定的鉴赏能力，在完成规定的工作时能灵活变通，但是他们缺乏专业知识赋予人们的预见能力。那么，我这次演讲的目的就是建议英国教育在培养专门型人才的同时，不要忽视业余型人才所具有的一些优点。我们的中等教育在应该富有弹性的地方却僵化刻板；在应该严格要求的地方却放任自流。每所学校都为了应付一套又一套的考试而不得不疲于教学，简直苦不堪言。有哪位校长敢于根据学校自己的机遇，放手自由地发展适合自己学校的一般文化教育或者专门知识教育呢？这种机遇一般源于学校的教师、学校环境、班级的学生特点、学校资金的充裕程度。我认为，任何校外考试制度如果主要是为了考查个体学生的学习情况，只会造成教育资源上的浪费，因而毫无裨益。

在教育中，首先要被考查的是学校而不是学生。每所学校都可以根据自己学校所开设的课程来颁发毕业证书，但是每所学校的课程标准都应加以核查或者修正。不管怎样，教育改革的首要之处就是要把学校视作一个独立的单位。学校应该可以开设经过批准的课程，这些课程应是学校教师根据学校的实际需要而开发出来的。假如我们做不到这一点，那么教育就会从一种形式主义陷入另一种形式主义，从一种惰性思维陷入另一种惰性思维。

第一章　教育的目的

　　为了保证学校教育的效率，不管在哪个国家每所学校都应被视为一个真正的独立的教育单位，而我曾设想过把针对个体学生的校外考试制度视作一种可被替换的制度。学校教育的独立性与校外考试制度这二者之间互为矛盾、并为两难，犹如处在斯库拉和卡律布狄斯之间[1]。更通俗地来说，学校教育的这个困境就像道路两边都有壕沟一样。假如我们不幸落到了某个管理部门的手中，而该管理部门单凭主观意愿，硬是把学校划分为两三种类型，然后要求每一种类型的学校采用某一门固定的课程，那么这种做法对教育的打击是相当致命的。当我说学校是一个独立的教育单位时，我的意思就是说，它应该是完完全全的独立的教育单位。根据实际情况，每所学校都应有各自不同的诉求。而只有在必要的情况下，有关的管理部门才可以将学校分门别类。不容许有过于僵化的课程，也不容许有未经学校教师完善的课程。这样的原则在经过恰当的修改之后，也适合于大学或者理工学院的教育。

　　教育面向的是国家的年轻一代，无论从历史的长度来看还是从现实的广度来看，它都是非常重要的。漫不经心地对待教育，从而导致生灵涂炭、希望破灭、国家危亡，肯定就会成为千夫所指。在现代生活条件下有一条规律是牢不可破的，即一个不注重智力教育的民族是注定要灭亡的。无论这个民族有什么样的英雄主义、什么样的文化魅力、什么样的聪明才智、什么样的战争功勋，只要它不注重智力教育，

---

[1] 处在斯库拉和卡律布狄斯之间（Every Scylla is faced by its Charybdis），英语中的习惯用语是"between Scylla and Charybdis"，比喻左右为难、腹背受敌、双重危险。斯库拉（Scylla）是希腊神话中的六头十二臂的女妖，象征危机四伏的礁石、悬崖；卡律布狄斯（Charybdis）为海王波塞冬（Poseidon）与大地女神该亚（Gaea）之女，后因化身为一个大漩涡，每天三次吞吐海水。在现实中墨西拿海峡（the Strait of Messina，意大利半岛和西西里岛之间的海峡）一侧有一块危险的岩石，称为斯库拉岩，而另一侧有一处漩涡，称为卡律布狄斯漩涡。
　　——译者注

那么就难逃失败的命运。如果我们今天故步自封，而明天的科学将会更进一步，那么届时未经良好教育的民族将不得不听候命运的裁判。

自人类文明开化之初，教育的本质就在于教育的宗教性。时至今日，我们依然应该坚守这一传统教育理念。

那么，到底该如何理解教育的宗教性？

宗教性的教育在于其培育了人们的责任感和敬畏感。责任感源自人们对事物发展过程的可能掌控，学习知识有助于取得改变，而无视知识则害莫大焉。敬畏感源自人们对当下所有存在的感知，存在于过去与未来之中，存在于时间的永恒之中。

第二章　教育的节奏

所谓"教育的节奏",我指的是一个基本的原理,每一个有教育经验的人在实践中对这个原理都是熟悉的。当然,我也知道在座诸位不少是英国杰出的教育家,因此我此次的演讲可能对大家来说少有新意。但是我必须指出,教育的节奏这个主题其实并没有得到透彻的论证,因其在实际应用中的影响因素较多。

首先请允许我用一种最简单明了的方法来阐述什么是教育的节奏,希望我的阐述能清晰地表达此次演讲的核心要点。所谓教育的节奏,就是在学生心智发展的不同阶段,寻找合适的时机,采用恰当的方法,实施相应的课程。大家肯定会认为这是老生常谈,无人不知,无人不晓。此次演讲的基本观点的确是明白易懂,但我还是非常想和大家深入探讨,一方面是因为大家对这个问题都有体会,另一方面是因为我认为这个显而易见的问题在教育实践中并没有得到妥善解决,特别是针对学生的心理特点。

幼儿期的任务

我首先要质疑的是关于课程安排前后顺序的一些理论的合理性。我的意思是,只有当这些理论本身能够自洽,它们才有可能被认为是正确的。首先思考一下难度的标准问题，并不是说简单的课程就一定要安排在困难的课程之前。与此相反，有的较为困难的课程恰恰就要安排在前面，因其与人的生活紧密相连，也因其与人的天性极为相关。对于幼儿来说，他们首先要习得的就是口头语言。在此过程中要把语义和语音关联起来，这其实是一个难度惊人的任务，因为这要求幼儿既要理解语言的意义，又要掌握发音的特点。然而，我们都知道幼儿的确能做到这一点，而且我们也都能解释这个奇迹背后的原因。尽管所有的奇迹都是可以解释的，但是对于智者来说奇迹就是奇迹[1]。我以此为例，就是想反驳那些要把较为困难的课程后置的奇谈怪论。

幼儿在学习口头语言之后，还要学习什么呢？他们还要学习书面语言，要把语言的发音和语言的形状联系起来。天哪！我们的教育理论家们都要疯了吗？[2] 大约6岁尚在学说话的孩子们要学会写字，即便是穷其一生苦苦求索的先师大哲对此也会感到震惊吧。再例如，数学教育中最难的是代数原理，而这个最为困难的学习任务也必须安排在较为容易的微积分之间来进行。

我不再就此赘述，而在此重申我的主要观点：面对教育实践的复杂性，要把困难后置的某些教育理论是靠不住的。

与此相对，教育理论中有的是关于课程安排中必要的前置原则，对于这一点我们一般都确信无疑。一个学生只有先学习识字，然后才能去读《哈姆雷特》[3]；一个学生只有先学习整数，然后才能去学习分

---

[1] 怀特海用的词汇如"the wise"（智者）、"miralce"（奇迹），带有一定的宗教意味，表示一些规律的不可抗拒性。——译者注

[2] 说明这依然是一个无比艰巨的学习任务，如果把这个学习任务与有关的教育理论相对照，那只能说有关的教育理论行不通了。——译者注

[3] 《哈姆雷特》（*The Tragedy of Hamlet, Prince of Denmark*，简称 Hamlet），英国诗人、剧作家莎士比亚的悲剧作品之一，又译为《王子复仇记》。——译者注

数。但是如果仔细审视，即便是这个大家都确信无疑的原则也不一定能站得住脚。这种前置原则的确有道理，但是这种原则必须要局限在某一特定的教学问题上。这个原则的危险之处就在于有时候这个原则是对的，而且是一个必需的、真实的条件，但是在其他时候又是错误的。一个人在识字之前的确是读不懂荷马史诗的。但是许多儿童，甚至许多过去不识字的成年人，却可以通过聆听妈妈的讲述或者吟游诗人的吟诵去领会《奥德赛》[1]的故事，从而徜徉在神话故事的美好想象之中。如果有某些愚钝之人在教育管理中不加批判地运用课程安排的前置原则，最终只能导致教育实践像撒哈拉沙漠一样干涸枯竭。

智力发展的各个阶段

此次演讲之所以以"教育的节奏"为主题，是因为我还想批判一下某些时下比较流行的观点。例如，人们常常认为学生的学习是一种步调一致、匀速前进的过程，是一种没有变化、没有起伏的过程。照此看来，如果一个学生在10岁的时候学习拉丁文，那么该学生在18岁或者20岁的时候就应该成为一个古典文化学者。我要指出，这是一个错误的教育理念，因其没有正确地认识到智力发展的实际心理过程，所以严重影响了我们的教学方法的有效性。生命其实是有其周期性的。生命在每天都有其周期性。我们既要工作，也要休息；既要活动，也要睡眠；既有春夏，也有秋冬；既有开学，也有放假。生命在每天有其周期性，以此类推，生命在每年也有其周期性。这样显而易见的周期我们都能理解，而在智力发展的过程中同样存在着周期性，只不过是比较难以察觉而已。智力发展的周期性在各个阶段各有不同，每个

---

[1]《奥德赛》（*Odyssey*），古希腊荷马史诗。——译者注

周期又各有细分。这就是我为什么选择"节奏性"一词来探讨教育中存在的问题的原因，其实"节奏性"指的就是这种看似不断重复的教育活动其实是千差万别的。如果我们不注意教育中应有的节奏，不理解智力发展应有的特征，那么我们的教育就不可能取得真正的进步。黑格尔[1]把事物发展的过程分为三个阶段，即正、反、合[2]，我们可以把这个哲学思想应用到教育实践中。套用黑格尔的哲学思想，我把智力发展的过程分为浪漫阶段、精确阶段、综合阶段[3]。

浪 漫 阶 段

学生在学习的浪漫阶段开始有所领悟。在这个学习过程中学生接触到了新的知识，新的知识蕴含着丰富的联系，启发着无限的可能，学生从直接学习中就可以清晰明了，另外也可从诸多材料中间接推理。在这个阶段，知识的学习是难成系统的，系统的学习只能通过专门的训练才能逐步形成。在这个浪漫阶段，学生的认识是直接的、感性的，学生偶尔才会进行一定的系统分析。先是认识到一些客观的事实，然后产生了某些初步的理解，于是学生的思想就会形成一定的联系，这就是该学习阶段的浪漫情感的缘由。举例来说，初看《鲁滨逊漂流记》[4]这部小说，只认为鲁滨逊·克鲁索就是一个男人，沙滩就是沙滩，脚印就是脚印，荒岛就是荒岛，欧洲就是一个人来人往、熙熙攘攘的地

---

[1] 黑格尔（Georg Wihelm Friedrich Hegel，1770—1831），德国哲学家，古典哲学集大成者，建立了世界哲学史上庞大的客观唯心主义体系，丰富了辩证法思想。——译者注
[2] 正（Thesis）、反（Antithesis）、合（Synthesis）。——译者注
[3] 浪漫阶段(the stage of romance)、精确阶段(the stage of precision)、综合阶段(the stage of generalisation)。——译者注
[4] 《鲁滨逊漂流记》（*Robinson Crusoe*），英国作家丹尼尔·笛福（Daniel Defoe）的作品，也有人翻译为《鲁滨孙漂流记》。——译者注

方。但是，如果把鲁滨逊与沙滩、脚印联系起来，再把与欧洲相隔离的荒岛联系起来，学生就会发现其间存在的若隐若现的可能，于是浪漫情感便油然而生。我举这个极端的例子，目的是为了清晰地说明我的主要意思，这个例子的寓意可以说明整个教育过程的第一个阶段的情况。教育在根本上就是要根据学生头脑中已有的所思所想来进行，如果面对空无一物的头脑，教育将无所作为。[1] 大家在一般意义上所理解的教育，通常指的是教育的第二个阶段，即精确阶段。但是，我们必须要搞清楚教育的整个过程，理解教育过程中学生的智力发展如何从懵懂到精确，终至开花结果。

精 确 阶 段

学生在学习的精确阶段，知识上也会日有增益。在这个阶段，学生的学习更为注重知识的精准一面，而不是像上个阶段一样注重知识的广泛联系。学生的头脑更为关注语言的语法体系，更为关注科学的结构条理。那么在这个阶段的教育中，学生就会逐渐形成一定的分析能力。学生学习新的知识，但是此时新的知识必须要经过他们自己的分析。

显而易见，如果没有前面浪漫阶段的基础，那么这个精确阶段就不会存在。学生总体上对一些事实有了大概的认知，因此他们的分析才具有了一定的意义。[2] 否则，那将是一些关于客观事实的无意义的、牵强附会的陈述，没有什么进一步的相关性。[3] 我重申一下，在这个阶

---

[1] 类似于《论语·述而》中所说的"不愤不启，不悱不发"。——译者注
[2] 只有在浪漫阶段的懵懵懂懂的认识之上，精确阶段的分析能力才能逐步形成。反过来说，如果没有一定的分析能力，前期所获得的认识就只能是一些客观事实而已。——译者注
[3] 如果这样的学习只是停留在客观事实层面，没有经过深入的分析思考，无法在知识系统中建立联系，它也就没有什么意义。——译者注

段中的学习任务不能仅仅局限于浪漫阶段所关注的客观事实。在浪漫阶段所学习的客观事实具有重要的意义，而在精确阶段要系统地学习更多的客观事实，从而对浪漫阶段的一般内容进行认识和分析。

综合阶段

教育发展过程中的最后一个阶段指向的就是黑格尔所说的"综合"概念。在教育的综合阶段中，学习的宗旨又回归到了浪漫主义，但是要基于各种知识和相关技巧的增益。这是精确训练所要实现的最终目标和所要达到的最终理想。对于以上这些内容，大家都是比较明白的，可能我的分析显得枯燥无味。以上这些内容的讲解也是必要的，下面我所要谈的内容与此相关，即浪漫阶段、精确阶段、综合阶段这三个周期的基本特点，大家要对此十分清楚。

循环的过程

教育就在于这三个周期的不断重复。微观上的每一节课应该形成一个循环流，引向随后的过程。较长的阶段应该引向一定的结果，然后形成下一个新的循环的起点。在教育中我们要摈弃不切实际的观念。教师的教育激励应该恰好满足学生节奏性的学习渴望，这样的教学才能成功，这样的学习才能不断获得成功的喜悦，然后从一个阶段迈向另一个阶段。

在幼儿智力发展的第一个浪漫阶段，他们开始对事物和事物之间的联系有所认识。幼儿的智力发育有一个显著特征，就是其思维发展活动与身体感知活动这二者之间是同时进行的。在幼儿智力发展的精确阶段，幼儿通过掌握口语来辨别各种事物、理解各种情感。在幼儿智力发展的第一个综合阶段，幼儿开始运用语言去学习、欣赏各种范畴的具体事物。

从获得感知到语言学习，从语言学习到分类思维和更为敏锐的感受，这是人的智力发展的第一个循环周期。这个循环周期值得我们进行更为深入的研究，因为这是我们唯一可以在自然状态下观察到的智力发育进程。而后期的智力发展过程就不太一样了，多多少少都会受到现今教育活动方式的影响而有所改变。这是一个显著的特征，即幼儿时期的智力发展可以说是非常成功的，而后期的教育则很难达到这一水平。在幼儿智力发展的最后，幼儿会说话了，具有了各种各样的知识，具备了相当敏锐的感知能力。如此看来，这个循环周期达到了既定的目标。从这个意义上说，这要比后期大多数学生所接受的大多数教育活动更为成功。这是为什么呢？一个新生儿看起来是那么娇弱无力，特别是考虑到新生儿所要面临的复杂的智力发展活动，这似乎太艰巨。我想这也许是因为自然在周围环境中设置了一个任务，而人的大脑发育刚好能够应对这个来自周围环境的任务。我的意思并不是说幼儿学习语言有多么神秘，或者说幼儿的思维活动有多么高级，但是从这个角度来看幼儿时期的智力发展过程，的确可以给我们带来很多的启发。

在后期的教育过程中，智力发展的过程就不会像幼儿期一样，不一定要在一定的时期内完成一定的任务，不一定就特定的任务达到一定的结果。在一定的时期内完成一定的任务，这是幼儿时期智力发展的特征。假如让一个学生在10岁的时候开始学习拉丁文，并希望通过系统的教育让其在20岁的时候成为一个优秀的人才，那么真实的结果肯定是失败的，学生既不会有兴趣学习下去，也不会学有所成。这里所说的失败，是与幼儿时期智力的自然发育过程——人的完美无缺的第一个自然周期——相对照而言的。学习拉丁文并不是一个多么艰巨的任务，而我们都知道幼儿时期的智力发展所面临的才是最为艰巨的任务。那么，为什么说学生后来学习拉丁文非常困难呢？这是因为后来学习拉丁文不是自然而然的，缺乏应有的教育节奏，缺少应有的成就激励，因而就没有了在学习上专心致志的执着精神。

其实在幼儿时期的智力发展过程中，幼儿的学习表现出了惊人的执着，这一点我在前文中并没有提及。幼儿全身心地投入到学习过程中，不会因为什么而改变他们既定的智力发展方向。如此对照看来，早期的、自然的智力发展过程与后期的、受到干预的智力发展过程是大相径庭的。由此也可以看出，人们的思维和头脑是自然而然发展的，形形色色的人们因此而适应了这个命中注定的、五彩缤纷的现实世界。在发现了智力发展的这个自然性之后，我们也可以借鉴幼儿时期智力发展的特点，在后期的教育过程中采取一定的措施，让学生能够做到一定程度上的专心致志。比如说，在教育中我们应该避免在智力发展的同一个阶段教授过多的、不同的知识。旧式教育体制针对某一知识领域，不加细分，不讲节奏，虽有所坚持，但终究难免失败。现代教育体制坚持了初级的一般教育，尽管总是把知识清晰地划分为不同的学科，但是同样不讲节奏，东拼西凑。我在这里呼吁，我们应该努力在学生的头脑中编织出一幅知识的和谐图景，协调教育中的各个因素达成各个周期，使每个周期对学生的当下学习都有内在价值[1]。古谚有云，在不同的季节要收割不同的庄稼[2]。

---

[1] 即重视学生的智力发展特点，把教育的方式和心智的周期相协调，适应每一个智力发展周期固有的内在要求。——译者注

[2] 对应原文为"We must garner our crops each in its due season"。——译者注

青春期的浪漫

现在我要谈谈关于前面讲到的"教育的节奏"这一主题的一些具体应用。

在幼儿期的第一个周期之后就是青春期的周期，青春期的智力发展是我们人类最重要的浪漫阶段。在这个阶段，一个人的品性基本上固化形成。一个人的青春期是怎么度过的，胸怀什么样的抱负，拥有什么样的梦想，将会决定这个年轻人后面一生的道路。在这个阶段，一个人会很快地掌握语言的表达和阅读，于是综合能力也就很快形成。幼儿期感知的浪漫信息较少，因此幼儿的综合时期也比较短暂。在幼儿期的智力发展周期之后，人们才开始真正去学习严格意义上的"知识"，这就引向了随后变化巨大的浪漫期。观点、事实、关系、故事、历史、可能、语言的艺术、声音的艺术、形状的艺术、颜色的艺术……这些都涌现在一个青年人的生活之中，焕发他的情感，激发他的思想，引发他的冲动，促使其去从事相似的活动。然而令人悲哀的是，这个黄金般的青春时光总是笼罩在死气沉沉的填鸭式教育的阴影之下。我所说的这个青春时光指的是8岁到12岁或者13岁的四年多时间，在此期间一个人开始熟练地运用母语，开始学会观察事物，开始学会安排事情。幼儿不会安排事情，不会观察事物，不会通过语言来回忆思想。然而，青春期的学生都是可以做到这些的，于是他们就进入了一个新的世界。

在青春期的智力发展周期中，精确阶段又不断重现，以小周期的形式循环往复。书写的完善，拼写的改良，算术的精进，以及对一连串简单事实（如英国历代国王）的背诵，这些都是精确阶段的学习任务。这样的学习任务既能训练学生的专注力，也能增益学生的知识。

虽然这些客观事实知识本身是不成体系的，但是青春期的智力发展在此基础上突飞猛进，给青春期的学生赋予了新的生命。

蒙台梭利教育法[1]的成功之处就在于其重视了青春期的浪漫阶段。按照这个逻辑，这也是蒙台梭利教育法的局限之处。从某种程度上说，蒙台梭利教育法在每一个浪漫阶段的教育中都是必需的。其要义在于让学生广泛浏览、鼓励大胆新颖，但是这样就缺乏了精确阶段应有的审慎。

语言的掌握

这个重要的浪漫期快要结束的时候，学生的智力发展达到了一定的程度，学生具有了学习精确知识的能力。这个时候，语言自然就成了学生专心学习的内容。学生对语言这种表达方式会非常熟悉，还会学习诸多故事、历史、诗歌，以便理解周围的人们，了解其他文化。这个年龄段开始于11岁，是一个特别专注于语言的智力发展周期。从12岁到15岁的三年间，通过对语言的不断学习和深入理解，一个学生就具备了熟练运用语言的能力，这是一个意义重大的学习任务。在这短短几年内，学生通过认真学习就会熟练掌握英语，简单理解法语，并且开始初步学习拉丁语。[2] 对于学习拉丁语来说，首要的是学习拉丁语的语法知识，特别是有关的句法知识，然后是阅读一些重要的拉丁文作品。所要阅读的拉丁文作品可以是简写本，也可以是优秀的翻译版本。通过对拉丁文原著的阅读，再辅以翻译版本的

---

[1] 蒙台梭利教育法（the Montessori system），创始者为意大利幼儿教育家玛利亚·蒙台梭利（Maria Montessori，1870—1952）博士，着重培养儿童的自觉主动学习和探索精神。——译者注
[2] 怀特海所讲的外语学习，针对的是英国的教育情况。——译者注

帮助，学生就会比较全面地理解该文学作品的主要内容。我认为这个阶段的一般学生都应该学习这三种语言，而且应该有一定的掌握，除非是有的学生因为努力地、精确地学习其他多个科目而分散了精力。有的学生的语言天赋特别好，那么这样的学生就会习得更多的语言知识。假如这样的学生愿意在以后的一段时间内继续学习语言，假如他们的确非常适合学习语言，那么在这个阶段结束以前，他们在学习拉丁语之后还可以学习希腊语。与语言学习相对应，其他的课程在学习的时间表中就应居于比较次要的地位，而且方法也应有所不同。比如说历史这样的类文学[1]课程，一般情况下就是通过语言学习的方式进行实施的。如果要学习欧洲历史，那么就不可能不去读一点英国文学、法国文学或者拉丁语文学。当然，我也不是说要放弃专门的历史教学。我的意思是，这个时期的教育应该符合这个时期的浪漫精神特质，特别是不要用某种大型考试来驱使学生在学习中死记硬背大量的、精确的细枝末节。

在这个智力发展的时期，科学知识的学习应处于一个浪漫阶段。学生在这一阶段的学习过程中应该独立观察、独立实验，虽然他们思维的精确性尚不完善。不管是从理论自身的角度来说，还是从技术应用的角度来说，科学的要义都在于具体实践中的应用。而且，科学的每一次的实践反过来都会提出一个新的研究问题。所以，科学知识的学习应开始于研究，结束于研究，科学知识应通过自然现象来进行掌握。在这个年龄阶段中，科学知识学习的恰当引导，或者科学实验的精确设定，都是可以具体情况具体分析的。不管怎样，我要提出一点，这个年龄的确适合以一种浪漫精神来学习科学知识。

---

[1] 类文学（semi-literary）。——译者注

专注于科学

到15岁的时候，智力发展就基本完成了语言的精确阶段和科学的浪漫阶段应该完成的任务。接下来，智力的发展就迈向了语言的综合阶段和科学的精确阶段。该发展周期比较短，但是意义十分重大。我认为这个发展周期大概有一年时间，这样就应该对以前课程中的均衡设置做出彻底的改变，要集中于科学课程而大幅减少语言课程。经过前面的科学知识学习的浪漫阶段之后，再经过这个大约一年的新阶段的学习，学生就会理解决定力学、物理学、化学、代数、几何等科学领域发展的一些重要原理。当然，这并不是说学生要进入这些专门的领域，而是说通过精确掌握各门科学的基本知识，学生开始系统地把以前所学的东西结合起来。以代数和几何为例，因为我对此还算有所了解。在前面阶段的三年学习中，学生会运用最简单的代数公式或者几何命题去做一些测量或者计算。在这样的数学学习过程中，通过计算精确的数据，学生强化了数学能力，熟悉了数学公式，明白了几何定理，领会了解题方法。那么在此基础之上，就应该抓紧时间加强学生对科学知识的学习。例如，学生应该充分掌握代数或者几何的一小部分理论。另外，假如有的学生在先前阶段中表现出了数学天赋，那么就应该在这一年加强他们的数学教育，甚至可以减少其他课程的学习来达到这一目的。在这里，我只是以数学为例来阐释在这个智力发展阶段的科学知识学习。

同时，语言能力的发展达到了综合运用的水平。学生在学习中不再特别关注语法知识的精确练习，不再特别关注作文的准确与否，而是开始深入地阅读文学作品。在深入阅读文学作品的过程中，学生学会了感悟思想、品味历史。而在学习历史的过程中，学生会对一个特定的、较短的历史时期做出深度学习，通过一些事件准确阐述一个重要时代，并对这个时代的一些人物或者政策做出简单的评判。

至此为止，我简要概括了从幼儿期到16岁半的教育过程，特别强调了教育过程中客观存在的生命节奏。如果以我所描述的节奏来实施教育，那么学生既能在特定的阶段专注于特定的知识学习，又能在不同的智力发展阶段表现出不同的学习兴趣。学生对有关知识点有所领悟，而且迫切需要深入认识，这样就要对该知识点进行精确学习。每一个学生在依次学习了各种不同的课程之后，就会明白自己的强项何在。最后，说一下我最为重视的一个目标：一个理科学生既要接受极其重要的文学教育，又要在最善于学习的年龄在科学领域开始培养独立思考的习惯。

16岁之后的教育又会出现新的情况。对于文科学生来说，科学课程的学习进入了综合阶段，他们一般是通过课堂学习科学领域的有关知识。文科学生的语言学习、文学学习、历史学习也都开始了新一轮智力发展周期的循环，但是已没有必要学习更多的细节问题了。对于理科学生来说，一直到中学毕业，先前的精确阶段都持续着，他们一直不断地学习着更多、更广的知识。

但是，这个阶段的教育往往是因人而异的，起码来说特殊的个案比较多，难以对这个阶段的教育进行整齐划一的概括。不过，我有必要强调一点，理科的学生如果以前没有学习外语，那么在这个阶段最好学好法语，也可以开始学点德语。

大 学 教 育

如果你们愿意，接下来我想再谈谈智力发展节奏在大学教育阶段中的重要性。

从幼儿期到成人期的整个智力发展阶段是一个大的循环周期。智力发展周期的浪漫阶段从幼儿期延伸到12岁左右，精确阶段体现在中学教育时期，而综合阶段体现在成人期的初始阶段。如果一个学生在接受中学教育之后还会接受高等教育，那么大学层次的教育过程主要针对的是智力发展周期的综合阶段。大学层次的教育应基于智力发展综合的理念。具体来说，大学生在学习某一门课程之前就应该对该门课程的基本知识、基本方法有所熟悉，熟悉先前所接受的训练，并且牢固掌握所学习的内容。形象地说，中学生一直在伏案学习，而大学生就要站起身来，并环顾四周。所以，如果在大学教育的第一年仍然固守中学的学习方法，仍然只是复习中学的学习内容，那就是一个严重的错误。一个中学生在中学阶段逐渐学会从特殊到一般的抽象概括，而一个大学生在大学阶段就要尝试从一般到特殊的具体应用。大学课程只有充分地、透彻地讲解普遍规律知识，才能被称为一门好的课程。当然，我并不是说大学课程要抽象到与具体事实相脱离，而是说学习具体事实的目的是为了对一般知识的适应性进行验证。

智力的培养

在大学教育阶段，学生的理论兴趣和实践应用统一了起来。无论你向学生教授什么样的知识，这个学生很可能在毕业以后都完全用不上以前所学习到的那些知识。即便是用上了那些知识，这个学生也很可能记不起来你到底教了他什么。大学教育之所以有用，就在于帮助学生充分理解一些基本的原理，并且促使学生将其灵活应用到具体实践中。大学毕业之后，一个人会忘记他在大学里学习的具体知识，但是他在无意识中会深深记住如何把理论应用到具体实践中。只有当丢掉课本、烧掉笔记、忘掉为考试而学习的零碎细节时，我们的学习才是真正有价值的。一个人会记住不断学习到的知识细节，这些知识细节犹如太阳和月亮一般亘古不变，而我们有时候所需要的信息可以在任何一本参考书中找到。大学教育的意义就在于让我们透过细枝末节来学习基本原理。这里所说的基本原理并不是简单地指那些书本上的、形式上的理论，而是指已经内化的、形成习惯的思维。这种思维可以帮助我们在相关的情境中恰当地解决问题，对相关的问题做出一定的反应，没有谁会径直照着书本知识去直面现实。以恰当的思维解决相应的问题，这是智力培养的终极目的。实际上，我们往往把学习当作一页一页地浏览我们曾经阅读的所有书籍，遇到了什么问题，我们似乎就能从某一本书的某一页中找到相应的答案。

当然，事实上我们都不至于这么肤浅幼稚，不至于被这种错误的教育观念误导。所以，学习纯粹的客观知识与发展专业能力之间也并不是完全对立的关系。换个说法来说就是，大学教育的理想目标在于传授知识，更在于赋予力量；大学的任务就是要把知识转化为力量，要把一个孩子培育为一个成人。

发展的节奏特点

最后，我想用以下两点评论来结束我的演讲，这两点评论也是我想提出的两个告诫。我的这次演讲的核心思想是关于智力发展过程中的节奏特点，但是我要指出，人的内在精神生活就像一张由很多线编织而成的网，这些线不会按照统一的标准向外延伸，因而人们的智力发展不可能是按照整齐划一的步调来进行的。我所提出的智力发展的节奏特点，适合于一般的学生，适合于理想化的情况。在理想的情况下，一般学生的智力是按照我所说的节奏得以不断正常发展。当然，现实生活复杂多样，在实际情况中可能存在违背这个规律的现象。但是，即使有违背这个规律的个别现象，也不会影响到我所论述的这个节奏性特点。人的智力发展的自身过程存在着一定的节奏，各个周期之间相互关联；在智力发展的整个过程中有大周期也有小循环，而不管是大周期还是小循环都有着相似的特征。另外，这个节奏性特点的一些主要规律是可以在教育实践中得到验证的，是适用于大多数学生的。那么在教育实践中，我们就可以根据这个节奏规律来进行教学，改变教学方式，提高教学质量，促进学生发展。课程的主要问题不在于诸多科目如何排列组织，而在于这些科目如何从根本上启发心智。真正需要排列组织的，是教育中的各个程序应该达成的相应素质。

另外，我还要指出，在智力发展过程中不要过分夸大三个阶段之间的差异。我非常怀疑一点，你们在听我讲解每一个循环的三个阶段的具体问题时可能会想：只有一个数学家才会划分这样的条条框框。我必须指出，这不关乎数学家什么事，而是关乎文字表达的局限，所以可能会让大家对我产生误解，对此我要提醒大家注意这一点。我的确一直都在不断强调，在智力发展的周期之中，浪漫阶段、精确阶段、综合阶段都是自始至终普遍存在的。但是，这三个阶段会交替居于主导地位，而正是这样的交替循环形成了智力发展的各个周期。

第三章　自由与规训的节奏

如果说我们人类的努力遭遇了什么挫败，让人感到悲哀的莫过于理想的消逝。回望过去，我们的先贤在学校里倾心传递智慧；再看现在，我们在大学里的目的变得如此卑微，仅仅是教授一些知识。从过去的神圣人类智慧降低到现今的若干学科知识，这标志着教育的失败，而且是一个长时间的失败。我并不是厚古薄今，不是说过去的教育就一定要比现在的教育成功。比如说，从卢奇安[1]的一系列作品中我们可以看出，古希腊的那些所谓的哲学家自命不凡、夸夸其谈，卢奇安对那个时代的知识分子冷嘲热讽。从这个历史故事中我们可以看出，那个时代的教育并不比当今时代的教育优越多少。我的意思是，在欧洲的文明曙光乍现的时候，我们的先贤胸怀理想从而教化育人，而渐渐地，我们现在的教育已无所谓"理想"一词，只有实践一面。

无所谓理想，只有实践，教化育人的进程就会停滞不前。假如我们的教育仅仅满足于一些非常机械的思维能力训练，或者仅仅停留在一些可资利用的条条框框的知识上，那么教育就不会有所进步。尽管从表面上看起来花样不少，但是课程安排比较盲目。虽想在时间有限

---

[1] 卢奇安（Lucian，约120—180），又译琉善，古希腊修辞学家和讽刺作家。他是无神论者，敌视所有的宗教；他谴责当时的社会制度，指出社会不公和暴力政治；他讽刺当时的哲学，认为其过于虚伪和愚昧。——译者注

的条件下有所作为,但终究不免失败。我们必须面对一个不可回避的现实,那就是:在上帝创造的世界中,我们所要学习的知识纷繁复杂,而我们的认识能力非常有限。假如说要一点一点地去学习所有需要学习的知识,那是根本不可想象的。这个世界的万事万物都有其存在的意义,都有值得我们学习的价值。也许,我们无法完全认识这个世界的万事万物也是有一定道理的。可能正是因为这样,我们才会乐于对一些重要的道理感到无知[1],我们的世界才会更有意义。我想说的是,知识的学习的确是智力教育的一个主要目标,但是智力教育还有一个目标,看似难以把握,实则意义重大,古人称之为"智慧"。没有知识的基础,一个人是不可能有智慧的;一个人虽然可以轻易地获得知识,但可能仍然没有智慧。

由此可以看出,智慧是掌握知识的方式。智慧关系着知识的运用、问题的解决、经验的升华,智慧是对知识的掌控,是我们所能获得的最本质的自由。简单地说,智慧主宰知识,古人对此很清楚,比我们现在还清楚。但是在追求智慧的教育实践中,古人也有令人遗憾的错误。他们总是以为智慧的传递是一件简单的事情,无非就是请几个口若悬河的哲学家给年轻人讲一讲,然后年轻人就获得智慧了。因此我们都知道,在那个时候的学校里面有不少不靠谱的哲学家。通往智慧的唯一道路是对知识的自由把握,通往知识的唯一道路是对学习的不断规训。自由与规训是教育过程的两个基本要素,所以我今天的演讲题目就是"自由与规训的节奏"。

在教育中,自由与规训并非我们所理解的字面意思和逻辑关系,并非像我们所想象的那样对立鲜明。学生的心智是一个不断发展的有机体,不是像一个空匣子那样可以随随便便地收纳什么新知识。但同

---

[1] 类似于《庄子》中所说的"相忘"。——译者注

时必须按部就班地学习新知识，这样才能给心智的发展提供足够的营养。在理想的教育之中，"规训"应该是学生的一个主动选择；在此基础之上，"自由"才能有所作为，才能促进学生的心智发展。如此看来，自由与规训之间并不是不可调和的。我们所要做的，就是协调好教育中的自由与规训，使之符合学生心智的发展变化。自由与规训不断调适于人的心智发展的自然过程之中，在前面的第二章中我把这个过程概括为"教育的节奏"。我一直坚信不疑，教育实践中的许多挫败都是因为没有注重教育中的这个节奏问题。从教育的节奏来看自由与规训的主题，我认为在教育的初始阶段和终结阶段，我们应以自由为基调；而在教育的中间阶段，我们应以规训为基调，辅以自由作为搭配。教育的过程不应是一个简单的周期循环——从自由到规训再到自由。实际上，在教育的过程中应该有许多这样的周期，而每一个大的周期之中又有许多小的周期。每一个小的周期都是一个细胞，教育发展的完整过程就是由这样的一个一个的细胞所构成。就教育过程的每一个细胞而言，我把初始的自由阶段称之为"浪漫阶段"，把中间的规训阶段称之为"精确阶段"，把最后的自由阶段称之为"综合阶段"。

  在此我要详细说明一下。首先，没有兴趣就没有心智发展，兴趣是注意和理解的先决条件。你可以通过鞭笞的方式激发兴趣，也可以通过哄诱的方式在愉快的活动中激发兴趣。无论如何，如果没有兴趣就不会有任何进步。生物体之所以能够自然而然地激发本能，从而迈向适宜的自我发展道路，是受快乐驱使的。一个幼儿能够长大以适应周围的环境，这是因为母亲的慈爱或者保姆的照料。我们需要吃东西，这是因为我们喜欢美食的味道。我们征服自然，这是因为我们有着无限的好奇心，总想有所发现。我们喜欢锻炼身体。[1] 我们痛恨危险的

---

[1] 原文如此，可能原稿有所遗漏。锻炼身体应是受健康的驱使。——译者注

敌人，这是因为我们总是沉湎于原始的快意恩仇。毫无疑问，痛苦也能作为激发行动的一个次要的驱动力，但是这只是在没有快乐的情况之下。一般情况下，快乐才是生命活力的自然的、健康的源泉。当然，我们也要避免沉迷于肤浅的快乐而不能自拔。我想要强调的是，在教育过程中应该以一种自然的、快乐的方式去发展心智。居于次要地位的严格规训要从教育的长远目标来予以考虑，同时这个长远目标也应该清晰可见，只有这样才能保证学生的学习兴趣不致丧失。

  我想说明的第二点是，空乏无用的知识是微不足道的，甚至是危害不浅的。知识的要义就在于知识的运用，表现为我们的灵活掌握，体现在智慧的光芒之中。而在平时的生活中，我们往往把知识和智慧分割开来，似乎拥有知识的人就是受人尊敬的。对此我不敢苟同，我不认为知识有着如此这般的神圣。尊重知识，首先要看谁有知识，其次要看怎么运用知识。知识之所以能够增益心智，就在于知识的运用能够改变心智发展过程中的直接经验。如此看来，为了学习知识而采取过分严厉的规训，在教育中是相当有害的。积极而富有创新精神的思维习惯只会在比较自由的氛围中产生，而胡乱的规训只会让学生的头脑更加混沌。如果你经常接触中学毕业生或者大学毕业生，你就会发现一个规律，思维迟钝的人在以往的教育过程中学习的都是一些惰性知识。而且，英国社会上关于知识学习的这种可悲腔调也是我们的教育失败的原因之一。另外，操之过急地灌输单纯的知识只会使教育适得其反，因为人的思想会拒斥灌输的知识。青年人内心里渴望走出书本，渴望走向实践，而通过规训强加于他们的教育只会扼杀他们的冲动。所以，规训的最终目的应该是为了满足学生对智慧的自然渴望，智慧会给原始经验增添价值。

  现在我们仔细思考一下人类心智的这些自然渴望的节奏特点。当一个人处于一个新的环境中时，头脑里首先就会出现一系列的活动，会联想一系列的知识和经验。这是一个发现的过程，一个开始习惯于奇思怪想的过程，一个提出问题的过程，一个寻找答案的过程，一个尝试新事物的过程，一个注意到新尝试之后的新结果的过程。这一系列的过程是自然而然的，同时也是极具吸引力的。8—13岁的学生往往表现出这样剧烈的心理过程，我们经常注意到这种现象。在这种心理活动中，好奇心占据着主导地位，不幸的是总有愚钝之人会磨灭学生的好奇心。毫无疑问，处于这个智力发展阶段的学生需要外界的帮助，甚至是外界的规训。例如，学生学习的环境需要认真营造。学习的环境要符合学生的智力发展水平和个人发展需要。从某种意义上说，这样的学习环境营造是无中生有的，但是实际上它呼应了学生智力发展的内在要求。例如，教师的教学活动意在让学生通过望远镜去观察星体特征，而也许学生会误解教师的意图，以为是让他们随便望望苍茫的宇宙。如果就像这样进行教育活动，面对不同层次的学生不做任何教学设计，即便是针对最笨的学生，也没有对以往的教学程序做出任何改变，那么学生是不可能学到新的知识的。请记住，教育不是往行李箱里塞东西，教育根本就不是那回事。教育的过程有其固有的特质，可以更为贴切地比喻为一个生物体吸收营养的过程。众所周知，在一定的情况下，美味可口的食物对于人的健康来说是多么重要。如果我们把鞋子放进行李箱里，然后再打开行李箱，鞋子还是鞋子。但是，如果我们给一个孩子吃错了东西，那就完全是另外一种情况了。

  儿童在浪漫阶段的初期需要我们用另一种方式予以引导。不管怎么说，儿童是人类漫长文明史的文化继承者，我们绝不可以让他们在冰川时代[1]的文化知识的迷宫里面迷茫、踟蹰，这是非常荒谬的。提出一些重大的事例，分析一些简要的思想，介绍一些核心的人物，只

---

[1] 冰川时代（the Glacial Epoch），怀特海用它来比喻对某些知识的学习脱离现实，并且在教育中没有得到充分引导。——译者注

有通过这样的方式才能强化学生自主的学习兴趣。总的来说，在教育的任何一个阶段，自由与规训都是不可或缺的。但是，在教育的浪漫阶段应该侧重于自由这一维度，让学生无拘无束地去观察、去行动。假如与此相悖，在学生的智力成长需要自由的时候，予以精确阶段才可以施加的规训，这就势必会造成思维发展的阻碍。简单地说，脱离了浪漫阶段的自由，就无所谓领会理解。在以往的教育中没有仔细研究浪漫阶段在一个人的智力发展阶段中的重要性，因而导致了过去的教育的失败，对这一点我是坚信不疑的。如果没有浪漫阶段的自由探索，那么从教育中所获得的只是一些僵化的惰性知识；更为糟糕的情况是，因为没有学到知识而被世人轻视。

　　如果对学生智力发展的浪漫阶段予以正确引导，就能促使他们产生另一种心智渴望。先前由于缺乏经验而产生的新鲜感消退了，对理论与事实的基本原理有了一些了解，而且开始独立地、大量地阅读，开始自主地对思想和行动进行探索。在这个时候，他们明白了精确知识学习的要义，并且通过熟悉的材料明白了常识的显著意义。那么此时就应该继续向前，精确地认识所学科目，牢牢地记住所学内容的显著特点，这就到达智力发展的精确阶段了。精确阶段是以往的教育体系中唯一强调的，不管是中小学教育还是大学教育。在以往的教育体系中，所谓教育就是让学生死记硬背书本知识，除此之外无他可言。过去的教育相当于是把智力发展的精确阶段过度延长了，其结果就是把学生教育成了书呆子。也许有个别学生幸免于此，避免了他们的才智被碾轧在毗湿奴的车[1]轮之下。在教育实践中，教师总是想向学生

---

[1] 毗湿奴的车（Juggernaut），这个词源自梵语 Jagannātha，印度教主神之一，意为"世界的主宰"。英语中常用"the car of Juggernaut"一词，意为"载有巨大印度神的偶像的巨大车子"，引申为不可阻挡的力量、压倒一切的力量。——译者注

多教授一点客观知识，多灌输一点精确理论，而其实学生在当时的学习阶段是无法完全消化吸收的。假如学生真的能消化吸收那么多的内容，那就是一种真正有效的教育。不管是中小学教师还是大学教授，都只能在学生的成长过程中起到次要的作用。一个人的学习具有一定的独立性，不管是在学校教育的过程中，抑或是在学生毕业之后的生活过程中。要促进一个人的心智发展，首先要遵循心智发展的既定基本规律。但是，一个不熟练的执业医生会轻易地损害一个敏感的有机体。[1]我们对此现象必须有所警惕，但是在教育中我们还是要做出应该做的事情。在这个阶段要让学生不断地理解一些基本的知识细节，认识一些主要的精确理论，还要学会一些容易掌握的技巧。对于已有的知识学生务必要有所学习，而且在当代社会中一个人的成功与否取决于他所具备的所有优秀的真才实干。要想吟诵诗歌，首先要学会运用韵律。要想建造桥梁，首先要懂得材料力学。希伯来[2]的先知想要传递福音，那么他们就要先学会写字，而在当时学会写字是很不容易的。没有谁的才智是与生俱来的，假如说有什么天生奇才，那么借用祈祷书[3]上的话来说，那肯定是虚构的、骗人的。

当智力发展的周期达到精确阶段之后，学习的浪漫精神就居于后位了。精确阶段中有一个无可回避的事实在这个阶段占据着主宰地位，即学生要学习什么是对的方法、什么是错的方法，还要学习精确的真理。但这并不是说浪漫精神就彻底消失了，在掌握特定知识的精确应用时，在教学中还要培养这种浪漫精神。浪漫精神务必要培养，其中

---

[1] 意即如果教师对此规律一知半解，就有可能在教育活动中有损于一个学生正常的心智发展。——译者注
[2] 希伯来（Hebrew），最早的犹太人被称为希伯来人，《圣经·旧约》描述的就是关于希伯来人的神话故事。——译者注
[3] 祈祷书（the Prayer Book），教徒用来礼赞、祈祷用的书。怀特海借用宗教中的教义指出人生来是没有智慧的，智慧需要后天的学习才能获得。——译者注

一个原因在于这是达成均衡智慧的一个必要因素，而均衡智慧是教育所要达到的一个目标。另一个原因是，一个学生只有在浪漫精神的活力之下，才能真正领会学习任务的要义。教育的要旨就在于在实践中发现自由与规训之间的精确平衡，从而以最快的速度让学生学习知识。但是应该怎么把握自由与规训之间的平衡，并没有一个放之四海而皆准的定理，因为课程不同、学生不同。但是我一直以来强调的心智发展的节奏规律是恒定的，即在教育过程的初始阶段要侧重于学生的自由探索精神，而在随后的中期阶段要侧重于学习精确的、各种各样的知识。我确信无疑的是，如果在初始的浪漫阶段中，教师的教学活动真正符合了学生的自由探索精神，那么在随后的精确阶段中学生的学习就会顺利得多，可以减少许多的规训。例如，学生就会知道该怎么学习新的知识，该怎么取得好的成绩，该怎么牢固地掌握要点。另外，我认为真正有效的规训是一种自我约束，而学生能不能做到自我约束取决于学生的心智是不是真的自由。教育中所要考虑的因素实在是繁杂而细微，所以我们还有必要让学生精神愉悦地完成既定的学习任务，并且形成一种习惯。这些因素能否得以实现取决于诸多因素，要看教育的实际过程是否符合学生在每一个阶段的内心渴求，学生是否全力以赴地学习，学生是否达到理应达到的水平，学生在实际的学习过程中是否被赋予一定的自由。

  一个娴熟的教师如何才能让他的学生保持浪漫精神的不断跃动，这是一个难以阐述的话题。一般情况下，需要用很长时间去解释清楚的事情，往往是在短时间内就做好了。如果要理解维吉尔的诗篇是多么高雅，从其语言表达之美即可感知，不需要哕里唆地论证。如果要强调数学的证明是多么迷人，可以应用其普遍原理去解决复杂的问题，这就是最快捷的方式。在这个阶段，一个教师的责任不可谓不重大。在我看来，一个教师在引导一个班级进行精确认知教学活动的时候，往往会削弱学生的学习兴趣。当然，也有个别极具天赋的教师能做到两者都不耽误。学生学习的主动性与训练都是必要的，但是训练往往会扼杀主动性，这是一个两难问题。

我们承认这是一个两难的问题，但这并不是说我们就可以完全无视对这个棘手的教育问题的解决。这个两难问题不是理论本身造成的，而是因为教育的实际情况各有不同，难以找到一个统一的、完美的应对策略。在过去的教育中，教育的方法扼杀了学生的学习兴趣。而迄今为止，我们尚在不断思考如何把这个矛盾降低到最小程度。我只是在此提醒大家，教育的确不是一件简单的事情，没有任何一个简单的办法能解决所有的教育问题。

在自由与规训的关系之间，有一个大家经常忽略的实际问题。浪漫精神的内涵比较宽泛，难以用一些明确的界限去界定和控制。学生在学习中自由探索的浪漫精神，有时候表现为其思维中瞬间闪过的灵感。与此相反，不管是在何种普通的教育体系之中，学生的学习是否完成了精确认知的知识习得，可以是也应该是清晰可见、明确无误的。如果你让它太过宽泛，你将扼杀学生的学习兴趣，让自己的教学目标落空；如果你让它太过狭窄，你的学生将对知识缺乏有效的掌握。[1] 因此，在每一个课程类型的每一门科目之中，应该先行激发学生最为好奇的思考，然后确定需要精确学习的知识。这一点在现在任何一种有效的教学方法中是看不到的。例如，有一些理科学生以后要从事科学研究的事业，我个人对这样的学生非常欣赏，如果他们要学习古典文化知识，那么就要确定：他们到底需要学习哪些拉丁语词汇？他们到底应该掌握哪些语法规则和结构？为什么不可以把这些问题都先确定

---

[1] 即如果太注重知识习得，过多强调精确认知，就可能会扼杀学生的学习兴趣，最终只会导致教育的失败。反过来，如果疏忽知识的习得，无视精确认知，就会削弱心智的发展基础。——译者注

下来，然后让他们集中精力去练习，好让他们牢牢记住这些语言知识，最终让他们理解这些语言知识在拉丁语或者法语、英语中的派生用法呢？在这种情况下，如果在阅读课文的过程中出现了一些新的语法结构或者词汇，那么教师就可以用最为简单的方式予以充分讲解。在教育中，像这样的完全的确定性是必需的。我认为，一个优秀教师的秘诀就在于明确知晓学生应该精确地掌握什么知识。如此一来教师就不会漫不经心地让学生去记忆一些不相干的、不重要的东西了。成功的秘密就在于对速度的把握，对速度的把握就需要专注于进程。但是对于需要精确掌握的知识来说，最为关键的是速度、速度、速度。要尽快地学习知识，然后应用知识。如果能够应用知识，那么就能掌握知识。

现在我们来看智力发展周期的第三个阶段，即综合阶段。在此阶段中有一种针对浪漫精神的反应。此时的学生已经学习了一些精确的知识，具备了一定的能力，清楚地理解了一些规则定理的公式和具体应用。现在，学生想要使用他的新武器了。每一个学生都是一个有效的个体，都想展现出一定的能力。在这个新的阶段，学生又开始了一系列浪漫阶段的那种自由探索。所不同的是，学生的思维不再是涣散松懈的"乌合之众"，而是训练有素的"作战军团"。从某种意义上说，所有的教育都应该在研究中开始，在研究中结束，都是为应对生活中的直接经验而做出准备，准备好相关的知识与合适的行动，从容度过生活中的每一时刻。反过来说，如果我们的教育没有开始于激发主动性并且结束于鼓励主动性，那么它肯定是错误的。教育的最终目的就是培养积极的智慧。[1]

我在大学教育工作中，常常痛心于学生思维的僵化。他们盲目地学习了一些精确的知识，但是那些知识是惰性的、无以为用。一个大

---

[1] 即教育应该培养富有行动力的智慧。——译者注

学教授的首要目的就是要展现他自己的真实特点——像一个无知之人一样地思考，并且积极地运用他自己的那一小部分知识。从一定意义上说，当智慧生长的时候，知识在缩减[1]，因为知识的细节将会被统摄到理论的体系之中。重要的知识在生活的每一个方面都能随处学到，但是一个人只有习惯于擅长运用大家都熟知的道理，才能说最终拥有了智慧。在智力发展周期的精确认知阶段，我们需要通过知识细节的学习来领会相关理论。进入综合阶段之后，我们不再对知识细节的学习感兴趣，而是会特别关注理论的灵活运用，此时的知识退入了无意识的习惯之中。例如在一般情况下，我们并不需要刻意去反复背诵"二加二等于四"。虽然以前我们不得不去这样背诵，但是现在我们都把这样的初级算术当成一个自动生成的思维习惯。这个阶段的根本意义就在于培养一个人从相对被动的规训跃升到比较自由的应用。当然，在综合阶段中依然需要学习精确知识，而且需要学习更多的精确知识。此时的思维感受到了精确知识的推动力量，因而得以掌握一般原理，并且能够广泛应用。但是知识的增长逐渐变得无意识起来，成为思想积极探索过程中的偶然事件。

　　以上都是关于人的智力发展过程中的三个阶段的节奏规律。一般来说，教育的整个过程取决于这个三段式节奏。13岁或者14岁之前是智力发展的浪漫阶段，14岁到18岁之间是智力发展的精确阶段，18岁到22岁之间是智力发展的综合阶段。这只是一个大致的节奏，从总体上影响着人的发展过程。我不认为所有的学生在所有的科目上都能同时达到某一个阶段。例如，我认为当学生开始进入学习词汇和语法这一语言学习的精确阶段时，他们对科学的学习恰恰进入了最旺盛的浪漫阶段。语言学习的浪漫阶段开始于幼儿学习说话的时期，这样可以

---

[1] 对应原文为"...knowledge shrinks as wisdom grows..."，怀特海此处所说类似于《道德经》中所说的"为学日益，为道日损"。——译者注

较早地进入到语言学习的精确阶段，但是科学知识的学习阶段要晚出现一些时间。所以，如果在早期教育中教授精确的科学知识，就会抹杀学生的探索精神和学习兴趣，最终学生也理解不了科学知识的丰富内涵。由此可以看出，在语言学习的精确阶段开始若干年之后，才能进入科学知识学习的浪漫阶段。

在学生心智发展的总周期中还有许许多多小的循环，每一个小的循环也同样体现着三个周期的变奏，这样的周期循环贯穿在一个人的学习的每一天、每一周、每个学期。在学习中，一个学生对某些主题的知识先是有大概的、模糊的领悟，然后开始掌握相关的知识点，最后在相关知识的基础上把整个问题融会贯通。如果一个学生不能持续不断地产生学习兴趣，无法掌握技巧，体会不到成功的激动，那么就不可能在学习上取得什么进展，注定要失去信心。总体来看，近30年的英国中学向大学输送了大批失去信心的年轻人，他们丧失了学习知识的热情。而大学教育反过来又强化了中学教育的这一缺失，加剧了失败。在这种情况下，英国年轻人的兴趣爱好就转移到了其他方面，这导致受过教育的英国人不再热衷于知识的学习。当我们谈到我们国家的一些伟大成就的时候——我们希望是除了战争之外——如果有的成就是在我们学校的教室里获得的，而不是在运动场上获得的，那么我们就会对教育的方式感到满意。

我以上的讨论都是针对智力教育这个方面，我的分析局限在一个限定的基础之上。然而，我们的学生都是活生生的人，不可以像拼图玩具一样随便拆解。机器的生产靠的是外在的构造能力，从而把一个个单独的零件组装上去。而一个活生生的人的成长靠的是自己的自我发展内在驱动，这就完全不同了。内在动力可以从外部予以激发和引导，也可以被消除掉。但是不论从外部予以什么样的激发或者引导，一个人发展变化的创生性的内在动力总是源于他自己的内心深处，而且每个人都有自己完全不同的特点。教育就是引导个体去认识生活的艺术。所谓掌握生活的艺术,就是当一个人在面对生活的真实情境的时候,他能充分发挥自己的潜能,灵活采用各种方式,熟练解决所遇到的种种问题。这就要求一种非常娴熟的技艺,把人的整个心智从低到高都联系起来。如此一来,科学、艺术、宗教、道德这些领域的客观存在就具有了价值和意义。每一个人的存在都需要一定的探索,生活的艺术就是要引导每一个人在探索中前进。我们人类文明中的几个主要宗教在最初的时候包含着一些思想元素,反对各种各样的世俗限制的道德教条的灌输。从"道德"这个词汇较为负面的意义上来说,道德是宗教的死敌。这就是为什么使徒保罗[1]强烈指责《律法书》,为什么《福音书》[2]猛烈批判法利赛人[3]的原因。人类宗教的每一次大传播,都会引起这样强烈的敌对行为。而当一个宗教慢慢消亡的时候,这样的敌对状态也会慢慢消失。从道德教育和宗教教育的发展历史来看,我们要特别关注其中的节奏性规律。无论一个宗教的教义如何表达,

---

[1] 保罗(Paul,3—67),原名"大数的扫罗"(Saul of Tarsus)。Tarsus 是其出生地,翻译为"大数"或"塔尔索"。又译为"保禄",天主教提到他时常称圣保罗,新教则通常称他为使徒保罗。他是犹太裔罗马公民,被公认为对早期基督教会发展贡献最大的使徒。但是他在早期参与迫害基督教活动,后转变成最热情的支持者。——译者注

[2] 《律法书》(*the Law*),《福音书》(*the Gospels*)。基督教圣经分为《旧约》和《新约》两个部分,基督教认为旧约是上帝通过摩西与以色列人所订立,而新约则是上帝通过耶稣基督与信者所订立。《律法书》是旧约的一部分,又称摩西五经,包括《创世记》、《出埃及记》、《利未记》、《民数记》和《申命记》,讲述希伯来传说中世界和人类的起源,以及以色列民族的形成和发展。《福音书》是新约的一部分,又称四福音书,包括《马太福音》、《马可福音》、《路加福音》和《约翰福音》,讲述耶稣生平与复活事迹。在这里,怀特海用宗教典故譬喻历史发展的否定之否定规律。——译者注

[3] 法利赛人(Pharisees),一个犹太人宗派,使徒保罗就是法利赛人,即"希伯来人所生的希伯来人"。法利赛人,包括转变之前的保罗,恪守摩西律法,反对耶稣基督的教义。——译者注

如果这个宗教在传播的过程中过早地强调教义的精确性，那么这个宗教就会消亡。只有在经过宗教教育的现实考验之后，宗教的教义才能表现出应有的活力。

我在这里不是要讨论教育中的宗教问题，这个问题太大了。我之所以提到宗教问题，是想请大家注意，我所阐述的这些规律不应被狭隘地理解。我们现在所分析的是生命高级阶段的节奏性发展的一般规律，表现在最初的觉醒，之后的规训，再到更高层次的成就。我在这里想要说的是，发展变化的本能是内生的，能否有所发现要靠自己的体会，能否有所约束要靠自己的规训，能否有所收获要靠自己的主动。一个教师有着双重的作用：一方面通过教师自己的学识来促进学生的思考，从而激发学生的学习热情；另一方面通过学习环境的营造来传授广博的知识，从而增强学生的学习信心。教师一定不能浪费，生命在较低的发展阶段中就要避免浪费，这是自然进化的一种方式。不管是科学、道德还是宗教，最终的驱动力都是价值感和重要性。这表现在很多形式上，例如惊讶、好奇、敬畏、崇拜、强烈渴望超越自我。这种价值感驱使人们付出辛勤的劳作，否则人们就不会有所进步，而会倒退到被动的、低级的类型之中。这种进步力量最突出的表现就是美感，即对已达到的完善程度的审美。我对此就要提出疑问：在我们现今的教育中，我们是否充分地强调了艺术的作用。

我们的公学[1]中最有代表性的教育模式曾经是针对那些来自富有的、有教养的家庭的男孩子。他们到处旅游，例如到意大利、希腊、法国，他们的家也往往布置得富丽堂皇。这种情况在我们现今公立的中小学教育中较为少见，即便是在现今的扩大化的许多公学中也不多见。但是我们绝对不能因此而忽略了艺术，因其是我们精神生活中的

---

[1] 公学（public school），英国收费昂贵的私立学校，学生的家庭背景较为优裕，如第一章中讲到的拉格比公学。——译者注

一个重要元素。我们的审美情感可以让我们获得最为生动形象的理解，而如果无视审美的价值，那么所有的思想认识就会大打折扣。在教育中，心智发展的自由境界是基于一个人的综合素质，对心智的所有方面都要有所重视，不可对其内在要求掉以轻心。在现今的经济状况下，人们常常会说我们的教育徒劳无益，甚至说要减少有关的教学活动。如果只是一味地开展知识教育，那么就只会培养出一大批的废品，而这恰恰就是我们国家的学校教育正在做的事情。我们做到了让学生有所启发，但是没有做到让学生有所满足。从历史经验中我们可以看出，当一个国家的艺术之花开始绽放的时候，这个国家才开始踏上文明之途。然而，面对这个显而易见的事实，我们却把艺术驱逐到了大众教育之外。这样的教育启发了又扼杀了学生的内心渴望，导致了教育的失败、人们的不满，难道不是吗？在教育中关闭艺术的大门是极其愚蠢的，因为我们其实并不需要费多少周章，就足以给学生提供各式各样的、简单易懂的艺术教育。你也许可以通过一些重大的改革以降低劳动强度、增强工作安全，但是你并不能大幅提高平均收入水平。这么看来，你就不可能实现乌托邦的梦想。然而你并不需要费太多周折就能培养学生的艺术情趣，让学生热爱音乐、喜欢戏剧、欣赏形状和颜色之美。我们也可以采取一些措施，达到人们普通生活之中的情感满足。如果你能想到一些最简单的方法，你就会明白所需物质资源简直可以忽略不计。如果你做到了这一点，当你的学生深刻理解了艺术所能赋予他们的一切——欢愉和畏惧——你就会知道先知、神父、政治家们将会更为有效地告知民众来自上帝的爱、责任的不可动摇、爱国热情的召唤。[1]

---

[1] 即由于在这个过程中的情感升华，人们将会更为深刻地感受到上帝之爱、责任之重、爱国之情，而这正是先知、神父、政治家们孜孜以求的教化目的。——译者注

莎士比亚创作戏剧的时候,英国人正生活在美丽的乡村,欧洲的历史从黑暗的中世纪刚刚迈入了多姿多彩的文艺复兴时期。跨越大西洋,新大陆与旧世界遥遥相望,开启了富于浪漫精神的历史发展新篇章。而如今我们面对的是居住在拥挤的城市中、生活在科学时代的英国人。我坚信一点,如果不能用新的方法迎接新的时代,不能用时代的精神教育人们,理想就会破灭,灾难就会发生,俄国的失败命运就会在英国重演。历史学家就会在英国的墓碑上刻下这样的墓志铭:她亡于她的统治阶层的思想盲目,亡于苍白的物质主义,亡于自以为是的零碎治国教条。

第四章　技术教育及其与科学和文学的关系

本次演讲的主题是技术教育。在此次演讲中，我想分析一下技术教育的核心要素，探讨一下技术教育和人文教育[1]的关系。这种探讨可帮助大家认识我们国家的技术培训体系，理解其成功运行所需的基本条件。另外，技术教育也是数学教师们特别关注的一个热点问题，因为大多数技术教育课程都包括数学科目。

在正式展开这个讨论之前，我们应该好好想想在技术教育中需要达到什么样的最佳目标。不管这个目标是高还是低，我们都必须予以明确。如果不对我们在这个工作中要实现的目标进行明确，那么我们的思考就有可能是不切实际的。

现在的人们似乎羞于谈理想。在此我们可以引用一位现代剧作家的作品[2]来谈谈这个话题，即我们的理想生活到底是什么样的。这位剧作家借一个疯狂的神父之口道出了我们应有的理想："我梦想一个理想的国度，国家即教会，教会即人民，三位一体，一体三位；我梦想

---

[1] 人文教育或文科教育（liberal education），指的是与理工科相对应的教育。——译者注

[2] 英国剧作家萧伯纳（George Bernard Shaw，1856—1950）的作品《英国佬的另一个岛》（*John Bull's Other Island*）。萧伯纳擅长幽默与讽刺，1925年获诺贝尔文学奖，同时他还是一个积极的社会活动家和费边社会主义宣传者。——译者注

一个理想的行业，工作即娱乐，娱乐即生活，三位一体，一体三位；我梦想一个理想的教堂，神父即信徒，信徒即上帝，三位一体，一体三位；我梦想一个理想的神性，生命即人性，人性即神圣，三位一体，一体三位。我所有的这些梦想，终究不过是一个疯子的梦想。"

在本次演讲中，我想着重阐释的一个思想就是其中的一句话："一个理想的行业，工作即娱乐，娱乐即生活。"这种三位一体的思想就是我们的技术教育的理想，当然这种理想听起来似乎怪诞不经。因为在我们的现实生活中，雇佣工人们劳作不止、愤懑不平、麻木不仁。我在这里并不是要做出一个详细的社会学分析，而是想告诉大家我们的现实距离我们的理想还有多远的路要走。其实我们都知道，假如有哪个雇主敢于实践"工作即娱乐"的原则，那么他的工厂肯定会在一个星期之内关门大吉。

不管是在文学故事中还是在现实生活中，我们都会看到一个无法逾越的规律[1]。这个规律告诉我们：只有辛苦劳动，人类才能繁衍生息。从理性和道德的角度来看，这个规律应该还有尚需完善的地方。比如说，早期本笃教派[2]的僧侣们是乐于劳作的，因为他们相信自己在劳作中与上帝同在。

先不考虑这个历史典故的宗教色彩，其中的基本思想是很有说服力的。人们的劳动应该与人们的心智和精神紧密结合，在相互渗透中共同发展。这样一来，劳动就成了一种快乐，不再是一种折磨。如果我们每个人都是这样的，在自己的具体工作中，按照自己的意愿把劳动的折磨变成劳动的快乐，将是怎样的一种情形？！这将彻底改变我们

---

[1] 原文是"curse"，直译为"诅咒"，即无可逃避的命运。——译者注
[2] 本笃教派（Benedictine），天主教的一个隐修会，又译为"本尼狄克派"，由意大利人本尼狄克于529年创立。本笃会遵循中世纪初流行于意大利和高卢的隐修活动，其隐修院的象征是十字架及耕地的犁。本笃会把一天的工作分为祈祷、读书和工作，三者并重，相互有关。——译者注

第四章　技术教育及其与科学和文学的关系

人类存在的基本规律，其中的方式可能迥异，但是只要我们在具体的工作中实现了其中的要义即可。从劳动的折磨变为劳动的快乐，不管是以什么样的方式，终将成为我们劳苦大众得以救赎的唯一希望。这个希望就掌控在从事技术教育的教师的手里，也掌控在那些掌控技术教育教师的教育活动的人的手里。这个希望能否实现事关重大，因为这将关系到我们能否重塑国民精神，能否让人们像早期本笃教的僧侣们一样在快乐中劳动。

现在我们的国家需要大量的熟练技工，也需要大量的富有创造精神的人才，更需要大量的思想上能够与时俱进的雇主。

要满足我们国家的这些现实需要，有且仅有一个办法。这个办法很简单，就是要让我们的工人、科技人员和雇主都在快乐中劳动，让他们享受自己的劳动。这个假设是基于人性的一般规律而言，我们仅凭常识就可以理解。比如说，无论一个技工的技艺是多么娴熟，如果他精神萎靡、身体疲倦，他有可能生产出大量高质量的产品吗？他的生产将会非常低效，他会经常敷衍了事，他会精于躲避监管，他会抵触新的方法，他会不断口出怨言。这样的工人会无视生产中的各种条件限制，因而会产生不切实际的所谓革命的天真想法。假如我们在技术教育中因循守旧、墨守成规，假如我们忘掉了本笃教的"劳动即快乐"的宗旨，那么我们很可能会在困难时期遭遇工人暴动，我们的社会终将得到应有的报应。

其次，有创造天赋的人才进行发明创造活动也需要快乐的精神状态。"需求是发明创造之母"[1]，我认为这句话并不准确，甚至是愚蠢的。严格地说，"需求是奇技淫巧之母"[2]，我认为这才是基本的事实。当代发明创造增多的基础是科学，科学的发展源于人们的好奇和探索，而

---

[1] 对应原文是"Necessity is the mother of invention"。——译者注
[2] 对应原文是"Necessity is the mother of futile dodges"。——译者注

这种智力上的活动必然要基于快乐的精神状态。

第三种人是雇主，他们也应该具有开拓创新的精神。我们会注意到，这些成功的雇主是我们社会中的重要人物，在全球各地建立了商业网络，经济上已经富甲一方。毫无疑问，商业总会有起落兴衰，如果各行各业的经济普遍不景气，就不可能有国家的繁荣可言。假如这些雇主只是把他们的经营完全当作发达的手段，以此猎取其他社会生活机会，他们就会丧失企业家应有的开拓意识。他们已经足够富裕了，在生意上赚的钱足以让他们颐养天年。如此一来，他们就不可能冒险去尝试新的方法，其灵魂就远离了生活的本真。对金钱的一味追求只会造成经营上的僵化保守，只会消弭应有的开拓创新。如果一个企业家在经营的过程中能感受到快乐，能享受开拓创新，那才是我们所希望看到的。如果一个企业家即便是在创建医院的过程中也体会不到快乐，只剩下生意上的烦恼，这就不是我们所希望看到的。

最后，假如雇主和技工在生产经营中的目的只有一个，即为了榨取利润从而获得财富，那么他们的生产经营肯定不会长久下去。生产经营不应只是为了赚取钱财利润、获得财富，而更应该服务于人们的福祉。只有从更为广阔的视野来看待生产和经营，劳资双方才有可能达成共识，从而达到和谐。

从以上的分析可以看出，无论是对技工而言还是对雇主而言，无论是就职业教育而言还是就科技教育而言，我们国家所真正需要的是一种自由的精神、一种思想的启蒙。这关乎我们如何理论联系实际，如何高效生产经营。从这个意义上说，在技术教育中教授学生学习几何和学习诗歌都是非常重要的，其意义不亚于教授学生如何操作车床。

大致来讲，柏拉图[1]的思想可以代表现代人文教育的精神，而

---

[1] 柏拉图（Plato，公元前428或427—公元前348或347），古希腊哲学家，与苏格拉底和亚里士多德共同奠定了西方文化的哲学基础。——译者注

圣·本尼狄克[1]的思想可以代表技术教育的精神。我们在此无意于对柏拉图和圣·本尼狄克的思想做出具体而详细的阐释，而是把这两位作为象征和代表，以此来分析两种看似对立的教育思想。就柏拉图的教育思想而言，我们所谈论的是其在当今时代产生的影响。

人文教育的本质就是对思维的发展和对审美的培育。人文教育着重于哲学思想、文学艺术的传授，最终落实于理论在实践中的运用。这其实是一种贵族式教育，要求有足够的闲暇时间来予以进行。这种柏拉图式的教育理想对欧洲文明的发展做出了不可磨灭的贡献：促进了艺术的发展，培养了作为科学之源的中立客观的求知精神，保持了精神自由在物质条件面前的尊严。柏拉图没有和其他的奴隶一起辛苦劳作，这一点与圣·本尼狄克不同，但是柏拉图同样属于人类的解放者之列。柏拉图的思想启发了欧洲思想开明的贵族，欧洲就是从思想开明的贵族那里继承了自由的精神，直至今天。几百年来，从教皇尼古拉五世[2]到耶稣会[3]学校，从耶稣会士[4]到当代英国公学的校长，他们的所作所为都深深地根基于柏拉图的教育理念。

对某些人来说，人文教育就是最好的教育，因为这种教育或许适合于他们的思想特征和生活环境。但是，人文教育的意义远非如此，其实所有的教育都可以以此为参照，按照达到人文教育的程度这一标准来判断该教育的好坏优劣。

---

[1] 圣·本尼狄克（St. Benedict，480—547），前文所讲到的本笃会的创始人。——译者注

[2] 教皇尼古拉五世（Pope Nicholas V，1397—1455），文艺复兴时期第一位教皇，兴建梵蒂冈图书馆，弘扬古希腊和古罗马的古典文化。——译者注

[3] 耶稣会，天主教的主要修会之一，1534年由罗耀拉（Ignatius of Loyola，1491—1556）创立，从事教育工作和非天主教地区的传教工作。中国耶稣会的开创者是意大利人利玛窦，于明朝万历年间进入中国，传播西方科学技术和人文科学。——译者注

[4] 耶稣会士（the Jesuit），天主教修道会耶稣会成员。——译者注

人文教育的要义在于传授数量庞大的、各种各样的、最有代表性的知识。如果以这样的方式来进行教育，一个人会学习到人类历史上最优秀的文化成果。最终，他将学会几种主要的语言，会理解世界历史的兴衰，会领会传情达意的诗歌，会通读若干传世佳作。特别是将会掌握几种主要的哲学流派，精读一些风格鲜明的哲学著作。

　　很显然，如果要完成这个学习任务，可能要耗尽一个人一生的时间，需要专心致志、皓首穷经地去学习这么多的内容。在这里会不由得让人想起卢奇安戏剧里面的一个典故：假如一个人想要去践行当下的某种伦理道德制度，那么他首先要花150年的时间去验证该制度的合理性。

　　当然，这样宏伟的理想并不适合于人们的实际教育。开展人文教育并不是要统统掌握人类的所有文明成果，从亚洲到欧洲，从欧洲到美洲，事无巨细，无一疏漏。人文教育所要关注的是人类文明成果中很小的一部分，当然也是最优秀的一部分。假如在人文教育中出现了希腊的色诺芬而遗漏了中国的孔子，我会认为这是不恰当的。[1] 而不管是色诺芬还是孔子，我其实都没有阅读过他们的原著。也就是说，看似体系庞大的人文教育其实并没有那么复杂，只需要学习由几种重要语言所记载的个别文献即可。

　　人类思想文化的表达并不仅仅局限于文学的形式，此外还有艺术的形式、科学的形式。同时，人文教育的过程也不仅仅局限于已有思想文化的被动接受，还应该强化其中的原创性。另外，原创性也不是单一维度的，可以细分为思考的原创性、行动的原创性、艺术想象的原创性，这三种原创性还可以再分为更细的分支。

　　学问的领域是如此宽广，而一个人一生的时光是如此短暂，转瞬

---

[1] 色诺芬（Xenophon，公元前431?—公元前355?），古希腊历史学家和作家。他是苏格拉底的弟子，其著作成为研究古希腊社会的必读文献。——译者注

即逝，一生的生活也是如此琐碎，难以专注。[1] 从这个意义上说，不管你是一个古典文化学者还是一个科学家，抑或是一个中小学校长，其实都是无知之人。

现在有一种奇怪的错觉，以为人们对某种文化的内容了解得越少，这种文化体系好像就越完美无缺。当然，这种错觉只会导致人们认识不到自己的无知。假如不读莎士比亚的戏剧，不学牛顿的定律，不懂达尔文的理论，那么即便掌握了柏拉图的哲学思想也没有什么意义。现在的人文教育没有像以前一样那么糟糕，原因就在于人们发现了这种似是而非的观点可能带来的危害，因而在教育中有所转变。

在我看来，没有什么大的学问或者小的理论能达到理想中的完美无缺境地。比如说柏拉图的文化发展理论中强调了认知的客观中立[2]，这就是一个心理学上的错误。我们的行为和我们在事物发展过程中所起的作用之间存在着因果联系，这是一个根本性的问题。而假如我们在教育中把智力活动或者审美活动与事物的发展脱离开来，回避这么一个根本性的问题，结果就有可能走向文明的衰退。从本质上讲，所有文化都是为了行动的文化，文化的意义就在于帮助人们摆脱劳动中的盲目折磨。很明显，艺术的存在就不是客观中立的，因为艺术可以让我们感受到这个世界的美妙，可以丰富我们的内在心灵世界。

所谓客观中立的科学精神其实是一种科学热情，这种热情期盼在复杂关联的事物之间寻找到一个井然有序的理论构架。这种科学热情的根本目的是为了让思想与行动结合起来，这就形成了具体行动在思想体系中的某种干预，而这一点在抽象科学理论研究中常常被忽略。

---

[1] 类似于《庄子》中所说："吾生也有涯，而知也无涯。以有涯随无涯，殆已！"——译者注

[2] "客观中立"的对应原文是"disinterested"，可以理解为"无利益驱动的"或是"大公无私的"。——译者注

没有哪个科学家在科学研究中只是为了认识而认识，科学家在认识的同时也满足了自己的科学探索热情。一个科学家并不是为了认识而去探索，而是为了探索而去认识[1]。在艺术创作的苦苦思索之中，或者在科学研究的孜孜以求之中，快乐来自既定目的的成功实现，由此而带来精神上的愉悦和享受，这就是艺术家或者科学家的快乐源泉。

把技术教育和人文教育对立起来看待是错误的。缺失了人文教育，技术教育就不可能完整；离开了技术教育，人文教育也不可能达成。也就是说，凡是教育就需要从这两个方面着手，既要传授技术，又要提升素养。简单地说，教育要培养一个学生并使其既懂得一些知识，又会做一些事情。知行合一，理论与实践之间的紧密结合将会有益于两个方向的同时发展。智慧不可能凭空产生，头脑里的创造性想法需要尽快付诸实践，这对于一个青少年来说尤应如此。如果在学习几何和力学的时候，能辅以工厂车间的具体实践，那么将会大有裨益。而如果没有这些理论与实践的结合，数学教育就只能是纸上谈兵了。

从宏观来看，一个国家的教育体系应该有三个基本的成分，即语文课程、科学课程和技术课程，而每一种课程都应该包含另外的两种课程。我想说的是，每一种教育形式都应传递给学生一种技能、一种理论、一种常识、一种审美，而诸多要素之间是相互依托、共生共长的。由于教育过程中时间上的限制，即便是最聪颖的学生也难以完全掌握每一门课程，所以在教育中就要有所侧重。例如，技术课程中的美育可以着重于某种工艺的训练或者某些工艺品的制作。但是，在语文课程和科学课程中，美育自始至终都是不可或缺的。

语文课程的教育方法在于语言的学习，学习我们相互传递思想的习惯表达方式。在语文课程的学习过程中，就技术层面而言，需要掌

---

[1] 对应原文是"He does not discover in order to know, he knows in order to discover"。——译者注

握的是语言表达技能；就科学层面而言，需要研究的是语言的结构或者语言与思想表达之间的关系。在语言使用的过程中，语言和情感之间的微妙关系，或是书面语言和口头语言所诉诸的感官的每一反应，都可以引向审美的教学目标。当然，语言课程中还需要我们学习的重要一点就是有代表性的文学著作，因为其中蕴含了太多的人生智慧。

语文课程的一个特点就是同质性，其中包含的各个要素之间是相互协调、互为补充的。语文课程一旦大体上建立起来，就几乎能够达到较为完善的程度，这在学校教育的各种课程之中是唯一的一种现象。语文课程中也普遍存在着一个缺陷，即在课程体系中过多地强调了语言本身的重要性。诚然，语言表达在我们的生活中是如此重要，语言使用在我们的生活中所起到的作用难以估量。但是，最近几十年来我们也看到了一个现象，即在我们的思想文化体系中，文学或者语言文字的作用正在慢慢衰减。如果我们人类想要真正作为大自然的服务者或者管理者，就不能只具备语言文字的能力，还需要掌握其他方面的技艺。

科学课程的本质在于训练学生掌握观察自然现象的方式方法，然后去认识自然规律，并且去推理自然规律。在科学课程中也会遇到前面所讲到的人文教育的一个问题，即时间的限制。与此相对，我们需要观察的自然现象不计其数，每一种自然现象背后都有其相应的观察方式、研究方法和科学理论。所以，我们不可能在科学课程的学习中面面俱到，只需要学习其中两三门有代表性的密切关联的科学。从这个意义上说，那些指责科学教育的片面和狭隘的言论也是有一定道理的。这样的指责的确是能够自洽的，因为现实中的科学教育的确很难做到全面和完善。反过来说，我们也要认真思考，如何才能在科学课程的种种局限之下发挥其内在的优势，从而避免走向片面和狭隘的危险。

针对科学课程的局限和优势，我们就自然地进入下一个话题，即技术教育。技术教育的本质在于训练学生把所学知识运用到物质产品的生产制造上。技术教育注重动手能力、手眼协调、随机判断,而生产制造过程中的判断能力来自知识的自由运用。因此,在技术教育中就需要一定的科学知识教育。在一个教育体系中,如果把科学教育局限到最小的范围,那就是要培养科学领域的专家人才;如果把科学教育延伸到最大的范围,那就是要培养具有一定科学素养的技术工人,当然同样重要的是,还要培养具有一定科学素养的企业主管或者经理。

技术教育需要与科学教育进行一定的结合,以达到理论知识的验证和应用。除此之外,技术教育还可以和美育相结合。比如说,在培养一个艺术人才或者一个工艺人才的时候,审美活动就要贯穿其中的整个过程。

柏拉图式的人文教育传统有一个重大缺陷,即完全忽略了技术教育的一面,而技术教育是理想人格得以全面发展的一个重要成分。柏拉图式的人文教育传统中的这个缺陷有其背后的根本原因,即自身体系中存在的两个错误的对立:心智和身体之间的对立,思想和行动之间的对立。为了避免误解,我在此需要澄清一点,古希腊人其实是非常注重人的形体之美和体育运动的。但是我们也可以看出,他们像柏拉图一样对哲学思想有着近乎狂热的追求,这可能是奴隶制度的一个必然结果[1]。

因此我始终信奉一条教育原理,如果我们在教育中把心智和身体分离,把思想和行动分离,忘记了学生有血有肉的躯体,那么我们的教育注定是要失败的。然而,后文艺复兴时代以来柏拉图式的教育模式却恰恰体现了这样的错误分离。凡是问题,总能找到解决问题的一

---

[1] 对应原文是"the nemesis of slave-owning"。"nemesis"的意思是报应、惩罚、不可逃避的惩罚、公正的惩罚。Nemesis 是古希腊神话故事中的复仇女神涅墨西斯。怀特海以此典故隐喻奴隶制度的束缚反而引向了思想自由的追求。——译者注

些办法，英国教育体制中的这个现实问题也不例外。英国的教育体制在分离了心智和身体、思想和行动之后，转而走向了体育竞技，意欲在运动中达到身心合一，从而弥补传统教育的这一缺失。

心智活动和身体活动之间的联系分布于各个感官之中，但主要集中于眼、耳、口、手。在感官和思想之间存在着相互的协调，在抽象思维活动和物质生产活动之间存在着相互的影响。在心智活动与身体活动之间的关联中，手的作用特别重要。究竟是手的活动决定了大脑的活动，还是大脑的活动决定了手的活动，迄今为止还是一个悬而未决的问题。不管怎么说，两者之间都是紧密相连、互为因果的。在过去的几百年里，有个别家族由于众所周知的特殊原因而停止了身体力行的劳动，但这并不是说心智活动和身体活动之间的关系就不存在了。

这么几个贵族由于停止了手工劳动，所以就导致了其思想的怠惰。作为一个补救措施，他们投入到了体育锻炼之中。但是一般情况下，体育运动中的思维活动不够丰富完整，体育运动中的感官活动也不够精细微妙。对于一些专业人员来说，他们需要经常动手写、开口讲，这样的活动其实也给了他们的思维活动一定的外部刺激。而对于某些读者来说，不管他们的知识多么渊博，如果他们只是被动地阅读，那么他们就不可能在专业领域出类拔萃。这样的读者往往思想保守、耽于空想，一方面是因为他们善于吸收知识而弱于付诸行动，另一方面是因为他们缺乏动手写、开口讲的感官活动，于是缺少了相应的大脑刺激。

在评价技术教育的重要性时，我们还要排除一个错误的想法，即学习就等于书本学习。从直接经验获得的一手知识才是心智发展的根本基础。但是从书本上获得的知识大部分都是间接的二手知识，远不能与从直接经验获得的一手知识相提并论。技术教育的目的就是要把生活中具体的、鲜活的事件看作一般的、抽象的知识的一个个案例。从书本上得来的知识往往是东拼西凑的二手信息，而这些二手信息其实也是源于另外一个地方的二手信息。因此，当今学术界的二手信息的本质就决定了其平庸无奇的结果。当今学术界难以有所作为，就在于其不敢直面现实的考验。弗朗西斯·培根[1]之所以伟大，并不在于他提出了科学归纳法，而在于他勇于对抗二手信息的束缚，因此成为一个学术领袖。

如果要发挥科学教育的优势，那就要根基于直接观察的实践经验。如果要发挥技术教育的优势，那就要根基于我们心智的瞬间火花，把大脑思维转化为手工操作，再把手工操作转化为思想意识。

在科学研究中，我们所必需的是逻辑思维。我们通常把逻辑思维分为两种方式，即发现的逻辑和被发现的逻辑[2]。

在发现的逻辑思维方式中，我们要权衡事物发生的概率，要剔除不相关的细节，要预设事物遵循的规律，要验证假设的成功与否。这样的思维方式也就是我们平时所说的归纳逻辑。

在被发现的逻辑思维方式中，我们通过演绎的方法来验证具体的事物，看该事物是否会遵循既定的自然规律。所以我们一旦发现了或者预设了某个自然规律，这个自然规律的具体应用就取决于演绎逻辑。如果没有演绎逻辑，科学也就毫无价值。科学就会成为无意义的游戏，从具体到一般，然后再反过来从一般到具体，犹如天使上下攀爬雅各的梯子[3]。当牛顿假设了万有引力定律之后，他立即开始计算地球对苹果的引力、地球对月球的引力。在此我们也要注意到，如果没有演绎

---

[1] 弗朗西斯·培根（Francis Bacon，1561—1626），英国文艺复兴时期的哲学家和作家，提出了唯物主义经验论的一系列原则，制定了系统的归纳逻辑。著有《新工具》（*Novum Organum*）、《学术的进步》（*The Advancement and Proficience of Learning Divine and Human*）、《亨利七世本纪》（*History of the Reign of King Henry VII*）等。——译者注

[2] 对应原文是"the logic of discovery and the logic of the discovered"。——译者注

[3] 雅各的梯子（Jacob's ladder），典出《圣经·旧约》中的"创世纪"，雅各梦中所见通往天堂的梯子。——译者注

逻辑，那么归纳逻辑也就不能成立。因此，牛顿所做的计算其实是对万有引力定律的一个归纳验证。

由此看来，数学其实就是演绎推理逻辑中较为复杂的部分，尤其是涉及数、量和空间的时候。

在科学教育中需要传授思维的艺术，例如，如何形成清晰的概念并付诸直接经验，如何有效地假设命题，如何验证所做假设，如何应用一般原理去解决特殊问题。另外，也需要培养科学阐释的能力，以从纷乱的观点中梳理出相关的问题，从而找出重点，分清主次。

如果一门科学课程或者几门科学课程是以这种恰当的方式实施的，特别重视思维的艺术，那么我们就可以克服科学教育中的所谓片面或者狭隘现象了。通常情况下，科学教育是基于一两门科学课程。假如这一两门科学课程的教师为了应付考试的要求，一味地向学生灌输这一两门科学课程的内容，那么这样的科学教育就真的是糟糕透顶了。在科学教育中，我们需要认识科学方法的普适性，并且把一般的原理应用到具体的问题中。如果一个人只懂得自己领域内的常规科学知识，故步自封，坐井观天，那么他其实并不真正懂得科学的要义。他的思想不够丰富，他的心智不够敏锐，捕捉不到来自其他学科的智慧光芒。他将一无所获，在面对实际问题的时候会茫然无措。

然而，在科学教育上把一般的原理应用到具体的问题中，这的确不是一件容易的事情，特别是针对低龄学生而言。古往今来，教育的艺术并非易事。如果要克服科学教育上的这个困难，特别是在教育的初级阶段，的确需要非凡的教育智慧。在一定程度上说，这样的教育活动也是对我们灵魂的锤炼。

在科学教育的过程中，如果数学能够教授得法，就能作为一种最为强大的工具来逐渐渗透一般原理。数学的精髓就在于不断地去伪存真，保留普适的、一般的知识和方法，舍去具体的、特殊的知识和方法。

比如说，我们可以用一个公式来解决一种特殊的问题，而其实这个公式可以用来解决上百个类似的、源于不同科学领域的问题。总而言之，普适的、一般的科学演绎是最有价值的一种推理，因为这是抽象思维的固有属性。

在此我们必须注意，事物都有两面性，对数学课程而言也是如此。假如我们仅仅就是为了传授一般的知识和方法，那么我们也会毁了数学课程。学习一般的原理是为了解决具体的问题，因为从根本上说我们所面对的就是这些具体的、特殊的个案。从这个意义上说，我们在运用数学来解决问题的时候，结果越具体越好，而采用的方法则是越一般越好。科学推理的本质其实就是把特殊概括为一般，然后再把一般具体到特殊。缺失了一般，就无所谓科学推理；而脱离了具体，任何科学也就失去了其应有的意义。

技术教育的优势就在于其具体性。在此请大家注意，一个缺乏高度概括性的一般原理并不等于一个具体的事实。例如，数学公式 $x+y=y+x$ 就比 $2+2=4$ 更具有概括性，但是"二加二等于四"也是一个高度概括的一般命题，也不存在任何具体的事实成分。而如果要获得具体的命题，就必须对涉及客体对象的原理有直觉的认识。例如，如果你对苹果有直接的感知或是直觉的印象，那么"这两个苹果和那两个苹果加起来就是四个苹果"就是一个具体的命题。

只有在技术教育中才能把科学领域的一般原理转化到具体应用中，从而避免所学知识停留在字面上。在一个人的心智发展过程中，仅仅做出消极的观察是远远不够的。只有动手去创造，并且通过所创造之物才能获得生动而深刻的认识。如果想要有所理解，那就必躬必亲，这是一条牢不可破的定律。只有在具体的实践中，也只有在现实的拘囿中，我们的潜能才会得以发挥，我们的思维才会跃然欲动，我们的知识才会有所增益。

实际上在小学教育中，我们一直以来都非常强调动手能力的培养。小学生在学校教育中要动手去剪裁、去分拣，通过这样简单的活动就可以去认识不同的形状和颜色。这也是一种实践活动，但不是我所想要深入分析的。在对小学生的这种教育方式中，实践先于思考，活动先于认知。这对小学生来说是很好的学习方式，但是我们所谈论的技术教育远不止如此。技术教育中的实践活动具有创造性，能够把头脑中的想法转化为眼前的现实，引向思维和行动的协调，达到思想意识、假设预见和最终结果之间的一致。也就是说，在技术教育中学生不但要知道理论有何用，而且要懂得理论在何处无用。

我们不能把技术教育看作柏拉图式人文教育的牵强补充，也不能把技术教育看作为了生活所迫而不得不学习的谋生手段。任何一个人穷其一生所能学习的知识、所能发展的能力都是极其有限的，不管是在人文教育中还是在技术教育中都是如此。那么在教育过程中，我们的心智和我们的性格如何发展才能真正成熟，如何平衡才能达成和谐呢？在我看来有三条道路可以遵循：语言文化、科学文化、技术文化。这三种素养的培育在一个人的教育过程中是缺一不可的，否则就会导致心智和性格在某些方面的严重缺失。但是，如果在教育过程中机械地灌输这三个方面的知识，学生就只能得到支离破碎的信息，相互之间缺乏有机联系，各个部分无法付诸应用。就语文课程而言，我们已经知道其中的一个优势就在于其课程体系内的协调一致。不管是语文课程、科学课程还是技术课程，每种课程在教育中都会有所侧重，同时也要融入另外两种课程的教育要素，这样才能达到和谐统一。

技术教育中的两个年龄段需要我们注意：一个是13岁，即小学毕业的年龄；另外一个是17岁，即校内技术教育结束的年龄。同时我们也需要注意到，如果是在一个初等技工学校培养一个技工人才，那么三年的学制就够了，但是，如果要培养一个航运人才或者一个管理人才，那么就要花费更长的时间。总的来说，我们在技术教育中要恰当地运用教育理论，有效地实施课程，从而保证一个学生在17岁毕业的时候能够学有所成，以其技艺服务于社会大众。

在技术教育中，学生的手工训练应开始于13岁，并且要保持手工训练和其他课业一定的比例，最终在技术教育的进程中达到比例的最大化。也就是说，在技术教育中不能过多地侧重于手工训练。针对某一特定行业的手工训练，如果能在车间内完成加工工艺和操作流程，那就直接在车间内进行教学。这样的实地训练不会占用学校课程的太多时间，同时学生在车间内也能迅速学会相应的技能。如果追问教育为什么会失败，我们往往会发现其根源在于教育理念的僵化。这对技术教育来说依然如此，如果我们认为所谓技术教育就是向年轻学生传授一种手工技艺，技术教育也是注定要失败的。我们国家需要劳动力的一定流动性，但是这种流动性不是说从一个地方到另外一个地方的流动性，而是说基于劳动力的综合素质，从一种工作切换到另外一种工作。我这样说可能会引起大家的误解，我并不是说在实际工作中一个工人必须不断地更换工种。具体怎么更换工种不是我们这些教育工作者所要关心的事情，而是他们工会组织的事情。我想要说的是，技术教育中的所有训练不应过于专门化，而应有所融合以培养较为综合的劳动技能，以适应复杂多变的现实需要，这样一来对工人、对雇主、对国家都是有益无害的。

基于以上考虑，技术教育的课程体系应该综合设置。与手工训练有密切联系的若干科学课程都要设置进去，不应单单设置某一门科学课程。即便与手工训练有直接联系的科学课程较少，也不能以狭隘片面的思维方式来实施课程。假如要划分技术教育的类型，我们可以大致根据每一种技术教育所主要关联的科学门类来进行。由此我们会发现六种类型的技术教育：(1) 几何技术型；(2) 机械技术型；(3) 物理技术型；(4) 化学技术型；(5) 生物技术型；(6) 商务和社会服务型。

这六种类型的技术教育分别需要特定的科学理论作为支撑，也需要其他门类的科学理论作为辅助，但也说明某一特定科学理论可以同时指导不同类型的技术教育。比如说，几何学可以指导木工工艺、五金工艺或者其他手工艺的技术教育，生物学可以指导农业技术教育。再比如说，烹饪、餐饮这一类的技艺需要生物学、物理学、化学这样的理论知识，不过坦白地说我对此也不甚明了。

对于商务和社会服务类型的技术教育来说，一方面需要数理、统计方面的专业知识，另一方面需要历史、地理方面的专业知识。商务和社会服务类型的技术教育所牵涉的学科知识较多，而且学科之间也有较大隔阂。但是不管怎么说，我们需要根据相关的科学知识理论来对技术教育进行分门别类。同时我们也要注意，在一定程度上一些核心科学课程能够指导几乎所有类型的技术教育。其实，我们国家的技术教育体系对于这些复杂关系都是比较清楚的，很多技术学院和初等技工学校在其教育实践中都很好地遵循了这些基本道理。

技术教育的理论支撑除了科学知识之外还有人文知识，而且科学知识和人文知识之间往往是相互关联的。例如，历史、地理这样的人文知识在技术教育中是非常必要的，但是我们要用科学的态度来确保我们所需要的历史、地理知识准确无误。再例如，如果我们要讲授科学定理或者训练科学思维，就需要一定的人文知识，因为我们需要以恰当的历史观来阐述相应科学知识的人文背景。也就是说，科学知识的价值取决于其在教育过程中对学生的智力发展所产生的影响，不要动辄以科学的名义夸大其词，而要从更为广阔的视野予以思考。

令人遗憾的是，技术教育中的语言文化素养没有得到足够的重视，只是强调了一定的语法学习。其中有一个历史原因：现在的柏拉图式人文教育其实是以拉丁语和希腊语为语言基础，然后才得以汲取古典文献的营养。但是我们再来思考这个问题，就会发现研习古典文献和学习语法之间并没有必然的联系。古希腊文化的伟大时代早已远去，然后才出现了那些亚历山大[1]的语法学家。当今世界的古典文化学者更是要跨越时间的漫漫长河，才能回到伯利克里时代[2]去聆听古希腊先哲的教诲。

当然，我们绝不能仅仅满足于让学生懂得一点语言文化知识。学生学习什么样的语言文化知识并不重要，重要的是如何学习。例如，文学可以展示我们的想象世界，可以构筑我们的内心王国。那么照此看来，在技术教育中教授文学就是为了让学生通过文学获得情感的快乐。教授什么样的文学并不重要，重要的是学生会产生什么样的愉悦感。可是在某些著名的英国大学的直接指导下，学生读了莎士比亚戏剧就要考试莎士比亚戏剧，学生从文学中获得的快乐体验被无情地剥夺，那些大学应该被控告谋杀了学生的灵魂。

精神上的快乐有两种，一种是创造的快乐，另一种是放松的快乐，两者之间并不是互不相干的。假如一个人换了一种工作，那么有可能会同时带来这两种精神上的最大愉悦。文学欣赏其实也是一种创造过程，遣词造句、节奏韵律、言内言外这些因素都是外在的刺激，内在的反应就是我们头脑中产生的意境想象。只有通过我们自己的文学感受才能让我们自己的现实生活灵动起来，除此无他。另外，除了职业文学创作者之外，文学还能给其他人带来身心放松的快乐，这样也就减轻了平时工作中的紧张压抑之感。艺术和文学一样，都可以给人带来这两个方面的精神享受。

---

[1] 亚历山大（Alexandria），埃及北部港口城市，曾是马其顿帝国埃及行省的总督所在地，后成为埃及王国的首都。在西方古代史中规模宏大，仅次于罗马，为古代世界文化中心之一。——译者注

[2] 伯利克里时代（the Periclean times），古希腊的一个历史时期，由雅典政治家伯利克里（Pericles，公元前495?—公元前429）统治，是希腊古典文化高度繁荣的时代，此时的雅典成为希腊的文化和政治中心。——译者注

如要获得放松的快乐，并无须额外的帮助，只要停止工作即可。身心放松是很重要的，甚至可以说是健康的一个必要条件。如果缺乏身心的彻底放松，那么给健康带来的危害也是显而易见的。人们保持健康的一种方式就是身心的放松，而身心放松最主要的形式就是深度睡眠。创造的快乐源于付出劳动而获得回报，这就需要经过一定的努力，因而这种情感体验对于高节奏的工作或者创新性的工作都是必不可少的。

如果一味地加紧生产，而工人在生产过程中得不到足够的休息，那么这样的经济管理方式是十分有害的。这样的企业可能会有暂时的经济繁荣，但是对于整个国家来说危害无穷。这些工人会因为身心受损而失业，那么国家就不得不保障他们以后的生活。另外，如果在生产过程中让工人高强度地劳动，然后再让工人长时间地放假休息，这也是一种不良的管理方式。如果不加以严格控制，这样长时间的放假休闲也有可能会造成工人的懈怠情绪。正常情况下，休闲和劳作应该交替进行，这样才真正符合人的内心需要。游戏就是一种休闲方式，因为游戏可以从工作中脱离开来。但是如果过度沉湎于游戏，也会让我们感到精神空虚。

从这个意义上说，文学和艺术在整个国家的有序组织中起着重要的作用。特别是对于一个国家的经济生产来说更是如此，犹如睡眠或饮食对于一个人的肌体健康一样重要。当然，我在这里并不是要讨论如何去培养一个艺术家，而是讨论如何把文学、艺术应用到我们的生活中，使之服务于我们的健康生活。文学和艺术对于我们的生活来说，宛如灿烂的阳光普照大地万物。

文学和艺术能带给我们愉悦和效率，因此我们应该在快乐中学习，而不是在苛责中学习。一旦我们明白了这个道理，就会发现其实并不存在什么困难，也不需要太多花费就能给学生带来艺术上的享受。我们可以给附近的剧院一定的补贴，让学生定期到剧院去看一些适宜的戏剧。也可以用同样的方法鼓励学生去听音乐会或看电影。可能画展对于学生没有那么大的吸引力，但如果展出的是一些有代表性的风景画或者写意画，而且学生已经有了一定的了解，那么他们可能就会对画展感兴趣。不管怎么样，在艺术欣赏的过程中学生必须亲自去体验。另外，还要培养学生大声朗读的艺术，例如艾迪生[1]所著的关于柯弗利绅士的系列随笔散文就特别适合学生练习朗读。

文学和艺术不但给我们的生命活力带来了间接的影响，更是直接地赋予了我们生活中的洞察力。我们生活在一个可以触摸到的物质世界之中，也生活在一个可以感受到的精神世界之中。在精神的世界里，我们的思想意识隐秘复杂，我们的情绪情感起伏波动。从文学和艺术中获得的洞察力是如此重要，可以帮助我们在现实世界中做出恰当的判断和控制。世界上各个民族之间的最终竞争不是在战场上，而是在工厂里。谁的工人训练有素、充满活力、教育得当，谁就会获得最后的胜利。而教育得当的其中一个基本条件，就是艺术的熏陶。

如果时间允许，我还想谈谈其他问题。例如，我建议在所有的教育体系中都增加一门外语。据我的直接观察，学习一门外语对于手工艺学生来说是行得通的。至于具体的教育原理，我已经在其他章节里讲得很清楚了。

最后，我要重温本笃教派的思想。本笃教派的僧侣们把知识、劳动和精神力量结合起来，为我们挽救了一个正在消失的古代文明模式。我们现在所面临的一个危险就是把现实世界看得太过黑暗，好像只有

---

[1] 艾迪生（Joseph Addison，1672—1719），英国散文家、诗人、剧作家和政治活动家。与斯梯尔（Richard Steele，1672—1729）先后创办杂志《闲谈者》（*Tatler*）与《旁观者》（*The Spectator*），产生了重大影响。《旁观者》杂志曾刊登关于柯弗利（Roger de Coverley）的一系列散文，提倡提高道德修养和倡导文学欣赏。——译者注

忘记理想才能取得成功。但是我相信这样的观念肯定是错误的，我们的现实实践会直接否定这种看法的。教育中的这个错误就在于我们没有理解技术教育的真正面貌。我们的祖先在历史的漫漫无边黑暗之中胸怀理想，众志成城，薪火相传。我们今天的任务不是因循守旧，而是大胆发挥我们的创造活力。

第五章　教育中的古典文化

古典文化[1]在我们国家的未来,并不取决于个别顶尖学者的孜孜以求,也不取决于众多专业人士的诲人不倦。几个世纪以来,古典文学教育和古典哲学教育给我们带来了心灵的愉悦,并且规训着人性的成长。而如今的古典文化却面临着一定的危险,这个危险并不是源于现在的古典文化学者不如前辈那样热爱古典文化。古典文化所面临的危险来自其他地方。在过去,古典文化在高等教育中独占鳌头,风光无限,因此学生在学校中往往专注于古典文化的研习。如果一定要找出一门能与古典文化相比肩的学问,那就只能是数学这门单独的学科。过去教育体系中的这个独特现象造成了一系列的后果。例如,在学校教育中需要大量的古典文化专家,以满足学生对古典文化的学习渴求;各个文化领域中弥漫着一种古典文化的腔调,好像不懂古典文化就显得没有学问;哪怕与未来的人生规划毫无关联,学生也要有意或者无意地去钻研古典文化。现如今所有这些现象都已远去,永远地消失在历史长河之中了。打个比方来说,童谣里唱到的矮胖子鸡

---

[1] 古典文化(classics 或者 classical studies),指的是有关古希腊和古罗马时期的文化研究,包括哲学、历史、语言、文学、法律、艺术等方面。英语单词"classics"的拉丁词源是"classicus",意思是"第一流的"或者"属于一流公民所有的"。
——译者注

蛋先生[1]在高高的墙头上得意扬扬，可一旦掉下来摔成碎片，谁也不能让他完好如初。在现在的教育中，还有其他许许多多的学科分支关涉到人们所关注的问题，相互之间存在着复杂的联系，并且在学科的发展过程中展现出人类智慧的杰出成就、想象的无限拓展、哲理的深入认知。现实生活中的各行各业也都是有学问的，每一个行业都需要一门或者几门学科作为相应的系列技术支撑。另外，人的一生倏忽而过，而一生之中适合于学习新知的时间更是短暂。因此，即便是所有的学生都适合学习古典文化，我们也不能先对他们进行系统的古典文化训练，然后再让他们学习其他的学科知识，这样的教育体系是完全行不通的。英国首相工作委员会中有一个"教育中的古典文化"特别委员会，我忝列其中。在这个委员会中的工作中，我听到了太多的牢骚，抱怨现在家长的教育动机是如何唯利是图、汲汲于功名。其实我觉得古人的教育动机未必淡然超脱，今人的教育动机也未必世俗不堪。在过去，通过学习古典文化才能追名逐利，因此大家都会去研习古典文化。而如今时过境迁，古典文化也就自然地被大家冷淡。亚里士多德曾经说过，学问之中自有丰厚利禄[2]。亚里士多德也是一个家长，也有孩子需要教育，他的这种教育动机不知道会不会让现在的公学校长感到讶异。以我有限的关于亚里士多德的知识来看，他的这种教育动机自有其道理。如果穿越时空，让亚里士多德和现在的公学校长就这个问题做一次辩论，那么胜者一方肯定是亚里士多德。其

---

[1] 矮胖子鸡蛋先生（Humpty Dumpty），也有直译为"汉普顿·邓普顿"，源自英语童谣：Humpty Dumpty sat on a wall, / Humpty Dumpty had a great fall. / All the King's horses, and all the King's men / Couldn't put Humpty together again.（矮胖子，坐墙头，栽了一个大跟斗。国王呀，骑兵啊，破镜难圆没办法。）这个童谣最早的时候是一个谜语，谜底就是"蛋"，Humpty Dumpty 比喻"又矮又胖的、傻乎乎的人"。——译者注

[2] 对应原文是"A good income is a desirable adjunct to an intellectual life"，类同于我国文化传统中的"书中自有黄金屋"。——译者注

实我一直以来都在思考一个问题，即古典文化在现今课程体系中的衰退到底有何意义。我得出的结论就是，在未来若干年如何进行古典文化教育，将取决于我国中学的做法；然后在未来一代人的时间内，各所公学将不得不效法，不管各所公学愿意与否。

关于古典文化教育，我们必须注意到一个事实，将来90%的学生在18岁毕业之后，将永远不会再读一本古典文化原著。而如果学生是在18岁之前更早地从学校毕业，那么将会有99%的学生不会再读什么古典文化作品。我曾经看过也曾经听过一些学者的动人叙述，诉说如何静静地阅读柏拉图或者维吉尔的作品，如何从这样的古典作品之中吸取伟大的精神力量。但是我们的这些年轻人似乎不可能再静下心来，读上一两本古典文化著作，从中获得有益的思想营养。在这种情况下，我们就必须为古典文化打一场保卫战，因为这关系到至少90%的学生。假如我们在教育过程中忽视了古典文化的重要作用，不再进行古典文化著作的研读，那么剩下的10%的学生也不会再与古典文化有什么接触了。进而言之，学校里面也不会再有古典文化的专业教师去传道授业了。这样看来，情况就不可谓不危急。

情况虽说危急，但是我们的专家学者依然对古典文化情有独钟，我们的工商领袖依然对古典文化重视有加，虽然工商界更侧重于教育品质与生产效率的关系。就教育中的古典文化这一话题，我曾经参加过多次公开的或私下的讨论。最近的一次讨论是在一所著名的大学内进行的，这次讨论虽然时间较短，但是收获颇丰。其中有三位理科教授极力鼓吹古典文化的重要性，他们认为古典文化应作为科学家们学习的基础学科。我之所以提到这件事情，是因为我本身也是一个科学家，我的个人经历就是典型的例证。

所有的教育中永远都存在着一个共同的问题，即时间的制约。《圣经》中的老寿星玛士撒拉[1]活了969岁，假如他在这么长的人生中没有学到足够渊博的知识，那一定是因为他自己不够用心或者他的老师不够尽责。而我们所面临的任务是在五年之内达到既定的教育目标，给中学生一定的古典文化教育。在这种情况下，我们进行古典文化教育的理由只有一个，即在限定的时间段内，在课业繁重的条件下，古典文化课程能够尽快地促进学生的思想成熟，尽可能地丰富学生的心智发展。就此而言，其他课程是很难做到的。

在古典文化教育中，我们首先要深入学习古典文化中的语言，然后才能学习古典文化体系中的逻辑学、哲学、历史，才能进行古典文化中的文学审美鉴赏。学习古典文化体系中的各种知识才是我们的根本目标，学习拉丁语和希腊语是达到这个目标的辅助手段。当目标达到以后，我们就可以丢掉这个语言工具，不再进行语言的研习。当然，如果有可能，学生还会继续学习拉丁语和希腊语，以更加深入地研究古典文化。但是在实际的教育情境中，我们往往会发现有不少聪颖的学生对于语言学习并无多大兴趣，他们仍然可以在某些领域学有所成。他们往往会钟情于别的事物，也许是一只蝴蝶，也许是一台蒸汽机，但就不是一句拉丁文。这种学生往往会有一点天分，善于观察活生生的现象，从而激发创造性的思考。对这些学生来说，抽象的语言表达形式往往难以把握，琐碎的字词和鲜活的生活难以建立直接联系。

但是总的来说，学习古典文化的必经途径就是对语言的分析。语言是所有学生掌握古典文化知识的一个最直接的工具，也是所有教师教授古典文化知识的一种最可行的方式。

对于古典文化教育这个问题，我会经常有所反思。例如：如果要

---

[1] 玛士撒拉（Methuselah），《圣经·旧约》（创世纪）中的犹太族长，活了969岁。怀特海以此指出时间的重要性，亦即教育的条件性。——译者注

让学生学习逻辑学，那么为什么不直接教授逻辑学？不用学习古典文化，而是直接学习逻辑学，不是更简单吗？在此我想起了不久前刚去世的奥多学校[1]校长桑德森[2]，他的离去是我们教育界的一个巨大损失。桑德森校长曾经这么说：学生通过"接触"[3]来学习新知。这句话道出了所有教育的根底，学生通过理解一个又一个具体的、特定的事件，然后逐渐形成抽象的、一般的概念。从这个意义上说，我们在教育中一定要避免向学生灌输与他们的体验无关的、干巴巴的教条。

理解了这个教育的基本原理之后，我们再来看到底如何有效地实施逻辑学的教育活动，帮助学生掌握思维的哲学分析活动。简单地说，我们该如何有效地让学生掌握逻辑学的基本思想和理论体系？一本逻辑学教材里面的条条框框与一个中学生的现实世界是没有任何直接联系的，逻辑学的内容适合于一个成年人的学习，比如说在大学教育阶段前后。学习逻辑学的时候，首先要剖析常见的英语句子的结构，这种语法分析活动在最开始的时候是极其枯燥无味的。另外，这样的语言分析往往是停留在英语语言的语言形式层面上，回避了语言的实质内容，例如字词的内在意义、思维的认知过程。但如果进而教授一门外语，那么情况就完全不同了。在学习一门外语的时候，自然就不会出现学习母语时的枯燥练习。这个时候，学生不会过多地关注语言的形式，而是会关注如何表达自己的意愿，如何理解别人的意图，

---

[1] 奥多学校（Oundle School），英国的一所全日制私立学校，位于英格兰的北安普敦郡，建于1556年。在英格兰的规模仅次于伊顿公学（Eton Public School）和米尔菲尔德公学（Millfield Public School）。——译者注

[2] 桑德森（Frederick William Sanderson，1857—1922），于1892年至1922年任奥多学校校长，建立实验室、天文台、图书馆、工厂车间和试验农场，增设自然学科科目的教学，对英国的中等教育的课程设置和教学方法都产生了重大影响。——译者注

[3] 这里所提出的"接触"（contact），强调了教育中的亲身体验，即做中学、用中学的基本教育理念。——译者注

如何领会书本上的意义。每一种语言之中都蕴含着一种独特的思维，那么让学生学习一门外语，就会引导他们去探索母语和外语之间存在的差异。一般来说，我们英国人可以尽早地让学生学习法语。如果条件允许，可以在家里请一位会说法语的女保姆来教孩子法语。如果没有这样的条件，可以等孩子到了大约12岁的时候在中学学习法语。建议在教授法语的时候采用直接法，让学生沉浸在法语的语言环境中，让学生直接用法语思考问题。在掌握法语的语言形式和相应意义的时候，不用经过英语的翻译过程。如果采用这种方式，一个智商平平的孩子也能学得很好，会很快地学会表达和理解简单的法语。学生在学习外语的过程中会有很大的收获，能体会到两种语言之间的不同之处，能掌握一种有用的工具以备将来之需。学生的语言意识得以发展，就能够深刻地感受到语言工具的结构特征。

当学生的语言意识有所发展，再进一步学习拉丁语就更能促进学生的思维进步。拉丁语的语言结构较为简单清晰，只要具备一定的语言意识，能对拉丁语的语言结构有所掌握，就能直观地理解其中的语言意义。拉丁语的这个特点在英语或者法语中是没有的。在语言交流的过程中，简单的、地道的英语往往会被翻译成蹩脚的法语，简单的、地道的法语也会被翻译成蹩脚的英语。对于一个正在学习法语的英国学生来说，他会很难察觉蹩脚的法语和地道的法语之间的细微差异，教师也很难向学生讲清楚其中的各种区分。其中的原因就是英语和法语之间的语言结构相似，都有现代语言的一些表述特征。再看英语和拉丁语之间的对比，就会发现这两者的语言结构差异较大，但也不是说大到让人无法逾越。

据一些中学校长亲自讲，拉丁语在中学其实是比较受学生欢迎的。就我的亲身经历来讲，我小时候也是很喜欢拉丁语的。在我看来，拉丁语之所以深受大家喜欢，是因为人们在学习拉丁语的过程中可以感受到思想的启蒙，可以从中发现什么有益的东西。学生会不断发现，拉丁语的语言结构与英语或者法语完全不同，由此而来的语言意义也是大相径庭。当然，拉丁语从本质上来说是一种较为古老的语言。与英语相比，拉丁语的语素在语篇结构中更具有句法意义。

由于拉丁语在古典文化教育中起着重要作用，我把哲学定位在逻辑学和历史学之间。我认为这应该是一个比较恰当的定位，因为通过拉丁语的学习可以启发我们的哲学思考。哲学思想来自逻辑学和历史学，同时也丰富着逻辑学和历史学。在拉丁语的学习过程中，学生经常要做语言翻译练习，从英语翻译成拉丁语，或是从拉丁语翻译成英语。在翻译的过程中，学生会分析语言之中蕴含的哲学思想，自然而然地也就进入了逻辑学的领域。如果一个人曾经在中学五年的青春时光里，每周写一篇拉丁语作文，每天翻译一些拉丁语著作，这将极大地有益于他以后的生活。如果这个人在中学毕业之后继续深造，从事学术研究工作，那么他肯定会感谢上帝让他在中学阶段接受了那样的教育。在任何一个科学领域里，都要经过自己的亲身体验才能登堂入室。对大多数人来说，这种体验式学习最直接的工具就是语言，通过语言来激发思维。从英语到法语再到拉丁语，间或学习几何和代数，一个人的教育过程就从语言学习迈向了思想启蒙的大道。我之所以对语言学习的重要性如此强调，可以从柏拉图那里找到依据，读者对此已然明了，在此不必赘述。[1]

从逻辑学再来看历史学，我依然引用桑德森校长的话：学生通过"接触"学习新知。那么一个学生到底该如何接触历史，通过体验来学习历史呢？历史资料中的原始文件、宪章纲领、法律文书、外交公函，

---

[1] 在第四章中，怀特海强调了语言学习对于古典文化的重要性。柏拉图式人文教育其实以拉丁语和希腊语为语言基础，然后才得以汲取古典文献的营养。——译者注

对于一个学生来说不啻于天书奇谈。千年之前的马拉松战役[1]的细节我们不得而知，但是可以从如今的一场足球比赛中隐约感知其大概的进程。我的意思是说，不管在什么年代中，不管在何种情形下，人类的活动都有着某种共通性。从这个意义上说，我们现在教授给学生的有关外交的、政治的历史知识，其实都是我们人类大历史的小细节。所以，我们在教育中所要注重的是漫漫历史长河中不断变化的观念和思想，纷繁复杂的审美意识和种族冲突，正是这些要素决定了、影响了我们人类的发展历程。例如，我们可以通过罗马帝国的兴衰史来看过去与现在之间的联系。我们可以把罗马帝国看作历史的一个瓶颈，这样历史就会从这个瓶颈缓缓倒出陈年佳酿。对于整个欧洲的文明发展史来说，关键的一点就是去研究罗马帝国的思想意识和运作机制。

再次从语言出发，我们可以通过古罗马的拉丁文去理解欧洲的历史变迁。古罗马的拉丁文负载着罗马帝国的思想观念，我们可以从中找到最简单的历史材料。其实，考察英语、法语、拉丁语之间的相互联系，其本身就是一个历史问题的哲学探究。例如，通过分析英语和法语之间的历史对比，我们可以研究欧洲的历史发展过程。就英语而言，英语在历史上曾经完全脱离了古代的不列颠文明，转而吸收了起源于地中海岛屿的语言，英语中的许多词汇体现了古代的地中海文明[2]。就法语而言，法语较为完整地保留了当地文明发展的连续性，同时也保留了这个过程中一些剧烈的文明冲突[3]痕迹。这并不是说语言、

---

[1] 马拉松战役（the Battle of Marathon），公元前490年秋季，希腊军队和波斯军队在希腊阿提卡东北部的马拉松平原进行的一场决战，雅典人以弱胜强，击退了波斯军队的入侵。——译者注

[2] 英语中体现的地中海文明，这里指的是英语语言在历史发展过程中借用了不少拉丁语词源，特别是一些科学技术专业词汇。——译者注

[3] 法语中体现的剧烈的文明冲突，这里指的是法国在历史上与英国和欧洲其他国家长期不断的战争历史，其反映就是在法语语言中也能发现不少外来词源。——译者注

文化、历史之间的关系有多么深奥，我也不想就此展开论述，其实大家心里也都明白这是一个简单的道理。那么，我们在我们的母语——英语——这个基础上，再初步掌握一定的法语和拉丁语，就可以通过现实生活中的语言联系去认识欧洲的历史发展过程，去理解欧洲历史上各个民族的迁徙流动。不同的语言是不同的民族在使用该语言的过程中的思想意识体现。每一种语言都体现着人们的所思所想、所作所为，每一个字词都来源于人们耕田犁地、养儿育女、修城筑堡的活动。如此看来，在不同的语言之间不存在真正意义上的同义词。我的所有论述都是基于这么一个主题，我的所有思考也都是基于这么一个要义。在英语、法语和拉丁语之间，我们就可以形成一个三角形。英语和法语占据着这个三角形的两个顶点，是现代思想意识的两种主要表现形式。英语和法语与第三个顶点——拉丁语——之间的联系，表示与古代地中海文明的历史渊源。这个语言文化的三角穿越时空，表达了彼此之间的鲜明对比。正是基于这个思考，我一再重申学习法语和拉丁语的重要意义。学习这两种语言是一种最为方便的手段，从而达到"接触"逻辑学和历史学的目的。而如果没有这样的亲身体验，那些所谓的逻辑思考、所谓的历史分析就只能是装腔作势、自娱自乐了。当然，我绝不是说这种教育方法是最简单的、最有效的，也绝不是说这种教育方法适合于大多数学生。教育之中应该因材施教，我对此非常清楚。但是我坚决认为这种教育方式能够取得最为满意的结果，能够带来最大的成效。另外，这种教育方式也经历了实践的考验。所以我认为可以对现行的这种教育方式进行一定的改革，使之适切于现实的教育情境。总的来说，这种语言教育方式体现着我们的文化传统精华，而且大多数训练有素的教师能够付诸教育实践。

大家也许已经注意到，我到目前为止只字未提古罗马文学，没有讲到古罗马文学的光辉灿烂历史。在拉丁语的教育活动中，我们要伴以拉丁语文学的教学，其中也可以应用一些古罗马文学作品。古罗马作家就罗马帝国的现实状况和思想意识做出了深刻的描绘，包括当时的古罗马人对古希腊哲学思想的理解和认识。但是古罗马作家中较少有挥洒不羁的创作天才，这是古罗马文学的一个显著特点。具体来说，古罗马作家较多地表现出创作的世俗性，较多地关注他们自己的国家问题。除此之外的话题，他们少有触及。除了古罗马的诗人和哲学家卢克莱修[1]之外，从其他许多作家的作品中我们都能感受到作家的世俗性局限。对于塔西佗[2]的作品来说，他侧重于对古罗马长老院顽固派的批判，由于没有看到古罗马行省执政官所做的工作，所以就描述了一些古希腊自由民在古罗马官僚体系中的表现。总而言之，当时罗马帝国的现实状况和思想意识被古罗马作家记载了下来，反映在古罗马文学作品之中。这就是为什么在古罗马文学作品中少见有天马行空的神话故事，而在当时的历史阶段中人们并未真正直面现实，往往从世俗转向了宗教。世界上其他国家的文学作品往往绘声绘色于宗教故事，比如在中国、希腊、法国、德国、意大利、英国。在这些国家的文学作品里，各路神仙津津乐道于生命的永恒、不朽。故事中的众神超然物外，不问世事，我想他们肯定对希伯来宗教故事中亘古不变的主题——与魔鬼撒旦的决一死战——早已心生厌倦。那么，众神肯定也对古罗马文学故事中广为流传的主题——听社会名流的广场演说——不屑一顾。

我们在教授拉丁语的时候伴以古罗马文学作品的讲解，并不是说学生可以借此精神食粮享用终生。其实我们英国的文学作品对学生来说更有意义，因为英国文学内容丰富、思想深厚、精妙绝伦。如果你

---

[1] 卢克莱修（Titus Lucretius Carus，公元前99?—公元前55?），古罗马诗人和哲学家，著有哲理长诗《物性论》（*On the Nature of Things*）。——译者注

[2] 塔西佗（Publius Cornelius Tacitus，55?—120?），古罗马历史学家，曾担任古罗马长老院议员，主要著作有《历史》（*Histories*）和《编年史》（*Annals*），今仅存残篇。——译者注

喜欢阅读带有哲学意味的作品,难道你会因为古罗马的西塞罗[1]而放过英国的培根、霍布斯[2]、洛克[3]、贝克莱[4]、休谟[5]、穆勒[6]吗?当然,假如你真的像大众一样喜欢英国的马丁·塔珀[7],那就不如去读一读西塞罗的作品。另外,如果你喜欢阅读世事人情之类的故事,难道你会不去读莎士比亚和其他英国作家的作品,而要去读古罗马的泰伦提乌斯[8]、

---

[1] 西塞罗(Marcus Tullius Cicero,公元前106—公元前43),古罗马哲学家、政治家、演说家。代表作有《论国家》(*On the Commonwealth*)、《论法律》(*On the Laws*)、《论神性》(*On the Nature of the Gods*)、《论演说家》(*On the Orator*)等。——译者注

[2] 霍布斯(Thomas Hobbes,1588—1679),英国哲学家和政治家,欧洲启蒙运动时期的杰出人物。代表作有《利维坦》(*Leviathan*)、《论人性》(*Human Nature*)、《对笛卡尔形而上学的沉思的第三组诘难》(*Third series of Objections*)等,晚年翻译《奥德赛》(*Odyssey*)和《伊利亚特》(*Iliad*)。——译者注

[3] 洛克(John Locke,1632—1704),英国哲学家,代表作有《论宽容》(*A Letter Concerning Toleration*)、《政府论》(*Two Treatises of Government*)、《人类理解论》(*An Essay Concerning Human Understanding*)、《教育漫话》(*Some Thoughts Concerning Education*)等。洛克就教育问题提出了著名的"白板说"。——译者注

[4] 贝克莱(George Berkeley,1685—1753),爱尔兰哲学家、科学家和主教,代表作有《哲学纪事》(*Philosophical Commentaries*)、《视觉新论》(*An Essay Towards a New Theory of Vision*)、《人类知识原理》(*Of the Principles of Human Knowledge*)等。——译者注

[5] 休谟(David Hume,1711—1776),英国哲学家,著有《人性论》(*A Treatise of Human Nature*)、《人类理解研究》(*An Enquiry Concerning Human Understanding*)、《道德原则研究》(*An Enquiry Concerning Human Understanding*)、《随笔与论文》(*Essays, Moral, Political, and Literary*)等。——译者注

[6] 穆勒(John Stuart Mill,1806—1873),英国哲学家、逻辑学家、心理学家和经济学家,代表作有《论自由》(*On Liberty*)、《功用主义》(*Utilitarianism*)、《逻辑学体系》(*A System of Logic*)等。——译者注

[7] 马丁·塔珀(Martin Farquhar Tupper,1810—1889),英国作家、诗人,代表作有《众所周知的哲学》(*Proverbial Philosophy*)等。——译者注

[8] 泰伦提乌斯(Publius Terentius Afer,公元前190?—公元前159?),古罗马喜剧作家。他的语言被奉为纯正的拉丁语典范,他的六部诗体喜剧对后世戏剧产生了重大影响。这六部喜剧为《安德罗斯女子》(*Andria, The Girl from Andros*)、《自责者》(*Heauton Timorumenos, The Self-Tormentor*)、《阉奴》(*Eunuchus*)、《福尔弥昂》(*Phormio*)、《两兄弟》(*Adelphoe, The Brothers*)、《婆母》(*Hecyra, The Mother-in-law*)。——译者注

普劳图斯[1]的作品,或者去看古罗马佩特洛尼乌斯[2]笔下的特里马乔宴会故事集吗?至于幽默风格的文学故事,你一定会读谢里丹[3]、狄更斯[4]等英国作家的作品,有谁会在读古罗马文学作品的时候开怀大笑呢?西塞罗的确是一个伟大的演说家,他在煌煌罗马帝国的政治舞台上举足轻重,而在泱泱大英帝国的历史上同样不乏这样的政治家指点江山。这样的对比可以无限罗列下去,或是诗歌或是历史,从英国作家到古罗马作家,我们都可以发现其中的诸多差异。我只是想表达一下我自己的立场,我不认同这么一个说法,即拉丁文学作品举世无双、无所不能。例如,我们很容易就能发现,拉丁文学作品里面既没有欢乐的笑声,也没有悲伤的哭泣。

对文学作品的判断不能脱离其所在的时代背景。古希腊文学或者英国文学善于表达普遍的人类情感,而古罗马文学作品与此格格不入。古罗马文学只善于表达一个主题,即罗马帝国本身,而罗马帝国是欧洲的母亲。罗马帝国堪称欧洲文明的巴比伦,《启示录》[5]描绘了巴比伦的兴衰沉浮,犹如一个妓女的坎坷身世,在末日来临之际她发出了

---

[1] 普劳图斯(Plautus,公元前254?—公元前184),古罗马喜剧作家,代表作有《俘房》(Captivi)等一百多部喜剧,但流传下来的只有二十多部。——译者注
[2] 佩特洛尼乌斯(Gaius Petronius Arbiter,27—66),古罗马政治活动家和作家,在其作品《萨蒂利孔》(Satyricon)中有关于"特里马乔宴会故事集"(The Banquet of Trimalchio)的内容,讽刺有钱而无趣味的暴发户。——译者注
[3] 谢里丹(Richard Brinsley Sheridan,1751—1861),英国剧作家和政治家,著有《造谣学校》(The School for Scandal)、《批判家》(The Critic)等。——译者注
[4] 狄更斯(Charles Dickens,1812—1870),英国作家,代表作品有《匹克威克外传》(The Posthumous Papers of the Pickwick Club)、《雾都孤儿》(The Adventures of Oliver Twist)、《双城记》(A Tale of Two Cities)、《远大前程》(Great Expectations)、《老古玩店》(The Old Curiosity Shop)、《我们共同的朋友》(Our Mutual Friend)、《大卫·科波菲尔》(David Copperfield)等。——译者注
[5] 《启示录》(Apocalypse),指《圣经·新约》中的"启示录"。在启示录中巴比伦被描绘成一个女人,人们通常认为它是指古罗马的首都。——译者注

第五章 教育中的古典文化

幽幽哀叹。

她远远地站在一旁,内心无比忧惧,喃喃低语。唉,唉,伟大的巴比伦,繁华的大都市!只消一个小时,你的命运将会改变。全世界的商人都会为你悲伤和哭泣,因为无人再来这里购买这些东西:

金器银器、珍珠宝石、紫色亚麻、红色丝绸、檀香木料、象牙制品以及木器铜器铁器,还有各种大理石用具;

桂皮、香料、油膏、乳香、美酒、油脂、面粉、小麦、野兽、绵羊、马匹、战车及奴隶,还有人的灵魂可供交易。

当时的古罗马文明就是以这种不可思议的方式呈现在早期的基督徒面前。但是基督教本身就是一种古代文化的结晶,而欧洲的古代文化恰恰发源于古罗马文明。也就是说,我们从古代的东地中海文明中同时继承了这两种文化属性[1]。

由此可以看出,通过阅读拉丁文学作品我们可以了解古罗马的历史事实。在了解古罗马历史的基础上,再去认识英国的历史或者法国的历史,就会形成扎实的文化底蕴。如果了解了古罗马的历史,自然也就了解了地中海文明的渊源,因为罗马帝国处在地中海文明最发达的历史阶段。再者,通过学习古罗马历史,我们也会自然地掌握欧洲的地理概况,很快地理解欧洲的诸多海洋、河流、山脉、平原在历史进程中所起到的作用。这种形式的古典文化教育能帮助年轻学生认识鲜活的历史发展过程,理解历史发展的背后动力,特别是让学生从外在形象和言行举止去判断人物伟大与否。从这些拉丁文学作品中,我们会发现古罗马人理想高尚,德行笃厚,同时他们又往往表现出非常邪恶的一面,他们在战斗中的血腥残暴也是众所周知的。我们必须不

---

[1] 即世俗性和宗教性的结合。——译者注

断反思到底什么才是真正的伟大与崇高，否则，道德教育就是空中楼阁，无据可依。如果我们在人性本质上无所谓伟大与崇高，那么我们的所作所为、所思所想也就无所谓道德不道德了。从这个意义上说，真正的伟大与崇高来自具体情境的直觉经验，而不是来自众说纷纭的最终结论。例如，一个年轻人在宗教皈依的过程中会有一种痛苦的体验，会感到自己像虫子一样渺小卑微，而不是像人一样伟大崇高。我们会认为这个年轻人是有道德的，因为他还保有伟大与崇高的基本信条，还存有对上帝威严的敬畏之心。也就是说，对伟大与崇高的认识是道德判断的基石。再例如，如今我们处在一个民主时代的历史开端，一个问题摆在我们面前需要思考，即关于人们的平等问题，到底应该是高水平的平等还是低水平的平等。诸如此类的问题就需要我们在教育过程中认真领会古罗马文明的智慧。罗马帝国的历史本身就是一出动人的戏剧，而启迪后世的哲学思想更是引人入胜。前面所讲都是关于拉丁文学作品的审美理解问题，因为其意义重大，所以我们必须对传统古典文化教育革故鼎新，使之适应新的教育情形。传统上的古典文化教育好像就是为了专门培养一些古典文化的专家学者，因此在初期阶段一门心思地实施语言教育，然后再培养古典文学兴趣，从而烘托古典文化氛围。然而在19世纪后半叶出现了其他许多新的课程，在学校教育中逐渐蚕食了古典文化的教育时间。因此，传统的古典文化教育方式往往浪费了学生大量的学习时间，最后只是停留在语言学习层面上。如今从英国中学毕业的很多青年学生几乎丧失了学习热情，对此我常常反思，这是否就是由传统古典文化教育带来的挫败感导致的。古典文化教育课程亟须改革，目标必须明确，因为在我们培养优秀人才的过程中已经出现了重大失误。

无论从事什么工作，我们都要恰当地控制两个基本要素：尺度和速度。例如，如果我们用显微镜来观察罗马的圣彼得大教堂[1]，那么这对大教堂的建筑师是不公平的。再如，如果我们以每天5行的速度来阅读《奥德赛》[2]，那么我们只会感到索然无味。其实这个问题同样适用于我们的古典文化教育。我们的学生不可能熟练地掌握拉丁语，不可能快速阅读拉丁语文献，而且从宏观的历史角度来看，学生需要研习的古典文化知识也是浩如烟海的。基于这个考虑，我们就有必要认真研究古典文化教育的尺度和速度，有必要梳理清楚教育工作中的各项要素。迄今为止，我尚未看到任何这方面关于教育心理学的研究文献。难道这个教育问题是共济会的一个秘密吗？[3]

我经常发现一个有意思的现象，一些大学者聚在一起的时候，如果碰巧谈到了古典文献的翻译问题，那些大学者简直就是避之唯恐不及，犹如一个翩翩绅士看到了肮脏下流的男女性事一样。我是一个数学家，对古典文献的翻译问题并没有感觉到有失斯文，所以接下来我想谈谈这个问题。

为什么要学习拉丁文呢？我们学习拉丁文就是为了理解其中的每一个字词，理解其中的句法结构，理解其中的内在意义，这就是学习拉丁文的基本要义，也是我就古典文化教育这个话题所持有的基本观

---

[1] 圣彼得大教堂（Basilica di San Pietro in Vaticano），又译为"梵蒂冈圣伯铎大殿"，位于梵蒂冈，意大利文艺复兴时期的艺术家米开朗基罗等人参与设计，被誉为世界第一大教堂。——译者注

[2] 《奥德赛》（*Odyssey*），古希腊荷马史诗。——译者注

[3] 这是怀特海的一个明知故问的反问，根本不是共济会的一个什么惊天阴谋，而是大家普遍忽略的一个教育问题。共济会（Free-Mason，或者 Free and Accepted Masons），字面意思是"自由石匠"，它是全球最大的一个秘密组织。共济会并非宗教，对入会申请者是否有宗教信仰或是什么宗教背景并没有要求，但申请者必须是有神论者，相信存在着一位神。历史上共济会曾参与社会改革运动，被一些持有阴谋论的人指责，认为其被用来控制世界的政治、经济活动。——译者注

念。如果我们在古典文化教育中眉毛胡子一把抓，不分主次，不分轻重，对语言的精致微妙之处视而不见，那么我们的古典文化教育就失去了应有的意义。假如教师在教育中采用古典文化的翻译版本教材，让学生绕过拉丁文的语言障碍，从而脱离解读拉丁文的思考过程，那么这是极其错误的。古典文化教育不只是传授古典文化知识，更在于培养学生准确、明晰、独立的思维能力。

我们要通过学习拉丁文去学习古典文化，但是其中也存在一个严峻的问题，即学习的速度，因为中学教育要在限定的4年或者5年之内完成。学习一首诗歌的时候也要在一定的时间之内进行。学习诗歌就要学习其中的对比、意象、情感，这就需要人的思想感受保持一定的节奏。但是人的思想感受具有一定的时间性，不可能无限延展，超出一定的时限。如果学生以蜗牛般的速度磕磕巴巴地学习，那么一首世间最为动人的诗歌最终也会变为一堆垃圾。我们设想一下一个学生是如何阅读古典文学作品的：读到"当……"，停下来查查词典；然后读到"一只雄鹰"，再停下来查查词典；读完"当一只雄鹰……"，再停下来思考思考句子结构。如此这般的古典文化学习能够让学生汲取古罗马的文化精髓吗？常识告诉我们这是不可能的，所以通常情况下我们会去找一个最好的翻译版本，一个尽可能地保留了原著的魅力与活力的翻译版本。然后我们就会比较流畅地阅读译文，还能写写画画自己的思想感悟。这种通过译文来学习古典文化的诉求相当于否定了拉丁文的实际应用价值，把拉丁文当作古董文物束之高阁，供人顶礼膜拜。

当然，肯定也会有人否定译文的价值，认为翻译的质量肯定赶不上原作。无论从哪个方面来说，译文肯定赶不上原文，这也是我们一定要让学生去读拉丁文原著的原因。一旦明白了原著的思想内容，阅读的速度也就不会太慢。所以我认为，在学习古典文化的初期阶段可以通过译文来迅速掌握其中的大意，然后再通过拉丁语原文充分、快速地理解其中的意蕴。华兹华斯[1]对科学家们有所批评，说他们"以解剖的科学名义犯下谋杀的罪恶行径"[2]。而在我们的古典文化教育的传统方式中，一些过去的古典文化学者还真像华兹华斯所说的凶手一样。[3]只有在阅读拉丁文原作时，我们才能真切地感受到其中深刻而热烈的思想之美，所以我们应以敬畏之心来对待原著之要义。但是我并不是说一定要仅仅局限于拉丁文原著的研习。除了古典文化原著之外，学生还可以通过其他途径来领略古罗马的思想智慧。例如，学生还可以通过英语看一看罗马帝国的兴衰历史，或者通过英语翻译版本去读一读维吉尔、卢克莱修、西塞罗的相关作品。我们能够通过拉丁文去研读的古典文化原著可能相对较少，但是很有必要通过这相对较少的原文去领略先贤的思想大厦，另外我们也可以借助其他途径进行学习和认识，不一定是通过作者自己的语言或者文字。但是，如果我们对作者的原著只字未读，那也是一个严重的问题。

以上谈的是关于古典文化学习的速度问题，至于尺度问题，主要是有关如何教授古典文化历史的复杂内容。就中学生的学习心理特点来说，他们所要学习的东西必须具体而鲜明。我们希望学生掌握古典文化时期诸多先师大哲的基本思想，可以让学生通过"接触"去进行学习。例如，我们可以用图片来展示当时的社会情景，观看当时的建筑、雕像、花瓶、壁画，从而让学生直观感受当时的宗教气息和家庭生活。通过这种方式，我们就可以把罗马帝国时期与之前的东地中海

---

[1] 华兹华斯（William Wordsworth，1770—1850），英国浪漫主义诗人，"湖畔派"诗人之一，被誉为"桂冠诗人"。——译者注

[2] 对应原文是"murder to dissect"，意指为了科学研究的医学解剖，在名义上光明正大，但是在方式方法上或者伦理道德上却不尽如人意。——译者注

[3] 怀特海指的是教育中的名实不一，以教育的名义做出反教育的行动。貌似进行古典文化教育，但是在实践中方法不得当，其实阻碍了古典文化学习。半生不熟地学习原文，或者投机取巧地学习译文，都无助于真正的理解。——译者注

文明进行对比，也可以与随后的中世纪文化进行对比。总之，这样的古典文化教育的目的就是要让学生在头脑中刻下历史的印记，让他们记住人们的服饰、房屋、技术、艺术、宗教都是如何嬗变的。从这一点来说，我们有必要效仿一下动物学家的做法，他们将所有的动物分门别类，展示动物样本供人参观学习。我们在古典文化教育中也可如此，通过展示文化样本来讲授罗马帝国的历史发展进程。

总的来说，人们的生活建构于技术、科学、艺术和宗教之上。这四个方面是相互联系的，都源于人们的思想意识。在科学和技术之间、在艺术和宗教之间分别存在着较为紧密的联系。没有这四个根本因素，就无法理解任何一个社会组织结构。现代的1台蒸汽机发动起来，相当于古代的1000个奴隶的工作量，而古代帝国主义扩展的核心目的就是劫掠奴隶。现代化的印刷出版机制是现代民主的一个必要条件，现代知识的核心要义就是科学的不断进步，并伴随着观念的不断改变和技术的不断完善。美索不达米亚[1]和埃及依赖水利灌溉成就了他们的古代文明，而罗马帝国的辉煌依赖出色地运用各种技术。古罗马的技术应用在各个方面，例如道路、桥梁、引水渠、隧道、下水道、宏伟建筑、商业船队、军事科学、冶金、农业。直到今天，我们依然可以看到这些技术广泛地应用在我们的生活之中。技术的应用就是古罗马文明得以形成和发展的秘密。我常常想：为什么古罗马的工程师没有发明出蒸汽机？他们其实随时都可以造出蒸汽机的。如果是那样的话，这个世界的历史就不知道要怎么改写了。古罗马人没有发明蒸汽机，我将

---

[1] 美索不达米亚（Mesopotamia）是古希腊对两河流域的称谓，意为"（两条）河流之间的地方"，这两条河指的是幼发拉底河和底格里斯河。美索不达米亚文明为人类最古老的文化摇篮之一，灌溉农业为其文化发展的主要基础。6000年前（公元前4000年）已有较发达的文化，曾出现苏美尔、阿卡德、巴比伦、亚述等文明。此后又经过波斯、马其顿、罗马与奥斯曼等帝国的统治。第一次世界大战后，其主要部分成为独立的伊拉克。

其归因于当时的温暖气候，在温暖舒适的气候中他们没有沏茶、煮咖啡的生活习惯。到了18世纪，人们习惯于围坐在火堆旁烧水，注意到了水壶里的水沸腾的现象。当然，我们都知道古代居住在亚历山大的发明家希耶罗[1]曾经发明过类似的一些小玩意儿。古罗马的工程师之所以没有发明出这类机器，只是因为他们缺乏机会看到水壶里的水沸腾这个普通现象，也就没有刻意去思考蒸汽的推动力量。

人类的历史发展依赖技术进步的推动力量，过去几百年来，先进的科学与发达的技术相结合，开创了人类历史的新纪元。

大约公元前1000年的时候，文字书写这种方式开始流行，开启了人类历史上第一个伟大的语言文化时代。在最初的朦胧发展阶段，书面文字主要用于宗教经卷、官府档案、历史记载。从文字的历史可以看出，过去的种种发明创造不是一蹴而就的，是需要经过一个漫长的发展过程的。即便在今天，我们在探索新知的过程中依然如此。在人类的历史发展过程中，新事物往往以一种不同的思维方式缓缓渗入到整个社会体系中。文字书写有助于记录人们的新思想，因此东地中海地区的人们慢慢掌握了文字书写这个工具。当古希腊人和希伯来人掌握了逐渐成熟的语言文字时，欧洲文明就开始了新的篇章。虽然希伯来的思想文化是在千年之后，即基督教传播开来之后，才逐渐为世人所知。在为世人所知的1000年前，希伯来的先知已经开始用文字记录他们的内心思想。而在彼时，古希腊文明也开始逐渐形成。

回到古典文化教育这个话题，我想说的是，如果要从宏观上把握历史的进程，理解古罗马在欧洲历史的前前后后所起到的作用，那么只是记住一些历史年代和政治事件是远远不够的，甚至历史教科书中

---

[1] 希耶罗（Hiero，10—70），古希腊数学家，其家乡是亚历山大。他发明了用蒸汽推动物体转动的设备，被称为"汽转球"，利用蒸汽的力量做出机械运动。——译者注

详细的语言描述也无济于事。因此，我们要运用一些模型、图片、示意图、图表等方式来展示技术发展过程中的一些典型例子，用以说明技术发展对我们的生活样态的具体影响。我们也可以用同样的方式进行艺术史的教育，艺术是实用性和宗教性的巧妙结合，表现着人们的内心世界，同时也改变着人们的所思所想。学生也可以通过模型、图片或者博物馆的实物去认识艺术的发展过程。总之，历史教育不应开始于历史的定论，而应开始于具体的案例，在一个一个案例中展现历史的缓慢进程，从一个时期到另一个时期，从一种状态到另一种状态，从一个民族到另一个民族。

对于源自东地中海地区的古典文化教育活动来说，我们应该采取同样较为具体的方式。古典文化教育的意义重大，因此一定要让学生通过具体的感知获得第一手的信息。古希腊和古罗马是欧洲文明的奠基者，如果要认识欧洲文明的历史，首先就要从古希腊人和古罗马人的哲学思想入手。为了让学生充分地认识古罗马的思想体系，我建议先让学生读一点古希腊文学的代表作品，当然只能是通过英语译本来进行阅读。请注意，学生需要读的是古希腊作家作品的英语译文，而不是英国人用英语写作的古希腊作家作品评论，不管英国人写的古希腊作家作品评论有多么精彩。古典文化教育要求阅读有关古希腊的著作，这些著作应该是古希腊人自己的著述。

就阅读古希腊著作的英语译文来说，可以让学生读一读史诗《奥德赛》的诗歌译文、希罗多德[1]的历史译文、英国作家吉尔伯特·默

---

[1] 希罗多德（Herodotus，公元前484?—公元前425），古希腊历史学家，被称为"历史之父"，著作为九卷本《历史》（*The Histories*），是第一部记叙体的史书。——译者注

雷[1] 翻译的戏剧中的合唱诗句、普鲁塔克[2] 的传记译文。特别需要提出的是，要让学生读一读希斯[3] 以学术文体翻译的古希腊科学史作品，例如阿基米德[4] 在马塞勒斯[5] 执政期间的生活片段，以及欧几里得[6]《几何原本》中的若干定义、公理、命题。在所要选择的这些译文中，要对相应古典文化原著所产生的时代文化背景做出适当说明。古罗马文明对欧洲文化发展具有极其重要的影响，核心就在于古罗马留给欧洲的两个文化遗产。古罗马文明吸收了希伯来的宗教思想，又融合了古希腊文明，这两个文化要素一起深深地影响了欧洲的历史发展。古罗马文明就是这样建基于形形色色的、蓬蓬勃勃的早期思想文化。例如，古罗马法之所以能够体现古罗马文明的博大精深，就在于它一方面构筑了罗马帝国钢铁一般的严刑峻法，另一方面包含了斯多葛式[7] 的人

---

[1] 吉尔伯特·默雷（Gilbert Murray，1866—1957），英国古典文化学者，精通古希腊时期的语言和文化，著有《希腊史诗的兴起》（*The Rise of the Greek Epic*）、《希腊宗教的五个阶段》（*Five Stages of Greek Religion*）等，用英语诗歌的形式翻译了大量古希腊戏剧。——译者注

[2] 普鲁塔克（Plutarch，46?—120），古希腊历史学家、传记作家和散文家，著有《希腊罗马名人比较列传》（*Parallel Lives*）、《道德论丛》（*Moralia*）等。——译者注

[3] 希斯（Thomas Little Heath，1861—1940），英国数学家、古典文化学者、翻译家。他擅长研究古希腊时期的数学历史，翻译了当时的一些数学著作，著有《希腊数学史》（*A History of Greek Mathematics*）、《希腊天文学》（*Greek Astronomy*）等。——译者注

[4] 阿基米德（Archimedes，公元前287?—公元前212?），古希腊数学家、物理学家、发明家、天文学家。——译者注

[5] 马塞勒斯（Marcus Claudius Marcellus，公元前268?—公元前208），古罗马军事领袖，曾五次担任罗马执政官。——译者注

[6] 欧几里得（Euclid，公元前300年左右），古希腊数学家，被誉为"几何之父"，著有《几何原本》（*Elements*）、《论图形的分割》（*On Divisions of Figures*）、《光学》（*Optics*）等。——译者注

[7] 斯多葛式（Stoic），斯多葛派源自古罗马雅典集会广场的一个派别，认为世界理性决定事物的发展变化，而人是其中的一部分，从而得出"天赋人权、人人生而平等"这样的西方人文主义的核心理论。——译者注

本关怀。在历史的长河中，由于文化遗产中各个不同成分的巨大差异，曾经导致了欧洲的四分五裂；也正是由于文化遗产中来自古罗马文明的和谐特质不断传承，欧洲往往是分久必合。纵观欧洲的历史可以发现，它其实就是古罗马文明渗透希伯来文明和古希腊文明，然后绵延至今的历史。各个文明之间存在着相互制约的复杂联系，一起影响着欧洲的宗教、科学、艺术、物质财富追寻、权力支配争夺。在每一个方面的历史发展之中，我们其实都可以依稀感受到内在的差异张力，犹如剑拔弩张。理解了古罗马，也就理解了文明的和谐本源。

第六章　数学课程

　　如今的教育正处在一个特殊时期，犹如几百年前的欧洲刚刚摆脱中世纪的黑暗。如今的学界和当时一样，尽管已经取得了不少成就，尽管其中不乏赫赫权威，但是它在历史发展的过程中逐渐显得狭隘，终难服务于人类的福祉进步。人们的期盼发生了改变，相应地就要求对教育的基础做出改革，从而适应学生的需要，向他们传授真正适合他们的、今后生活中必需的知识。纵观人类的历史进程，但凡出现一次思想意识的伟大变革，就必然会有一场教育革命随之而来。教育革命往往也会推迟发生，甚至拖上一代人的时间。一方面是因为既得利益者的阻碍，另一方面是因为一些学界领袖因循守旧，他们固守自己在求学时期所接触和研习的思想流派。但是历史发展的客观规律不容抗拒，教育必须是鲜活的、有效的，必须向学生传递新的知识、培育新的能力，只有这样才能帮助他们跟上时代的思想潮流。

　　任何一个行之有效的教育体系都不能产生于真空之中，也就是说，教育实践不能脱离当下的思想背景。教育必须是现代的，否则就会像一个有机体一样最终枯萎凋谢，难逃失败的命运。

　　但是，如果仅仅停留在"现代"这个冠冕堂皇的字眼上，那也只是敷衍塞责，无济于事。所谓现代的教育，就是用现代的思想去传递现代的知识、培育现代的能力。从这个意义上说，即便是昨天才刚刚发现的新事物，到了今天也就难称其为现代了。昨天发现的新事物也许是来自以前所流行的思想体系，因而往往显得深奥艰涩。我们所要求的教育的现代应该体现在思想意识层面，即在文明社会中广泛传播的观念。我今天下午演讲的主题，就是要探讨一下教育中深奥艰涩的课程是如何地不合时势。

对于数学家来说，这的确是一个复杂的问题。局外人往往会抱怨数学课程深奥艰涩，对此我们最好予以承认，在一般人的观念中数学的确让人感到高深莫测。但是我觉得深奥艰涩并不意味着数学课程有多难，只是说数学课程的应用有着较大的局限性，与人们的思想意识较少发生直接联系。

人们对数学课程的这种抱怨导致了一个不良的后果，即数学课程在人文教育中总是没有得到应用。数学是教育过程中不可缺少的一个环节，但在现实情境中我们往往发现人们的数学素养普遍偏低。我对此现象感到非常担心，认为在教育中应该加强数学教育。加强数学教育并不是说要盲目地学习更多的数学知识，而是首先要理解问题所在，找出阻碍数学广泛应用的真正原因。

数学课程到底是不是深奥艰涩呢？总的来说，应该是这样的。世界公论是起决定性作用的[1]，人们的一般判断还是靠得住的。

不管是就科学领域的理论知识而言，还是就学校教材的教学内容而言，数学的确都是一门深奥艰涩的学科。从一般的数学原理出发，经过演绎得出无数的数学推论，每一个推论都比上一个推论更加复杂。我在这里并不是要论证数学有多么复杂，数学学科本身就是这样发展形成的。我在这里想要强调的是，数学吸引学生学习的原因也正是阻碍数学作为一个教育中的工具得以应用的原因，例如，一般原理的演

---

[1] 对应原文是"Securus judicat orbis terrarum"，这是圣·奥古斯丁（Saint Augustine，354—430）的话。——译者注

绎推论，推论之间的复杂关联，演绎过程的似非而是，计算方法的五花八门，完全抽象的理论特质，而正是数学的抽象特质赋予了数学永恒的真理。

数学的这些方面对人们来说具有极其重要的价值，从古至今吸引了众多天资聪颖之士为之孜孜不倦。我在此有必要澄清一点，除了那些天资聪颖之士，一般人对数学的这些方面都是难以掌握的。之所以难以掌握，是因为数学中的诸多原理和定理纷繁复杂，与宏观理论或者日常思想都缺乏明显的关联。如果在数学教育中一味地教授数学中的细枝末节，这将是下下之策。

由此可以看出，如果要使数学在教育中得以应用，就要严格筛选数学课程知识，就要认真改变数学教学方式。我认为只要付出了一定的努力，即便是智商一般的学生也能有所收获。即使是为了一点点的进步，我们也要对数学教育做出改变。在数学教育的任何一个阶段，我们都要严格排除一些不合时宜的因素。呈现给年轻学生的科学不应显得深奥艰涩，科学教育应该直接地、简单地传递若干具有重要意义的一般原理。

就数学教育的改革而言，我们这一代的数学教师的确取得了令人骄傲的成就。我们在改革中表现出了巨大的活力，在短时间内完成了令人不可思议的工作。特别是在公共考试体系的桎梏之下，对既有的数学课程做出一定的改变，一般人是无法体会到其中的困难程度的。

虽然困难，但是我们在数学教育中还是取得了巨大的进步，至少打破了传统上僵化的数学教育模式。那么我今天下午着重要谈的，就是关于我们该如何重建数学教育体系。对此问题，我认为在教育中一定要祛除数学课程的深奥艰涩，"祛除深奥艰涩"是我对这个问题的简单概括。

在教育过程中，我们应该有条不紊地传授一系列具有重要意义的知识，坚决避免一些看似花里胡哨实则离题千里的教学活动。数学教育的根本目的是为了让学生熟悉抽象的思维方式、懂得理论的实际应用、掌握方法的恰当使用。如果不是为了这个根本目的，在数学教材中盲目罗列各种各样的数学公理，强迫学生死记硬背，还要这样那样地考试，那真是糟糕透顶了。数学教材的编写非常重要，关系到学生能否从中理解数学的基本知识。数学教材中的例子应该直接明了地证明相应的数学公理，所举的例子可以是抽象的情境，也可以是具体的现象。只要教师觉得合适，这样的例子就多多益善。需要强调一点，数学教材中的这部分内容万万不可简而化之，数学考试中往往也会考查类似问题的解决，这就需要学生通过诸多例题来掌握复杂数学知识的实际应用。人们往往存在一种错误的观念，认为卷面试题能甄别一个人的资质禀赋，而书本知识能检测一个人的死记硬背。对此我不敢苟同，我的个人经历并非如此。如果一个学生为了争取奖学金而认真学习书本知识，那么他一定也可以赢得卷面考试。数学教材只要编排得当，提供丰富的练习题目，而不是盲目地东拼西凑，照样可以测试学生的数学能力。不过，这是针对考试对教学的不良影响而说的一点题外话。

数学的主要知识点其实并不高深莫测，只能说是比较抽象。在人文教育中开展数学教育，其中的目的之一就是为了训练学生的抽象思维能力。数学中包含着许多抽象的知识形式，是人们进行精确思维的重要基础。在我们的教育过程中，数学一般体现为三个方面：数的关系、量的关系、空间的关系。当然，学校教育中的数学并不等同于科学研究中的数学，后者的内容要更为宽泛。我们现在所谈论的是学校教育中的数学课程，数、量、空间这三个方面是相互联系的。

在教育过程中，我们的教学顺序是从特殊到一般。那么在数学教育中，我们就要让学生通过简单的例题的练习来掌握相应的知识点。也就是说，数学教育不应该是盲目地教给学生一个又一个数学公理。而应该让学生认识到，他们以前所学习的各种知识其实都是与数、量、空间有关系的，这才是数学教育的要义所在。从特殊到一般，这种教育方式是形成所有哲学思想的根本基础。实际上，任何一个人只要恰当地掌握了数学的基础知识，他都能具备哲学思想的基本素养。但是在数学教育中我们务必要避免一点，即数学知识点的盲目累加。不管做多少例题，不管学多长时间，所学习的例题必须要用于掌握数学课程的核心知识。通过这种方式，也只有通过这种方式，我们才能祛除数学的深奥艰涩。

这里所谈到的数学教育并不特别针对两类学生：一类学生将来会成为专业的数学家；另一类学生在将来的专业中需要运用比较复杂的数学知识。我们指向的是所有学生的人文素养，包括前面所说的两类学生。因此，数学课程应该围绕一些简单的知识点展开，通过具体的例题进行讲解。数学教育必须目的明确，要和前面所讲的专业数学研究严格区分开来。当然，数学教育为数学研究做出了必要的准备。在数学教育的最终阶段，学生通过练习会掌握基本的公理。在我们英国现今的数学教育中，最终阶段是让学生掌握圆和三角形相连的关系证明。数学家往往会对这样的数学题很感兴趣，但是这难道不够深奥艰涩吗？这与人文教育的理想不是相距甚远吗？在古典文化教育中，学生学习拉丁文法的目的就是为了阅读维吉尔和贺拉斯[1]的作品，从这些最为伟大的历史人物身上汲取最为崇高的人文思想。对于数学教育的存在意义而言，难道我们仅仅满足于学生会掌握九点圆[2]的几何性质吗？坦率地说，这难道不是妄自菲薄吗？

对此大可不必担心，我们的数学教师在教育中尽职尽责，对数学

---

[1] 贺拉斯（Horace，公元前65—公元前8），古罗马诗人、批评家，著作有诗体长信《诗艺》（*Ars Poetica*）等。——译者注

[2] 九点圆（nine-point circle），三角形三边的中点，三高的垂足和三个欧拉点（连接三角形各顶点与垂心所得三线段的中点）九点共圆。通常称这个圆为九点圆，或欧拉圆、费尔巴哈圆。——译者注

课程做出了许多改革。我们的数学课程决不会满足于让学生懂得"两义情况"[1]之类的数学概念。

在基础教育结束的时候，对那些天资比较聪颖的学生来说，该如何复习总结呢？首先，学生应该能够对已经学习的数学知识有一个总体的把握。不一定是面面俱到、无一疏漏，但是要清楚核心的知识，懂得数学的要义，为将来的进一步学习打下扎实的基础。另外，对于分析数学和几何学这两类知识来说，学生可以直接应用于物理实验室，设置一个简单的力学实验，验证所学的相关知识。这样的应用具有双重的意义，一方面学习物理知识，一方面学习数学知识，两者互为印证。

数学知识在力学原理的精确验算中是非常关键的。通过数学的应用，学生就会逐渐明白精确的自然规律，那些规律在我们的经验中在多大程度上得以验证，以及抽象思维在自然规律的验算中所起到的作用。这个过程的目的就是让学生通过翔实而具体的例证来掌握知识要点，而不是死记硬背一些条条框框。

然而，在复习总结的时候，如果只是拘泥于所学数学知识点的直接讲解，那将是非常错误的。我的意思是说，我们对基础数学教育的最后阶段应该仔细斟酌，让学生明了所学数学知识的基本要点，从而让学生温故而知新。例如，数的概念和量的概念是精确思维的基本要素，但是在数学教育的基础阶段这两个要素并没有严格区分开来，因此学生可能在学习代数的过程中并没有意识到量的运用。对于禀赋较好的学生来说，他们经过数学学习会在思维上取得巨大的飞跃，会体会到量的概念对于数字度量的重要意义。从数的概念到量的概念的跨越，有的书专门讲到了这一点，例如欧几里得的《几何原本》第五卷就被公认为古希腊数学在这个方面的杰出成就，针对这个问题做出了详

---

[1] 两义情况或二义情况（ambiguous case）。——译者注

细的阐述。而传统的数学教育往往忽略了这本书的价值，简直可以说是肤浅无知，《几何原本》第五卷所讲到的数学知识没有得到足够的重视。要仔细选择其中的关键命题，要认真思考其中的证明过程。我们不是要把第五卷的整本书引用到课堂中，而是要学习其中能够反映基本思想的若干命题。这对一些学习程度较为落后的学生来说并不合适，但是对一些学习程度较好的学生来说则是非常有意思的学习内容。对于量的性质和有关量的精确测算，会给学生带来很多有意思的讨论。这样的数学教育工作不应该是不着边际的泛泛而谈，而应该在每一个阶段采用真实的案例予以解释说明，让学生认识量的特征是否缺失、是否模糊、是否可疑、是否确凿，诸如温度、热度、电流、喜悦与痛苦、质量与距离，这些都可以用来思考。

除了数量关系之外，另一个需要实践证明的数学知识是函数关系。数学中的一个函数相当于物理学中的一个定律，或是相当于几何学中的一条曲线。当一个学生在数学课程中学习作图的时候，他就开始了学习函数与曲线的关系。近些年的数学课程对作图教学做了不少改革，但是到目前为止，这种改革要么是过于激进，要么是过于保守。数学教育的意义不在于作图本身，而在于作图背后的教育理念。就像一支枪背后的那个持枪人一样，教育行为的有效性取决于相应的教育理念如何定位。但是回望我们的数学教育实践，其中存在着为作图而作图的倾向，如此一来我们的教育意义也就荡然无存了。

在学习简单的代数函数和三角函数时，我们其实也开始了学习物理定律的精确表达。例如，曲线可以视作物理定律的一种数学表现形式。在数学函数的物理定律演绎中，有一些是需要避免的，例如平方反比函数或者直接距离函数[1]。需要实际演绎的数学函数应该是简单易懂的，也应该是能够证明物理定律的具体运用的。对此我特别提出一

---

[1] 平方反比（the inverse square），直接距离（the direct distance）。——译者注

点，我们可以利用微分学里面的一些函数知识去做简单的曲线性质证明。在这个过程中，学生就会发现变化率的概念其实没有那么难；x的数次幂（例如 x^2、x^3 等）求导，很快就能算出来；如果借助几何学，还可以对 $\sin x$ 和 $\cos x$ 进行求导。如果像这样的话，我们就不会再给学生灌输他们既不能懂也不会用的数学公理，而是把学生吸引到一些具有重要意义的问题解决中。如果我们让学生通过这种方式熟悉数学概念的演绎过程，那么他们的思维肯定会有所改变。

在数学教育中，我们可以如此这般地把函数应用于物理定律的演绎之中。除此之外，数学知识还可以运用在其他的实践领域，只要在这个实践领域中存在着精确的客观规律，而这个客观规律无法通过自然观察得出准确结果，但是可以通过简单的数学计算而得出。同时，这样的数学计算过程往往就成了数学知识客观应用的代表性案例。统计学就是其中的另外一个代表性案例，凡是统计都要牵涉大量的数据，却可以通过数学轻而易举地解决和验证。一般情况下，只要稍微学点统计方法就可以对社会现象进行统计分析，这就是一个最简单的数学知识应用案例。

除此之外，学生还可以通过数学史来学习数学。我们不应把数学史仅仅看作年代、人名的简单拼凑，数学史的要义在于阐述过去的数学思想潮流，那些思潮什么时间首次出现，并得到了人们的关注。我之所以提出数学史这个问题，是因为我觉得我们可以运用数学史进行教学，也许可以帮助我们取得最为理想的效果。

到目前为止，我们讨论的是两个主要的问题，即量的概念和自然规律，人文教育体系中的数学课程必须要重视这两个问题。另外，数学还有一个方面不容忽视，即作为逻辑方法训练的必备工具。

那么，什么是逻辑方法呢？如何训练一个人的逻辑方法呢？

逻辑方法不仅仅是进行有效推理的知识，抑或是集中精力进行推理有关知识的活动。即便是停留在这样的知识或者活动层面，那也是十分可贵的。因为在人类的早期发展历史上，人们的心思主要用在摘果打猎、充饥果腹上，并无多少闲暇去归纳演绎、推理验证。所以，如果没有经过扎实的训练，很少有人专门从事逻辑推理。

如果要想成为一个娴熟的逻辑推理者，或者只是想用逻辑推理的基本知识启发普罗大众的心智，一般的推理知识或者推理活动是远远不够的。逻辑推理的要义在于准确把握关键问题、抓住核心证明要点、不断提出相关事实。只有经过长时间的练习，学会牢牢抓住中心思想，一个人才有可能领会逻辑推理的艺术。就此而言，我认为几何比代数更适合用于训练人们的推理能力。相对来说，代数公式运算难以一目了然，而几何空间图形则是直接醒目的。在几何的运算过程中，颜色、味道、重量诸如此类不相干的物质属性统统被忽略掉，这样的简化过程或者抽象过程本身就十分具有教育意义。另外，几何中的定义或者未经证明的命题都需要相应的几何问题事实清楚、关系明晰，所下定义或者所做命题只是证明几何问题的开端而已。随着几何问题的不断证明，其中的逻辑推理就愈发明显。在几何的学习过程中，学生也不会像学习代数一样面对问题的符号抽象，不管是什么样的抽象符号都会干扰规律的记忆。在几何学习中只要引导得当，在每一个阶段的每一个要点上，学生的逻辑推理就能逐步展开。通过这样的方式，逻辑方法的精义就能得以直观展现。

我们现在暂不考虑一般学生学习较慢的问题，也暂不考虑其他科目的时间占用问题，来思考一下几何在人文教育中能带来什么效果。我把几何学习的过程分为五个阶段，当然在教学实践中并不一定是按照我说的这五个阶段进行。第一个阶段的任务是学习"全等"[1]。我们对几何中的全等的认识取决于我们的判断，即当外部情形改变的时候，

---

[1] 全等（congruence）。——译者注

其内在性质保持不变。不论是什么几何图形的全等，全等的本质是两个几何图形之间点对点的对应关系，所以两个图形之间相对应的长度、角度都是相等的。其实，所谓长度相等、角度相等，在本质上就是长度、角度的全等。我们采用各种测量单位计算的长度、角度相等，都是判断全等的各种方法而已。在数学教育中，我们需要认真学习全等的概念和表现，更要认真领会全等所蕴含的逻辑推理思想和科学理论价值。通过学习全等，学生就能掌握一些几何图形（例如三角形、平行四边形、圆形）的性质，也能理解两个平面之间的相互关系。数学中的概念和公理太过纷繁复杂，我们在数学教育中必须选择其中具有重要意义的内容进行教学。所以，就全等教学来说，我们最好仅仅局限在这些经过证明的若干命题之中。

第二个阶段的任务是学习"相似"[1]。在几何的学习过程中，对相似性的学习可以集中在3~4个关键的命题上。相似概念是全等概念的延伸，同样是基于空间图形之间的点对点关系。如果要掌握几何的相似概念，那就一定要学习相似的或者处于相似位置的直线图形，分析其中的一两个简单特性。我们可以利用平面图或者地图来帮助学生掌握几何的相似概念。另外，我们也可以利用三角学的方法，通过三角学来帮助掌握其中的若干定理。

第三个阶段的任务是学习三角形原理[2]。三角学研究相似图形的关系问题和图形旋转中的周期性问题。在三角学中我们开始运用一些代数分析知识，用数量关系去研究几何图形。在数学中，我们可以用几何图形去证明相关函数的周期性。函数周期性最简单的证明就是利用三角，这一证明方式在测量活动中往往是必不可少的。三角学中有很多公式，有的公式虽然很重要，但是在数学教育中根本就用不着。数

---

[1] 相似（similarity）。——译者注
[2] 三角形原理（the elements of trigonometry）。——译者注

学教材中的三角学公式应该加以审慎选择，必须能够被学生通过实例予以证明。

针对三角学的学习，我们需要对其中的公式做出一定的选择，排除一些不适宜的内容，这在数学教育中是非常突出的一个现象。当然，就我个人对数学教育的理解而言，也许我对其中某个内容应该保留或者应该排除的判断是错误的。数学教育中的三角学内容不应太过复杂，可以通过一个角的各种运算来进行学习。但是如果三角运算太过繁复，超过了正弦、余弦、两角之和这样的内容，那就应该排除在数学教育之外。通过作图让学生证明三角学中的函数，通过运算让学生解决三角学中的问题。由此可以看出三角学有如下的意义：（1）验证全等和相似中的一些定理；（2）解决测量中的一些问题；（3）演绎有关周期和波动的一些函数。围绕这三个方面，通过数学教材的学习和实际应用的锻炼，学生就会在三角学中有所收获。

如果还想进一步拓展学生的三角学知识，传授其他更多的三角学公式，我们就要小心谨慎，一定要排除那些相对复杂的、较为系统的公式。所谓"排除"，我的意思是指学生不需要花费时间和精力去熟练地运用那些公式。对此而言，数学教师也许会觉得有必要在课堂上通过若干例子予以讲解，但是学生没有必要非得掌握具体的运算过程。另外，我特别提出一点，有关外切圆和内切圆的所有公式都应该被排除在三角学的教学范围之外，排除在整个几何科目的内容之外。这样的公式尽管在几何学中非常重要，但是在基础的、非专业的数学教育中意义不大。

如此看来，关于三角学的教学内容应该有所控制，使之切实可行。我听说美国的一所大学要求学生熟练掌握三角学的90个公式或定理，我们英国的数学教育尚不至于如此糟糕。就三角学而言，我们英国的基础数学教育基本上达到了我们预期的目标。

第四个阶段开始学习解析几何[1]。在代数函数的学习过程中，我们有时候可以运用图形予以证明，已经涉及了数形结合的基本思想。解析几何中的针对性更为明显，借助于相应的方程式去分析直线、圆、三种圆锥曲线。在此我特别提出两点。第一，在数学教育中，有时候我们的确没有必要把传授给学生的所有数学知识都予以证明。例如，在平面解析几何中如何化简一般二次曲线方程，这个问题对于基础阶段的学生来说难度太大，他们无法掌握具体的运算过程。但是我们要向学生讲授圆锥曲线的基本内容，梳理三种圆锥曲线的基本特征。

第二，我建议不要在数学教育中专门讲授"圆锥曲线几何"[2]。在一定条件下，我们对一些简单的几何图形不断演绎，从而进行解析几何运算，这是数学教育的常见方式。圆锥曲线几何分析计算圆锥曲线根据焦点和准线的变化而变化的问题，这对学生来说难以把握，因而明显不适合于我们的数学教育情境。较为常见的圆锥曲线解析几何公式是 $SP = e \cdot PM$，这在数学教育中就存在着很大的问题，既复杂难懂又毫无意义。我们究竟为什么要学习圆锥曲线的这种几何运算公式呢？为什么不去学习圆锥曲线的其他诸多解析式呢？当我们熟悉了笛卡尔方法论[3]之后，我们就会知道对于圆锥曲线的计算来说，首要的是一次方程和二次方程的运用。

---

[1] 解析几何（Analytical Geometry）。——译者注
[2] 圆锥曲线几何（geometrical conics）。——译者注
[3] 笛卡尔方法论（the Cartesian methods）。笛卡尔（Rene Descartes，1596—1650）在方法论中指出，研究问题的方法分四个步骤：(1) 不接受任何自己不清楚的道理，尽量避免偏见，要根据自己非常清楚和确定的判断。不管是什么权威的结论，都是可以怀疑的；(2) 如果要研究的问题复杂，就尽量将其分解为多个比较简单的小问题，一个一个地解决；(3) 把小问题从简单到复杂进行排列，先从容易解决的问题入手；(4) 问题解决之后，再综合起来检验。近现代西方科学研究的方法基本上是按照笛卡尔的方法论进行的，笛卡尔方法论对西方科学的飞速发展起了极大的促进作用。——译者注

按照这个过程，接下来的第五阶段就要学习有关投影几何[1]的内容。投影几何的核心概念是交比和投影[2]。投影是一种点对点的常见几何形式，也是前面所讲的全等和相似中的一对一的点对点关系。在教授投影几何的时候，我们一样要避免陷入旁枝末节之中而不分主次轻重。

只要任何图形之间存在着共同的性质，就可以推理证明相关图形之间的相互关系，这就是投影几何的理论意义。经过投影变换后，几何图形的投影性质保持不变，这是投影几何中的一个核心思想。交比概念主要是用来对几何图形的投影变换进行计算和度量。我们要针对若干少量命题来展开投影几何的教学，以此让学生学习其中蕴含的两个有紧密联系的过程。第一个是简化过程，这种简化是心理上的而不是逻辑上的，因为一般情况下几何投影中的逻辑关系是最为简单的，而学生需要证明的投影关系往往是他们都已熟知的或是明白易懂的。第二个是演绎过程，只要学生能够借助一定手段发现某种投影，或者能够通过一定的标准检验某种投影，就可以遵循从一般到具体的原则进行充分演绎。

在数学教育中，我们也可以对圆锥曲线投影和一般二次曲线方程进行简单讲解。但是，这两个方面是投影几何的边缘内容，因此我们在教学中不必做出详细的证明，只需直接告诉学生相关的公式就可以了。

以上所罗列的五个教学步骤并不复杂，属于一种理想化的几何教学模式，但是理想就是理想，往往不能真正实现。在我们实际的几何教学中，数学教材就每一个阶段所展示的演绎推理甚为寥寥。对此我们必须予以充分重视，让学生通过具体的例子认识每一个几何命题的重要意义。演绎推理过程可以通过教师的讲解进行演示，也可以通过学生的运算进行证明，只要能够帮助学生理解相关演绎推理的意义即

---

[1] 投影几何（Projective Geometry）。——译者注
[2] 交比（cross ration），投射（projection）。——译者注

可。只有这样，学生才会懂得如何分析空间图形的主要性质，也才会懂得基本方法的实际运用。

如果以这样的理想来实施数学教育，学生就能从中得到一些基本的数学知识，用于对客观世界做出科学的探究和哲学的思索。在此过程中，学生的逻辑方法也能够得以锻炼。我们的数学课程改革已经取得了不少进展，那么在此基础上我们能否再进一步，能否开拓教育视野、强化哲学思维？坦白地说，我认为单凭个人的努力是很难达到这个目的的。现实教育中存在着诸多困难，我对此已有说明。任何改革在实践中都会阻力重重。但是只要广大教师明白教育改革的目标，只要大家能够一起不断努力，我们就能在数学教育中大有作为，最终带来令人意想不到的改变。改变数学教育需要一步一步地进行，例如先编写必要的新教材，然后改革数学考试，强化数学中非技术性的一面。实际上，在我们的教育实践中大部分数学教师早已跃跃欲试，争取消除人们对数学教育的责难，让数学不再是一门枯燥无味的课程。

第七章 大学及其功用

一

　　大学的不断扩张是当代社会生活的一个显著特征。世界上的所有国家都参与到了这个时代潮流之中,而美国在高校建设中取得了尤为突出的成就。但是我们也有可能因为这个成就而看不到其中可能存在的问题。大学的数量不断增长,大学的规模不断扩大,大学内部的院系机构日益分化,在这个历史过程中我们必须牢记大学服务于国家的要旨。否则,大学的不断扩张也许会消弭大学的本质意义。因此,我们有必要反思大学的功用,这个反思适用于所有发达国家的高等教育,特别是美国的高等教育。美国的高等教育在全世界处于领先地位,只要引导得当,就能推动人类文明向前迈进,取得最为可喜的进步。

　　关于大学的功用,本文所述仅限于一般原理,并不涉及大学院系内部的诸多具体问题。既然是一般原理,就需要论证说明,在这里我就以商学院为例来谈谈我对大学的思考。之所以选取商学院为例,有三个原因。首先,商学院是大学发展中的一个新事物。其次,商学院与现代国家的主要社会活动关系密切,是高等教育改变国家面貌的一个经典范例。最后,就我个人而言,我现在有幸执教的哈佛大学规划了一所气势恢宏的商学院,建筑的基础工作正在接近尾声。

在这样一所全球领先的著名学府里，建立这样一所规模宏大的商学院，这本身就有一定的新意。哈佛大学商学院的建设标志着一个运动的高潮，在持续了多年的运动中，类似的院系风靡于美国高校。这是高等教育里面的一个新现象。面对新的情况，我们就需要对大学的功用做出新的思考，以深入理解大学造福社会的要义。

我们千万不要夸大商学院的新意，大学在历史上的任何时候都不曾拘囿于纯粹抽象的教育活动。例如，意大利的萨勒诺大学[1]是欧洲最早的大学，曾是专门进行医科教育的。再如，1316年的英国剑桥曾建立一所学院专门培养"为国王服务的工作人员"。大学培养出了神父、医生、律师、工程师，而如今的商业活动已经高度知识化，也需要大学教育的参与。商学院的所谓新意在于其课程与教学的诸多方面尚处于试验阶段，从这个意义上说，反思商学院的教育理念就具有特别重要的意义。但是我并不是要去探讨商学院的具体教育内容或者具体运作方式，我对这些内容并不熟悉，没有发言权。

二

大学既是实施教育的组织，也是进行研究的单位。但这并不是说大学的作用就是仅仅向大学生们传授客观知识，或者只是给大学教师们提供科研条件。

如果是单纯为了学习客观知识或者获取科研条件，那其实可以以更为经济的方式来实现，用不着耗费巨资国帑创办大学。书本并不是多么昂贵，师傅带徒弟的传承方式也是由来已久。15世纪印刷术普及之后，信息传播变得更为迅捷，那么大学似乎就更没有存在的理由了。

---

[1] 萨勒诺大学（Università degli Studi di Salerno），又译"萨莱诺大学"，位于意大利南部的萨勒诺市。——译者注

但实际上，建立大学的主要动力正是出现在15世纪之后，到了近代以来大学的兴建更是如火如荼。

大学存在的理由在于紧密联系年轻人和老年人，发挥想象，为学为道，搭建知识生长与生命热望之间的桥梁。大学的确是要传授知识，但必须是以一种充满想象力的方式来传授知识。这是大学服务于社会的应有之义，否则就不能成其为大学。只有展开想象的翅膀上下求索，方能激发灵感、求得新知。如此一来，所见事实就不再是简单的事实，而能从中发现无限的可能。所学知识也不再是记忆的负担，而是鲜活灵动、蓬勃欲发，犹如诗人一样吟诵我们的内心梦想，犹如建筑师一般勾画我们的人生蓝图。

想象不能脱离事实，必须用以阐明事实。通过自由想象，发现一般规律，检验于既存客观事实，应用于未知的新的疆域。有赖于如此这般的想象，我们才得以用知识去构筑一个新的世界，才得以用智慧去追寻人的生生不息。

年轻人总是富于想象力的，如果经过大学教育的强化，那么他们的想象力就可以让他们受用终生。一般情况下，富于想象力的人往往经验不足，而经验丰富的人往往想象力贫乏，这是世界的一个悲剧。没有知识，只有想象力，那是傻瓜；而没有想象力，只有知识，那是学究。[1] 大学的功用即在于此，把想象力与经验完美地融合在一起。

年轻人的想象充满活力，在大学教育的初期引导过程中，不要勉强年轻人立即诉诸实践。如果要求年轻人的想象一定要有条有理、切实可行，那么无偏见的思维习惯就无法养成，从一般规律到具体演绎之间的种种可能就会被遮蔽。面对这个大千世界，年轻人必须自由地思考，或正确或错误，无须畏惧危险。

---

[1] 类似于《论语·为政》里所说的"学而不思则罔，思而不学则殆"。——译者注

从这个意义上说，我们也可以把大学的一般功用当作商学院的特殊功用。如果有人指责商学院的作用就是为了培养喜欢经营生意的人，对此我们也不必在意。因为这是对人性的根本污蔑，把经商创业看成了追求狭隘物质享受的庸俗行为。我们都需要创业立家，我们的生活多姿多彩，对于此等胡说八道不足为信。

在现代的复杂社会机制中，各行各业的发展都离不开一定的思想探索。在较为原始的情况下，一个拓荒者可以依据内心本能判断大致方向，然后从高山一路走向远方。但是现代商业的状态是如此复杂，如果想要从中取得任何成就，必须先行予以分析思考，然后寻找可能的契机。原始的商业关系简单明了，人与人之间是直接接触的，物与物之间是相互对应的。今天的商业组织需要深刻洞悉各行各业的人们的心理特点，这些人生活在不同的城市、山川，来自海洋上、矿井下、森林中。今天的商业组织需要深入了解热带地区、温带地区的经济情况怎么样，大型集团的管理方式是如何地盘根错节，又是如何地牵一发而动全身。今天的商业组织需要熟练掌握各个地方有关政治、经济的法律法规，绝不仅仅是纸上谈兵，必须能够实打实地恪守法律条文开展相关活动。今天的商业组织需要懂得政府的运作机制，悉知在具体的条件下会有什么样的灵活变化，也需要领会各种团体机构的社会影响，学会倾听人们的疾苦从而服务于大众的福利。今天的商业组织需要不断认识如何保持健康、如何防止疲劳、如何追求长寿。今天的商业组织需要充分理解工厂的生产如何影响人们的生活，科学理论知识如何改变社会的进步。今天的商业组织需要训练有素地做出正确判断，是或者不是，不是出于夜郎自大，而是出于自知自信，对诸多可能能够做出清醒的评估。

大学培育出了我们文明世界中的知识先驱——神父、律师、医生、政治家、科学家和文学家，他们高举理想的旗帜，引领人们在时代的洪流中不断向前。清教徒[1]逃离英国,根据他们自己的宗教信仰在新大陆重建理想社会,创办于美国坎布里奇的哈佛大学就是早期清教徒的杰作之一。"坎布里奇"[2]意即"剑桥",根据远在英国的古老的剑桥而命名。不少清教徒曾经在剑桥接受高等教育,那里是英国的思想圣地。与那些早期的知识先驱所从事的各行各业一样,现代的商业行为也需要充满智慧的想象力。而大学恰恰就能够培育这种想象的智慧,因而欧洲的各个民族才能够得以不断前进。

在中世纪的早期历史上,大学的萌芽看起来是模糊不清的,甚至是难以察觉的。大学的历史发展是一个非常缓慢的、自然而然的过程,但是欧洲历史的诸多方面因此而取得持续的、快速的进步。通过大学的推动作用,人们行动上的探索与思想上的创新相互融合。然而,在历史的初期,人们可能无法判断一所大学到底能起到什么样的推动作用。即便在今天,人们有时也难于理解大学到底有何功用。大学毕竟是人的创造物,难免存在不完善的甚至是失败的地方。但总体来看,大学在全世界各地都取得了非凡的成就。各个国家或地区的文化史都证明了大学的巨大影响,例如意大利、法国、德国、荷兰、苏格兰、英格兰、美国。这里所说的"文化史",并不特指专家学者的思想史,而是泛指社会成员的生活史。他们投身于国家建设,也许是法国、德国抑或其他国家,燃烧着生活的热情,做出了卓越的贡献,凝聚了爱国的精神。我们每一个人都愿意成为这样的一分子,为社会发光发热。

---

[1] 清教徒(Pilgrim Fathers),这里指的是从英国到美国的清教徒前辈移民,早期清教徒(Puritan)信奉加尔文教义(Calvinism),为了逃避当时英国的宗教迫害,为了他们宗教自由,于1620年搭乘"五月花"(the Mayflower)号货船到达美国的普利茅斯(Plymouth),开始建立殖民地。——译者注

[2] "坎布里奇"(Cambridge),与英国的剑桥同名,这里为了避免混淆把美国的"Cambridge"翻译为"坎布里奇"。由于美国和英国的历史关系,美国和英国的不少地名相同或者相似。——译者注

但是有一个巨大的困难摆在眼前，妨碍了我们高尚理想的可能实现。在现代社会中，这样的困难甚至会成为一个危害。例如，在任何一个大的机构组织中，作为职场新人的年轻人必须要服从安排，在指定的岗位上做既定的工作。没有哪个大公司的总裁会在自己的办公室里与一个最年轻的新人商讨公司大事，年轻人往往是该干什么就得干什么，也许偶尔会看到他们的总裁出入办公大楼。对于年轻人来说，他们每天所做的工作也是一种锻炼，从中获取知识，从中磨砺品性。更直白地说，这也是他们自己作为新人唯一能做的工作，也是公司雇用他们需要他们做的工作。从这个意义上说，我们对此也无可厚非，公司文化传统就是这样的。但是再仔细想想，这样的公司传统会产生一个不良的后果，因为长期按部就班地工作会磨灭人的想象力。

想象力被早早地磨灭，一个人在职业生涯后期所必需的这种素质就过早地被扼杀了。我以此为例来说明一个常见的情况：一个人的专业技能必须经过长期培训，但这往往有损于他的思想活力，而专业技能的发展是建立在一定的思维想象的基础上的。这是我们教育中的一个关键问题，也是所有困难的症结所在。

大学培养现代商务的从业者，或者是其他类型的专业人员，就需要提升他们的想象力，让他们充满想象地把握各行各业之中潜藏的种种规律。如此一来，大学毕业生在见习阶段就能具备一定的想象力，因而能从工作的烦琐之中发现专业的窍门。如果年轻人能从工作之中发现规律、验证规律，那么他们按部就班的工作就有了新的意义。所以，一个人只有经过恰当的训练方能获得一定的想象力，从而养成管中窥豹的习惯。否则，就只能日复一日地循规蹈矩，慢慢地总结经验教训。

综上所述，大学的功用就在于培养学生通过想象获取知识的能力。如果不是为了这个特定的想象力，商务人士或者其他专业人士就没有必要上大学了，不如在实践中一点一点地积累经验教训。如果离开了想象，大学将无一是处，或将百无一用。

三

想象力会在人与人之间传染。想象力无法用尺码丈量，无法用磅秤称重，无法直接搬运给学生。只有通过沟通和交流，教师才能让学生懂得如何想象，而这样的教师的学识中必须含有充满智慧的想象。关于这一点，其实我只是在重复前人说过的话而已。两千多年前，古人把教育比喻为一把火炬代代相传，而我所说的想象力就是那把点燃的火炬。大学存在的根本意义就在于大学的教师队伍，他们的为学问道都应被想象力的火炬熊熊点燃，这是大学教育的重中之重。如果没有正确对待这个问题，那么不管大学规模如何扩张、学生数量如何增长、课程设置如何多样，不管我们对这些表面现象多么引以为傲，大学最终都将难以达成其教育理想。

想象力与学问的结合需要放下思想包袱，摆脱束缚，无忧无惧；需要灵活变通，借他山之石琢己身之玉，认真学习别人的不同观念和见解；需要好奇心的驱使，需要自信心的支持，而自信源于学问的不断更新，以及而后推动的社会进步。我们无法一劳永逸地获得想象力，接着无限期地储存在保鲜盒里，然后想什么时候取就什么时候取，想取多少就取多少。于想象之中为学问道是一种存在的方式，而不是一件可以买卖的商品。

大学教师的卓越之处就在于能够充分认识和熟练掌握想象力与学问的结合，而正是基于这一点，大学的育人功能和科研功能才会有机地融合在一起。想要大学教师充满想象力吗？那就鼓励他们做研究吧。想要大学科研人员充满想象力吗？那就鼓励他们教学吧，让他们与年轻的学子展开思想的对话，当这些年轻人正处在一生之中最为好奇、最富于想象力的阶段，当这些大学生的心智刚刚成熟而需要恰当引导的时候。面对这些思想活跃的大学生，科研人员的课程讲授应该张弛有度、娓娓道来；面对思想活跃的科研人员，大学生的大学生活一定能收获颇丰、获益匪浅。所谓教育，其实就是引导人们探索生活；所谓研究，其实就是思想的历险；所谓大学，其实就是年轻人和老年人一起迈向未来的场所。教育的成败在很大程度上取决于有关知识是否新颖，知识的新颖可以体现在知识自身的更新换代上，也可以体现在知识应用的与时俱进上。鱼儿一刻也离不开水，知识一日也离不开"新"[1]。有的知识讲的是古老的生物物种，有的知识讲的是祖辈的传统道理，但是不管知识的内容有多么久远，在将其传授给学生的时候务必赋予其当下的新意，使之像刚刚从大海里捕捞上来的鱼一样新鲜无比。

学者的作用就是唤起生活中的智慧与美，如果没有学者的思想魔力，智慧与美就要被湮灭在往昔的岁月之中。一个不断前进的社会需要依靠这三种人：学者、发现者和创造者。除了这三种专才之外，社会的进步也依靠每一位受过教育的社会成员，每一位社会成员都应具备一定的知识素养、一定的探索精神、一定的创新能力。所谓探索精神，指的是不断认识大道之理；所谓创新能力，指的是弘理求实，于现实实践之中贯以相关真理。知识素养、探索精神、创新能力这三者之间是相辅相成的。从一定程度上说，一个人如果能在日常实践中有益于社会进步，那么他就是一个不折不扣的创造者。尺有所短，寸有所长，每一个人的自身境况不同，因而所做贡献不一。那么对于国家来说，就需要综合协调各种社会推动力量，例如，通过学术研究发展

---

[1] 怀特海用英文单词"new"、"novelty"和"freshness"表示"新"，类似于《大学》中所讲到的"苟日新，日日新，又日新"。——译者注

商业实践，或者反过来，通过商业实践深化学术研究。协调进步力量，推动社会进步，这正是大学的功用，大学就是这样的一个有效地推动社会进步的中介。虽然大学谈不上是唯一的社会文明发展中介，但是纵观当今世界，没有哪一个发达国家的大学不是欣欣向荣的。

如何衡量一所大学的知识产出？一所大学的思想创新绝不仅仅体现在一些署名发表的论文和书籍中。人各有异，知也不同，行也不一，大学的知识贡献无法用单一的尺度来衡量。例如，一些极具思想影响力的学者几乎没有发表过什么文章，甚至没有写下过什么只言片语。实际上在每一所大学里，我们也总会看到一些优秀的大学教师著述甚少。这些优秀教师的创新思想体现在他们的课程讲授中，体现在师生的讨论互动中，通过这些方式在教育中发挥着巨大的影响力。时光荏苒，他们培养的学生会一个一个地年老而逝去，这些教师的名字也会逐渐被人忘记。在众多被人忘记的、曾经做出伟大贡献的优秀教师之中，其中有一位大家都熟知能详，他就是苏格拉底[1]。

所以，如果仅仅通过署名发表的论文书籍来衡量一位大学教师的贡献多寡，那将是一个极大的错误。现今存在着这样的一个趋势，可能会导致这么一个错误。对此我们有必要提出坚决的反对意见，抗议有关当局一意孤行，有损于高等教育的效应，有害于无私奉献的风气。

除了上述比较特殊的情况之外，总体而言，评估一位大学教师的效率应该落实于其公开发表的学术思想。学术贡献应该用思想影响来衡量，而不是用作品字数来衡量。

由此我们可以看出，高校教师管理与商业组织管理不可同日而语。大学教师的社会公共参与精神和对高等教育事业的热忱决定了一所大

---

[1] 苏格拉底（Socrates，公元前470/469—公元前399），古希腊哲学家，西方哲学奠基人。苏格拉底并无著述流传，他的思想记载于他的学生柏拉图（Plato）和色诺芬（Xenophon）的作品中。——译者注

学的水平高低。大学教师就应该是一支学术队伍，相互学习，自由决定他们的教学、研究活动。对大学教师的教学科研活动可以设定一定的规章制度，例如授课的时间、师生的考勤，但是教学科研的核心内容应该由他们自主决定。

谈到大学教师的学术自由，并不是说就有悖于教师工作的法律公正。在一定的合法条件下，例如工作量与工作薪酬这样的法律规定，雇用一个人提供合法的服务，这都是合情合理的。只有当一个人愿意从事这项工作的时候，他才会接受这个工作岗位。[1]

那么关于大学教育就只剩下一个问题了：在什么条件下才能培养出合格的大学教师队伍，从而建设好一所大学呢？现实之中的危险就在于很有可能培养出完全不合格的大学教师，例如有的学究貌似学问高深，实则迂愚无用。如果是这样误人子弟，那么可能再过几十年，公众就会慢慢发现这样的大学是如何地欺世盗名。

绝不能仿照一家公司的章程来管理一所大学，这是最高教育当局务必谨记的一条原则，也是现代民主国家的现代大学体制的应有要义。对于一所大学的商学院的建设发展来说，这个原则同样适用。其实就如何管理一所大学这个话题来说，美国许多大学的校长已经在公开场合做出了详细阐明，我对此不必赘言。但是对于美国或者其他国家的公众来说，到底有多少人真正懂得这个道理，恐怕也是个疑问。大学培育人才的根本问题就在于如何聚集一批富有想象力的学者，然后让年轻学子感受他们的思想智慧。而如何培养这样的学者，需要我们予以认真思考。实践证明，我们对此万万不可大意。

---

[1] 怀特海为大学教师的学术自由提供辩护，认为它是合法的、合理的。——译者注

四

巴黎大学和牛津大学是欧洲的两所名校,历史悠久,蜚声世界。我在这里只谈英国的牛津大学,因为我是英国人,对此比较熟悉。在过去的历史之中,牛津大学也许曾经有过不当之处。尽管牛津大学有一些问题,但是它有一个最大的优点贯穿了历史的始终,与这个优点相比,它曾经的不足之处犹如尘埃一样微不足道。这个优点就是:几百年来,牛津大学在漫长的历史发展过程中造就了一批又一批学者,他们的为学问道充满了想象的智慧。对于这一点,但凡热爱文化的人都会心存感念。

跨越大西洋,从欧洲来到美国,我们同样能发现许许多多诸如此类的例子。《独立宣言》的作者杰斐逊[1]先生被举世公认为最伟大的美国人,他成就卓著,彪炳史册。杰斐逊创建了一所大学,倾其所能精心育人。校舍古朴,环境优美,学者博雅,管理有方,这所大学的方方面面都贯穿了一个核心要点,即激发想象力。

还有其他许多美国大学都可以用来佐证我的观点,但是我最后要说的是哈佛大学,特别是因其作为清教徒运动的一所代表性大学。17和18世纪美国新英格兰地区的清教徒非常具有想象力。虽然他们惯于克己复礼、生活质朴,虽然他们厌恶浮华虚伪、矫揉造作,但是在追求真理的道路上,他们极具智慧的想象力。那个时期的哈佛大学培养出了许多世界著名的思想大师,足以证明当时的清教徒教授们充满想象的智慧。在清教徒运动式微后期,在新英格兰文学[2]的黄金时代,爱

---

[1] 杰斐逊(Thomas Jefferson,1743—1826),美国开国元勋之一,美国第三任总统,《独立宣言》(*Declaration of Independence*)(1776)的主要起草人,创办了弗吉尼亚大学(University of Virginia)。——译者注

[2] 19世纪30年代前后出现在美国东北部新英格兰地区的文学和哲学运动,被称为"新英格兰文艺复兴"。——译者注

默生[1]、洛威尔[2]、朗费罗[3]都曾在哈佛大学执教。在随后的现代科学时代中，威廉·詹姆斯[4]这样的学者出现在哈佛大学，同样也是富于想象力的典型代表。

如今的哈佛大学成立了商学院，商学院依然需要传承历史悠久的智慧的想象力，接过这把代代相传、熊熊燃烧的火炬。从一定意义上说，这是一把危险的火炬，因为它曾经多次引燃大火[5]。假如我们胆怯于此，那就干脆直接关闭大学算了。想象的智慧传承于希腊、佛罗伦萨、威尼斯这样的商人中，传承于荷兰的学术中，传承于英国的诗歌中。商业与想象共生共长，没有谁不会期盼他的国家富于这样的智慧，从而重现雅典曾经达到过的那种辉煌：

彼之民兮，威仪堂堂，
观往来兮，引风领尚。[6]

总之，美国的教育也应追求如此一般的光荣与梦想。

---

[1] 爱默生（Ralph Waldo Emerson，1803—1882），美国诗人、作家，美国超验主义（Transcendentalism）文学运动领导者，著有《论自然》（*Nature*）、《英国人的性格》（*English Traits*）等，演讲辞有《论美国的学者》（*The American Scholar*）等。——译者注

[2] 洛威尔（James Russell Lowell，1819—1891），美国诗人、批评家、编辑、外交官，著有《比格罗诗稿》（*The Biglow Papers*）、《生命中的一年》（*A Year's Life*）等。——译者注

[3] 朗费罗（Henry Wadsworth Longfellow，1807—1882），美国诗人、教育家，著有《夜吟》（*Voices of the Night*）、《歌谣及其他》（*Ballads and Other Poems*）等。——译者注

[4] 威廉·詹姆斯（William James，1842—1910），美国哲学家、心理学家，被誉为"美国心理学之父"，"实用主义"（pragmatism）倡导者。著有《心理学原理》（*The Principles of Psychology*）、《彻底经验主义论文集》（*Essays in Radical Empiricism*）等。——译者注

[5] 即多次引燃思想的火花，多次燎原我们人类的文明历史。——译者注

[6] 对应原文是："Her citizens, imperial spirits, / Rule the present from the past."直译为："她的公民，帝国的精神；从过去统治到现在。"——译者注

译者后记

《教育的目的》这本书看起来不算厚,但是翻译起来真的是难。在翻译过程中,我们往往是枯坐一整天,而翻译出来的只有寥寥几百个汉字。回顾此译本形成的前前后后,我们不禁总是想起董桥的感叹,看来文字还真是肉做的。

怀特海先生是一位卓越的数学家和哲学家,其皇皇巨著、巍巍学问于近百年来在全世界有着深刻的影响。因其在自然学科领域的成就,当选为英国皇家学会院士;因其在人文学科领域的成就,当选为英国人文和社会科学院院士;因其在哲学上的杰出贡献,当选为亚里士多德学会的会长。他曾在英美两国的著名学府任教,从剑桥到哈佛都撒播了他的思想火种。巍巍乎可畏,煌煌乎可敬。于敬于畏,如履薄冰,这是整个翻译过程的基本心态。把怀特海的教育哲理之思引介给读者,该如何做到"信达雅",该如何融通"隔与不隔",该如何协调"形似与神似",这样的问题一直纠缠在每一个字词或句读之中。

如果太过形似,那么翻译出来的东西颠三倒四、佶屈聱牙、支离破碎、莫名其妙,读者一定会说:这是机器翻译出来的吧。如果太过神似,那么就是欺上瞒下,偏离怀特海的原本思想,戏弄读者的学习体验,仰望头顶三尺之上,万万不敢造次。其中之困难,翻译专业人士常比喻为戴着镣铐的舞蹈。

其学理思想高深复杂，其学术文体晦涩难辨。怀特海在论述教育问题的时候，往往会跨界到其他领域中去，从教育到心理、从哲学到宗教、从人文到科学，怀特海的每一次倏忽转换都会让人撵得气喘吁吁。在怀特海的语言表达之中，诸如对文艺复兴时期莎士比亚有关作品的引用已经算是比较好懂的了，其随手拈来的古希腊、古罗马时期的一个又一个历史典故，只能让人一次又一次地望洋兴叹。那么，准确而流畅地把怀特海的思想传达给读者就不是一件容易的事情。在当今信息时代，读者的心理期待可能会更高，读者需要理解怀特海的教育思想，也需要掌握其中的细枝末节。同时，读者需要的是简单明了、一目了然，而不是拗口难懂、艰深生僻，所以在翻译的过程中，对待一字一词都不得不小心谨慎。因此，在能够直译的地方我们尽量直译，而当我们发现直译实在是无法表达其内在思想时，就不得不以其意义为核心来遣词造句。同时，为了弥补貌似脱离原文的意译，我们添加了大量的注释，希望能帮助读者了悟其间的文与思、形与意。

在翻译这本书的过程中，我们一直不断地反思：一方面，是否背叛了怀特海，是否误解了怀特海，是否没有传达出怀特海高屋建瓴的大师风范，是否没有领悟到怀特海教化育人的深邃广博；另一方面，有没有做到思想内容的通达，有没有做到语言文字的顺畅，能不能经受读者在阅读中的批判眼光的考验，能不能面对读者在阅读中的种种质疑或发难。对于翻译的优雅而言，这是一个尽量靠近的理想；对于翻译的忠实而言，这是一个必须坚守的底线。然而，在作者、读者和译者之间，一直存在着微妙的关系，想要达成翻译的"黄中通理"就必需读者的参与。与其说请教于方家之类有心无感的客气话，毋宁邀请大家一起来解读怀特海的思想和语言。在读者的参与过程中，互文见义就会逐渐产生，每一个人心中的哈姆雷特就会慢慢浮现，每一个人诉求的大道之理就会不断清晰。那么，教育的目的不就这样实现了吗？

译　者
2015年11月于西南大学

怀特海生平简介

1861年2月15日出生于英国肯特郡萨尼特岛上的拉姆斯盖特（Ramsgate, Isle of Thanet, Kent, England）。

1880年在剑桥大学三一学院（Trinity College, Cambridge）学习数学专业，1884年毕业。

1885年在剑桥大学三一学院获得奖学金，并成为三一学院的教师，从事数学专业和物理专业的教学和研究工作。

1903年当选为英国皇家学会院士（Fellow of the Royal Society）。

1911年于伦敦大学学院（University College London）从事教学、科研和管理工作。

1914年于帝国理工学院（Imperial College of Science and Technology）教授应用数学。

1922年当选为亚里士多德学会会长（President of the Aristotelian Society）。

1924年于哈佛大学（Harvard University）教授哲学。

1931年当选为英国人文和社会科学院院士（Fellow of the British Academy）。

1937年于哈佛大学退休。

1947年10月30日逝世于美国马萨诸塞州的坎布里奇（Cambridge, Massachusetts, USA）。

怀特海主要著述目录

1898. *A Treatise on Universal Algebra*, Cambridge: Cambridge University Press.

1902. "On Cardinal Numbers," *American Journal of Mathematics*, 24: 367–394.

1906a. *The Axioms of Projective Geometry*, Cambridge: Cambridge University Press.

1906b. "On Mathematical Concepts of the Material World," *Philosophical Transactions of the Royal Society of London*, Series A, 205 (1906): 465–525.

1907. *The Axioms of Descriptive Geometry*, Cambridge: Cambridge University Press.

1910–1913, *Principia Mathematica* (with Bertrand Russell), Cambridge: Cambridge University Press.

1911. *An Introduction to Mathematics*, London: Williams and Norgate.

1917. *The Organisation of Thought, Educational and Scientific*, London: Williams & Norgate.

1919. *An Enquiry concerning the Principles of Natural Knowledge*, Cambridge: Cambridge University Press.

1920. *The Concept of Nature*, Cambridge: Cambridge University Press; reissued Mineola, NY: Dover Publications, Inc., 2004.

1922. *The Principle of Relativity with Applications to Physical Science*, Cambridge: Cambridge University Press.

1925. *Science and the Modern World*, Cambridge: Cambridge University

Press, 1926.

1926. *Religion in the Making*, New York: Macmillan.

1927. *Symbolism, Its Meaning and Effect*, New York: Macmillan.

1929a. *The Aims of Education and Other Essays*, New York: The Macmillan Company.

1929b. *The Function of Reason*, Princeton: Princeton University Press.

1929c. *Process and Reality*, New York: Macmillan.

1933. *Adventures of Ideas*, Cambridge: Cambridge University Press; New York: Macmillan.

1934. *Nature and Life*, Chicago: University of Chicago Press.

1938. *Modes of Thought*, New York: Macmillan.

1947. *Essays in Science and Philosophy*, New York: Philosophical Library.

The Aims of Education
教育的目的
（英文版）

Alfred North Whitehead

CHAPTER 1

THE AIMS OF EDUCATION

Culture is activity of thought, and receptiveness to beauty and humane feeling. Scraps of information have nothing to do with it. A merely well-informed man is the most useless bore on God's earth. What we should aim at producing is men who possess both culture and expert knowledge in some special direction. Their expert knowledge will give them the ground to start from, and their culture will lead them as deep as philosophy and as high as art. We have to remember that the valuable intellectual development is self-development, and that it mostly takes place between the ages of sixteen and thirty. As to training, the most important part is given by mothers before the age of twelve. A saying due to Archbishop Temple illustrates my meaning. Surprise was expressed at the success in after-life of a man, who as a boy at Rugby had been somewhat undistinguished. He answered, "It is not what they are at eighteen, it is what they become afterwards that matters."

In training a child to activity of thought, above all things we must beware of what I will call "inert ideas" — that is to say, ideas that are merely received into the mind without being utilised, or tested, or thrown into fresh combinations.

In the history of education, the most striking phenomenon is that schools of learning, which at one epoch are alive with a ferment of genius, in a succeeding generation exhibit merely pedantry and routine. The reason is, that they are overladen with inert ideas. Education with inert ideas is not only useless: it is, above all things, harmful — *Corruptio optimi, pessima.*

Except at rare intervals of intellectual ferment, education in the past has been radically infected with inert ideas. That is the reason why uneducated clever women, who have seen much of the world, are in middle life so much the most cultured part of the community. They have been saved from this horrible burden of inert ideas. Every intellectual revolution which has ever stirred humanity into greatness has been a passionate protest against inert ideas. Then, alas, with pathetic ignorance of human psychology, it has proceeded by some educational scheme to bind humanity afresh with inert ideas of its own fashioning.

Let us now ask how in our system of education we are to guard against this mental dryrot. We enunciate two educational commandments, "Do not teach too many subjects," and again, "What you teach, teach thoroughly."

The result of teaching small parts of a large number of subjects is the passive reception of disconnected ideas, not illumined with any spark of vitality. Let the main ideas which are introduced into a child's education be few and important, and let them be thrown into every combination possible. The child should make them his own, and should understand their application here and now in the circumstances of his actual life. From the very beginning of his education, the child should experience the joy of discovery. The discovery which he has to make, is that general ideas give an understanding of that stream of events which pours through his life, which is his life. By understanding I mean more than a mere logical analysis, though that is included. I mean "understanding" in the sense in which it is used in the French proverb, "To understand all, is to forgive all." Pedants sneer at an education which is useful. But if education is not useful, what is it? Is it a talent, to be hidden away in a napkin? Of course, education should be useful, whatever your aim in life. It was useful to Saint Augustine and it was useful to Napoleon. It is useful, because understanding is useful.

I pass lightly over that understanding which should be given by the literary side of education. Nor do I wish to be supposed to pronounce on the relative merits of a classical or a modern curriculum. I would only remark that the understanding which we want is an understanding of an insistent present. The only use of a knowledge of the past is to equip us for the present. No more deadly harm can be done to young minds than by depreciation of the present. The present contains all that there is. It is holy ground; for it is the past, and it is the future. At the same time it must be observed that an age is no less past if it existed two hundred years ago than if it existed two thousand years ago. Do not be deceived by the pedantry of dates. The ages of Shakespeare and of Molière are no less past than are the ages of Sophocles and of Virgil. The communion of saints is a great and inspiring assemblage, but it has only one possible hall of meeting, and that is, the present; and the mere lapse of time through which any particular group of saints must travel to reach that meeting-place, makes very little difference.

Passing now to the scientific and logical side of education, we remember that here also ideas which are not utilised are positively harmful. By utilising an idea, I mean relating it to that stream, compounded of sense perceptions, feelings, hopes, desires, and of mental activities adjusting thought to thought, which forms our life. I can imagine a set of beings which might fortify their souls by passively reviewing disconnected ideas. Humanity is not built that way — except perhaps some editors of newspapers.

In scientific training, the first thing to do with an idea is to prove it. But allow me for one moment to extend the meaning of "prove"; I mean — to prove its worth. Now an idea is not worth much unless the propositions in which it is embodied are true. Accordingly an essential part of the proof of an idea is the proof, either by experiment or by logic, of the truth of the propositions. But it is not essential that this proof of the truth should constitute the first introduction to the idea. After all, its assertion by the authority of respectable teachers is sufficient evidence to begin with. In our first contact with a set of propositions, we commence by appreciating their importance. That is what we all do in after-life. We do not attempt, in the strict sense, to prove or to disprove anything, unless its importance makes it worthy of that honour. These two processes of proof, in the narrow sense, and of appreciation, do not require a rigid separation in time. Both can be

The Aims of Education

proceeded with nearly concurrently. But in so far as either process must have the priority, it should be that of appreciation by use.

Furthermore, we should not endeavour to use propositions in isolation. Emphatically I do not mean, a neat little set of experiments to illustrate Proposition I and then the proof of Proposition I, a neat little set of experiments to illustrate Proposition II and then the proof of Proposition II, and so on to the end of the book. Nothing could be more boring. Interrelated truths are utilised *en bloc*, and the various propositions are employed in any order, and with any reiteration. Choose some important applications of your theoretical subject; and study them concurrently with the systematic theoretical exposition. Keep the theoretical exposition short and simple, but let it be strict and rigid so far as it goes. It should not be too long for it to be easily known with thoroughness and accuracy. The consequences of a plethora of half-digested theoretical knowledge are deplorable. Also the theory should not be muddled up with the practice. The child should have no doubt when it is proving and when it is utilising. My point is that what is proved should be utilised, and that what is utilised should — so far as is practicable — be proved. I am far from asserting that proof and utilisation are the same thing.

At this point of my discourse, I can most directly carry forward my argument in the outward form of a digression. We are only just realising that the art and science of education require a genius and a study of their own; and that this genius and this science are more than a bare knowledge of some branch of science or of literature. This truth was partially perceived in the past generation; and headmasters, somewhat crudely, were apt to supersede learning in their colleagues by requiring left-hand bowling and a taste for football. But culture is more than cricket, and more than football, and more than extent of knowledge.

Education is the acquisition of the art of the utilisation of knowledge. This is an art very difficult to impart. Whenever a textbook is written of real educational worth, you may be quite certain that some reviewer will say that it will be difficult to teach from it. Of course it will be difficult to teach from it. If it were easy, the book ought to be burned; for it cannot be educational. In education, as elsewhere, the broad primrose path leads to a nasty place. This evil path is represented by a book or a set of lectures which will practically enable the student to learn by heart all the questions likely to be asked at the next external examination. And I may say in passing that no educational system is possible unless every question directly asked of a pupil at any examination is either framed or modified by the actual teacher of that pupil in that subject. The external assessor may report on the curriculum or on the performance of the pupils, but never should be allowed to ask the pupil a question which has not been strictly supervised by the actual teacher, or at least inspired by a long conference with him. There are a few exceptions to this rule, but they are exceptions, and could easily be allowed for under the general rule.

We now return to my previous point, that theoretical ideas should always find important applications within the pupil's curriculum. This is not an easy doctrine to apply, but a very hard one. It contains within itself the problem of keeping knowledge alive, of preventing it from becoming inert, which is the central problem of all education.

The best procedure will depend on several factors, none of which can be neglected, namely, the genius of the teacher, the intellectual type of the pupils, their prospects in life, the opportunities offered by the immediate surroundings of the school, and allied factors of this sort. It is for this reason that the uniform external examination is so deadly. We do not denounce it because we are cranks, and like denouncing established things. We are not so childish. Also, of course, such examinations have their use in testing slackness. Our reason of dislike is very definite and very practical. It kills the best part of culture. When you analyse in the light of experience the central task of education, you find that its successful accomplishment depends on a delicate adjustment of many variable factors. The reason is that we are dealing with human minds, and not with dead matter. The evocation of curiosity, of judgment, of the power of mastering a complicated tangle of circumstances, the use of theory in giving foresight in special cases — all these powers are not to be imparted by a set rule embodied in one schedule of examination subjects.

I appeal to you, as practical teachers. With good discipline, it is always possible to pump into the minds of a class a certain quantity of inert knowledge. You take a text-book and make them learn it. So far, so good. The child then knows how to solve a quadratic equation. But what is the point of teaching a child to solve a quadratic equation? There is a traditional answer to this question. It runs thus: The mind is an instrument, you first sharpen it, and then use it; the acquisition of the power of solving a quadratic equation is part of the process of sharpening the mind. Now there is just enough truth in this answer to have made it live through the ages. But for all its half-truth, it embodies a radical error which bids fair to stifle the genius of the modern world. I do not know who was first responsible for this analogy of the mind to a dead instrument. For aught I know, it may have been one of the seven wise men of Greece, or a committee of the whole lot of them. Whoever was the originator, there can be no doubt of the authority which it has acquired by the continuous approval bestowed upon it by eminent persons. But whatever its weight of authority, whatever the high approval which it can quote, I have no hesitation in denouncing it as one of the most fatal, erroneous, and dangerous conceptions ever introduced into the theory of education. The mind is never passive; it is a perpetual activity, delicate, receptive, responsive to stimulus. You cannot postpone its life until you have sharpened it. Whatever interest attaches to your subject-matter must be evoked here and now; whatever powers you are strengthening in the pupil, must be exercised here and now; whatever possibilities of mental life your teaching should impart, must be exhibited here and now. That is the golden rule of education, and a very difficult rule to follow.

The difficulty is just this: the apprehension of general ideas, intellectual habits of mind, and pleasurable interest in mental achievement can be evoked by no form of words, however accurately adjusted. All practical teachers know that education is a patient process of the mastery of details, minute by minute, hour by hour, day by day. There is no royal road to

Chapter 1 The Aims of Education

learning through an airy path of brilliant generalisations. There is a proverb about the difficulty of seeing the wood because of the trees. That difficulty is exactly the point which I am enforcing. The problem of education is to make the pupil see the wood by means of the trees.

The solution which I am urging, is to eradicate the fatal disconnection of subjects which kills the vitality of our modern curriculum. There is only one subject-matter for education, and that is Life in all its manifestations. Instead of this single unity, we offer children — Algebra, from which nothing follows; Geometry, from which nothing follows; Science, from which nothing follows; History, from which nothing follows; a Couple of Languages, never mastered; and lastly, most dreary of all, Literature, represented by plays of Shakespeare, with philological notes and short analyses of plot and character to be in substance committed to memory. Can such a list be said to represent Life, as it is known in the midst of the living of it? The best that can be said of it is, that it is a rapid table of contents which a deity might run over in his mind while he was thinking of creating a world, and has not yet determined how to put it together.

Let us now return to quadratic equations. We still have on hand the unanswered question. Why should children be taught their solution? Unless quadratic equations fit into a connected curriculum, of course there is no reason to teach anything about them. Furthermore, extensive as should be the place of mathematics in a complete culture, I am a little doubtful whether for many types of boys algebraic solutions of quadratic equations do not lie on the specialist side of mathematics. I may here remind you that as yet I have not said anything of the psychology or the content of the specialism, which is so necessary a part of an ideal education. But all that is an evasion of our real question, and I merely state it in order to avoid being misunderstood in my answer.

Quadratic equations are part of algebra, and algebra is the intellectual instrument which has been created for rendering clear the quantitative aspects of the world. There is no getting out of it. Through and through the world is infected with quantity. To talk sense, is to talk in quantities. It

The Aims of Education

is no use saying that the nation is large, — How large? It is no use saying that radium is scarce, — How scarce? You cannot evade quantity. You may fly to poetry and to music, and quantity and number will face you in your rhythms and your octaves. Elegant intellects which despise the theory of quantity, are but half developed. They are more to be pitied than blamed. The scraps of gibberish, which in their school-days were taught to them in the name of algebra, deserve some contempt.

This question of the degeneration of algebra into gibberish, both in word and in fact, affords a pathetic instance of the uselessness of reforming educational schedules without a clear conception of the attributes which you wish to evoke in the living minds of the children. A few years ago there was an outcry that school algebra was in need of reform, but there was a general agreement that graphs would put everything right. So all sorts of things were extruded, and graphs were introduced. So far as I can see, with no sort of idea behind them, but just graphs. Now every examination paper has one or two questions on graphs. Personally I am an enthusiastic adherent of graphs. But I wonder whether as yet we have gained very much. You cannot put life into any schedule of general education unless you succeed in exhibiting its relation to some essential characteristic of all intelligent or emotional perception. It is a hard saying, but it is true; and I do not see how to make it any easier. In making these little formal alterations you are beaten by the very nature of things. You are pitted against too skilful an adversary, who will see to it that the pea is always under the other thimble.

Reformation must begin at the other end. First, you must make up your mind as to those quantitative aspects of the world which are simple enough to be introduced into general education; then a schedule of algebra should be framed which will about find its exemplification in these applications. We need not fear for our pet graphs, they will be there in plenty when we once begin to treat algebra as a serious means of studying the world. Some of the simplest applications will be found in the quantities which occur in the simplest study of society. The curves of history are more vivid and more

Chapter 1 The Aims of Education

informing than the dry catalogues of names and dates which comprise the greater part of that arid school study. What purpose is effected by a catalogue of undistinguished kings and queens? Tom, Dick, or Harry, they are all dead. General resurrections are failures, and are better postponed. The quantitative flux of the forces of modern society is capable of very simple exhibition. Meanwhile, the idea of the variable, of the function, of rate of change, of equations and their solution, of elimination, are being studied as an abstract science for their own sake. Not, of course, in the pompous phrases with which I am alluding to them here, but with that iteration of simple special cases proper to teaching.

If this course be followed, the route from Chaucer to the Black Death, from the Black Death to modern Labour troubles, will connect the tales of the mediaeval pilgrims with the abstract science of algebra, both yielding diverse aspects of that single theme, Life. I know what most of you are thinking at this point. It is that the exact course which I have sketched out is not the particular one which you would have chosen, or even see how to work. I quite agree. I am not claiming that I could do it myself. But your objection is the precise reason why a common external examination system is fatal to education. The process of exhibiting the applications of knowledge must, for its success, essentially depend on the character of the pupils and the genius of the teacher. Of course I have left out the easiest applications with which most of us are more at home. I mean the quantitative sides of sciences, such as mechanics and physics.

Again, in the same connection we plot the statistics of social phenomena against the time. We then eliminate the time between suitable pairs. We can speculate how far we have exhibited a real causal connection, or how far a mere temporal coincidence. We notice that we might have plotted against the time one set of statistics for one country and another set for another country, and thus, with suitable choice of subjects, have obtained graphs which certainly exhibited mere coincidence. Also other graphs exhibit obvious causal connections. We wonder how to discriminate. And so are drawn on as far as we will.

But in considering this description, I must beg you to remember what I have been insisting on above. In the first place, one train of thought will not suit all groups of children. For example, I should expect that artisan children will want something more concrete and, in a sense, swifter than I have set down here. Perhaps I am wrong, but that is what I should guess. In the second place, I am not contemplating one beautiful lecture stimulating, once and for all, an admiring class. That is not the way in which education proceeds. No; all the time the pupils are hard at work solving examples, drawing graphs, and making experiments, until they have a thorough hold on the whole subject. I am describing the interspersed explanations, the directions which should be given to their thoughts. The pupils have got to be made to feel that they are studying something, and are not merely executing intellectual minuets.

Finally, if you are teaching pupils for some general examination, the problem of sound teaching is greatly complicated. Have you ever noticed the zig-zag moulding round a Norman arch? The ancient work is beautiful, the modern work is hideous. The reason is, that the modern work is done to exact measure, the ancient work is varied according to the idiosyncrasy of the workman. Here it is crowded, and there it is expanded. Now the essence of getting pupils through examinations is to give equal weight to all parts of the schedule. But mankind is naturally specialist. One man sees a whole subject, where another can find only a few detached examples. I know that it seems contradictory to allow for specialism in a curriculum especially designed for a broad culture. Without contradictions the world would be simpler, and perhaps duller. But I am certain that in education wherever you exclude specialism you destroy life.

We now come to the other great branch of a general mathematical education, namely Geometry. The same principles apply. The theoretical part should be clear-cut, rigid, short, and important. Every proposition not absolutely necessary to exhibit the main connection of ideas should be cut out, but the great fundamental ideas should be all there. No omission of concepts, such as those of Similarity and Proportion. We must remember that, owing to the aid rendered by the visual presence of a figure, Geometry is a field of unequalled excellence for the exercise of the deductive faculties of reasoning. Then, of course, there follows Geometrical Drawing, with its training for the hand and eye.

But, like Algebra, Geometry and Geometrical Drawing must be extended beyond the mere circle of geometrical ideas. In an industrial neighbourhood, machinery and workshop practice form the appropriate extension. For example, in the London Polytechnics this has been achieved with conspicuous success. For many secondary schools I suggest that surveying and maps are the natural applications. In particular, plane-table surveying should lead pupils to a vivid apprehension of the immediate application of geometric truths. Simple drawing apparatus, a surveyor's chain, and a surveyor's compass, should enable the pupils to rise from the survey and mensuration of a field to the construction of the map of a small district. The best education is to be found in gaining the utmost information from the simplest apparatus. The provision of elaborate instruments is greatly to be deprecated. To have constructed the map of a small district, to have considered its roads, its contours, its geology, its climate, its relation to other districts, the effects on the status of its inhabitants, will teach more history and geography than any knowledge of Perkin Warbeck or of Behren's Straits. I mean not a nebulous lecture on the subject, but a serious investigation in which the real facts are definitely ascertained by the aid of accurate theoretical knowledge. A typical mathematical problem should be: Survey such and such a field, draw a plan of it to such and such a scale, and find the area. It would be quite a good procedure to impart the necessary geometrical propositions without their proofs. Then, concurrently in the same term, the proofs of the propositions would be learnt while the survey was being made.

Fortunately, the specialist side of education presents an easier problem than does the provision of a general culture. For this there are many reasons. One is that many of the principles of procedure to be observed are the same in both cases, and it is unnecessary to recapitulate. Another reason is that specialist training takes place — or should take place — at a more advanced stage of the pupil's course, and thus there is easier material to work upon. But undoubtedly the chief reason is that the specialist study is normally a study of peculiar interest to the student. He is studying it because, for some reason, he wants to know it. This makes all the difference. The general culture is designed to foster an activity of mind; the specialist course utilises this activity. But it does not do to lay too much stress on these neat antitheses. As we have already seen, in the general course foci of special interest will arise; and similarly in the special study, the external connections of the subject drag thought outwards.

Again, there is not one course of study which merely gives general culture, and another which gives special knowledge. The subjects pursued for the sake of a general education are special subjects specially studied; and, on the other hand, one of the ways of encouraging general mental activity is to foster a special devotion. You may not divide the seamless coat of learning. What education has to impart is an intimate sense for the power of ideas, for the beauty of ideas, and for the structure of ideas, together with a particular body of knowledge which has peculiar reference to the life of the being possessing it.

The appreciation of the structure of ideas is that side of a cultured mind which can only grow under the influence of a special study. I mean that eye for the whole chess-board, for the bearing of one set of ideas on another. Nothing but a special study can give any appreciation for the exact formulation of general ideas, for their relations when formulated, for their service in the comprehension of life. A mind so disciplined should be both more abstract and more concrete. It has been trained in the comprehension of abstract thought and in the analysis of facts.

Finally, there should grow the most austere of all mental qualities; I mean the sense for style. It is an aesthetic sense, based on admiration for the direct attainment of a foreseen end, simply and without waste. Style in art, style in literature, style in science, style in logic, style in practical execution have fundamentally the same aesthetic qualities, namely, attainment and restraint. The love of a subject in itself and for itself, where it is not the sleepy pleasure of pacing a mental quarter-deck, is the love of style as manifested in that study.

Here we are brought back to the position from which we started, the utility of education. Style, in its finest sense, is the last acquirement of the educated mind; it is also the most useful. It pervades the whole being. The administrator with a sense for style hates waste; the engineer with a sense for style economises his material; the artisan with a sense for style prefers good work. Style is the ultimate morality of mind.

But above style, and above knowledge, there is something, a vague shape like fate above the Greek gods. That something is Power. Style is the fashioning of power, the restraining of power. But, after all, the power of attainment of the desired end is fundamental. The first thing is to get there. Do not bother about your style, but solve your problem, justify the ways of God to man, administer your province, or do whatever else is set before you.

Where, then, does style help? In this, with style the end is attained without side issues, without raising undesirable inflammations. With style you attain your end and nothing but your end. With style the effect of your activity is calculable, and foresight is the last gift of gods to men. With style your power is increased, for your mind is not distracted with irrelevancies, and you are more likely to attain your object. Now style is the exclusive privilege of the expert. Whoever heard of the style of an amateur painter, of the style of an amateur poet? Style is always the product of specialist study, the peculiar contribution of specialism to culture.

English education in its present phase suffers from a lack of definite aim, and from an external machinery which kills its vitality. Hitherto in this address I have been considering the aims which should govern education. In this respect England halts between two opinions. It has not decided whether to produce amateurs or experts. The profound change in the world which the nineteenth century has produced is that the growth of knowledge has given foresight. The amateur is essentially a man with appreciation and with immense versatility in mastering a given routine. But he lacks the foresight which comes from special knowledge. The object of this address is to suggest how to produce the expert without loss of the essential virtues of the amateur. The machinery of our secondary education is rigid where it should be yielding, and lax where it should be rigid. Every school is bound on pain of extinction to train its boys for a small set of definite examinations. No headmaster has a free hand to develop his general education or his specialist studies in accordance with the opportunities of his school, which are created by its staff, its environment, its class of boys, and its endowments. I suggest that no system of external tests which aims primarily at examining individual scholars can result in anything but educational waste.

Primarily it is the schools and not the scholars which should be inspected. Each school should grant its own leaving certificates, based on its own curriculum. The standards of these schools should be sampled and corrected. But the first requisite for educational reform is the school as a unit, with its approved curriculum based on its own needs, and evolved by its own staff. If we fail to secure that, we simply fall from one formalism into another, from one dung-hill of inert ideas into another.

In stating that the school is the true educational unit in any national system for the safeguarding of efficiency, I have conceived the alternative system as being the external examination of the individual scholar. But every Scylla is faced by its Charybdis — or, in more homely language, there is a ditch on both sides of the road. It will be equally fatal to education if we fall into the hands of a supervising department which is under the impression that it can divide all schools into two or three rigid categories, each type being forced to adopt a rigid curriculum. When I say that the school is the educational unit, I mean exactly what I say, no larger unit, no smaller unit. Each school must have the claim to be considered in relation to its special circumstances. The classifying of schools for some purposes is necessary. But no absolutely rigid curriculum, not modified by its own staff, should be permissible. Exactly the same principles apply, with the proper modifications, to universities and to technical colleges.

When one considers in its length and in its breadth the importance of this question of the education of a nation's young, the broken lives, the defeated hopes, the national failures, which result from the frivolous inertia with which it is treated, it is difficult to restrain within oneself a savage rage. In the conditions of modern life the rule is absolute, the race which does not value trained intelligence is doomed. Not all your heroism, not all your social charm, not all your wit, not all your victories on land or at sea, can move back the finger of fate. To-day we maintain ourselves. To-morrow science will have moved forward yet one more step, and there will be no appeal from the judgment which will then be pronounced on the uneducated.

We can be content with no less than the old summary of educational ideal which has been current at any time from the dawn of our civilisation. The essence of education is that it be religious.

Pray, what is religious education?

A religious education is an education which inculcates duty and reverence. Duty arises from our potential control over the course of events. Where attainable knowledge could have changed the issue, ignorance has the guilt of vice. And the foundation of reverence is this perception, that the present holds within itself the complete sum of existence, backwards and forwards, that whole amplitude of time, which is eternity.

CHAPTER 2

THE RHYTHM OF EDUCATION

By the Rhythm of Education I denote a certain principle which in its practical application is well known to everyone with educational experience. Accordingly, when I remember that I am speaking to an audience of some of the leading educationalists in England, I have no expectation that I shall be saying anything that is new to you. I do think, however, that the principle has not been subjected to an adequate discussion taking account of all the factors which should guide its application.

I first seek for the baldest statement of what I mean by the Rhythm of Education, a statement so bald as to exhibit the point of this address in its utter obviousness. The principle is merely this — that different subjects and modes of study should be undertaken by pupils at fitting times when they have reached the proper stage of mental development. You will agree with me that this is a truism, never doubted and known to all. I am really anxious to emphasise the obvious character of the foundational idea of my address; for one reason, because this audience will certainly find it out for itself. But the other reason, the reason why I choose this subject for discourse, is that I do not think that this obvious truth has been handled in educational practice with due attention to the psychology of the pupils.

The Tasks of Infancy

I commence by challenging the adequacy of some principles by which the subjects for study are often classified in order. By this I mean that these principles can only be accepted as correct if they are so explained as to be explained away. Consider first the criterion of difficulty. It is not true that the easier subjects should precede the harder. On the contrary, some of the hardest must come first because nature so dictates, and because they are essential to life. The first intellectual task which confronts an infant is the acquirement of spoken language. What an appalling task, the correlation of meanings with sounds! It requires an anlysis of ideas and an analysis of sounds. We all know that the infant does it, and that the miracle of his achievement is explicable. But so are all miracles, and yet to the wise they remain miracles. All I ask is that with this example staring us in the face we should cease talking nonsense about postponing the harder subjects.

What is the next subject in the education of the infant minds? The acquirement of written language; that is to say, the correlation of sounds with shapes. Great heavens! Have our educationists gone mad? They are setting babbling mites of six years old to tasks which might daunt a sage after lifelong toil. Again, the hardest task in mathematics is the study of the elements of algebra, and yet this stage must precede the comparative simplicity of the differential calculus.

I will not elaborate my point further; I merely restate it in the form, that the postponement of difficulty is no safe clue for the maze of educational practice.

The alternative principle of order among subjects is that of necessary antecedence. There we are obviously on firmer ground. It is impossible to read *Hamlet* until you can read; and the study of integers must precede the study of fractions. And yet even this firm principle dissolves under scrutiny. It is certainly true, but it is only true if you give an artificial limitation to the concept of a subject for study. The danger of the principle is that it is accepted in one sense, for which it is almost a necessary truth, and that it is applied in another sense for which it is false. You cannot read Homer before you can read; but many a child, and in ages past many a man, has sailed with Odysseus over the seas of Romance by the help of the spoken word of a mother, or of some wandering bard. The uncritical application of the principle of the necessary antecedence of some subjects to others has, in the hands of dull people with a turn for organisation, produced in education the dryness of the Sahara.

Stages of Mental Growth

The reason for the title which I have chosen for this address, the Rhythm of Education, is derived from yet another criticism of current ideas. The pupil's progress is often conceived as a uniform steady advance undifferentiated by change of type or alteration in pace; for example, a boy may be conceived as starting Latin at ten years of age and by a uniform progression steadily developing into a classical scholar at the age of eighteen or twenty. I hold that this conception of education is based upon a false psychology of the process of mental development which has gravely hindered the effectiveness of our methods. Life is essentially periodic. It comprises daily periods, with their alternations of work and play, of activity and of sleep, and seasonal periods, which dictate our terms and our holidays; and also it is composed of well-marked yearly periods. These are the gross obvious periods which no one can overlook. There are also subtler periods of mental growth, with their cyclic recurrences, yet always different as we pass from cycle to cycle, though the subordinate stages are reproduced in each cycle. That is why I have chosen the term "rhythmic," as meaning essentially the conveyance of difference within a framework of repetition. Lack of attention to the rhythm and character of mental growth is a main source of wooden futility in education. I think that Hegel was right when he analysed progress into three stages, which he called Thesis, Antithesis, and Synthesis; though for the purpose of the application of his idea to educational theory I do not think that the names he gave are very happily suggestive. In relation to intellectual progress I would term them, the stage of romance, the stage of precision, and the stage of generalisation.

The Stage of Romance

The stage of romance is the stage of first apprehension. The subject-matter has the vividness of novelty; it holds within itself unexplored connexions with possibilities half-disclosed by glimpses and half-concealed by the wealth of material. In this stage knowledge is not dominated by systematic procedure. Such system as there must be is created piecemeal *ad hoc*. We are in the presence of immediate cognisance of fact, only intermittently subjecting fact to systematic dissection. Romantic emotion is essentially the excitement consequent on the transition from the bare facts to the first realisations of the import of their unexplored relationships. For example, Crusoe was a mere man, the sand was mere sand, the footprint was a mere footprint, and the island a mere island, and Europe was the busy world of men. But the sudden perception of the half-disclosed and half-hidden possibilities relating Crusoe and the sand and the footprint and the lonely island secluded from Europe constitutes romance. I have had to take an extreme case for illustration in order to make my meaning perfectly plain. But construe it as an allegory representing the first stage in a cycle of progress. Education must essentially be a setting in order of a ferment already stirring in the mind: you cannot educate mind in *vacuo*. In our conception of education we tend to confine it to the second stage of the cycle; namely, to the stage of precision. But we cannot so limit our task without misconceiving the whole problem. We are concerned alike with the ferment, with the acquirement of precision, and with the subsequent fruition.

The Stage of Precision

The stage of precision also represents an addition to knowledge. In this stage, width of relationship is subordinated to exactness of formulation. It is the stage of grammar, the grammar of language and the grammar of science. It proceeds by forcing on the students' acceptance a given way of analysing the facts, bit by bit. New facts are added, but they are the facts which fit into the analysis.

It is evident that a stage of precision is barren without a previous stage of romance: unless there are facts which have already been vaguely apprehended in their broad generality, the previous analysis is an analysis of nothing. It is simply a series of meaningless statements about bare facts, produced artificially and without any further relevance. I repeat that in this stage we do not merely remain within the circle of the facts elicited in the romantic epoch. The facts of romance have disclosed ideas with possibilities of wide significance, and in the stage of precise progress we acquire other facts in a systematic order, which thereby form both a disclosure and an analysis of the general subject-matter of the romance.

The Stage of Generalisation

The final stage of generalisation is Hegel's synthesis. It is a return to romanticism with added advantage of classified ideas and relevant technique. It is the fruition which has been the goal of the precise training. It is the final success. I am afraid that I have had to give a dry analysis of somewhat obvious ideas. It has been necessary to do so because my subsequent remarks presuppose that we have clearly in our minds the essential character of this threefold cycle.

The Cyclic Processes

Education should consist in a continual repetition of such cycles. Each lesson in its minor way should form an eddy cycle issuing in its own subordinate process. Longer periods should issue in definite attainments, which then form the starting-grounds for fresh cycles. We should banish the idea of a mythical, far-off end of education. The pupils must be continually enjoying some fruition and starting afresh — if the teacher is stimulating in exact proportion to his success in satisfying the rhythmic cravings of his pupils.

An infant's first romance is its awakening to the apprehension of objects and to the appreciation of their connexions. Its growth in mentality takes the exterior form of occupying itself in the coordination of its perceptions with its bodily activities. Its first stage of precision is mastering spoken language as an instrument for classifying its contemplation of objects and for strengthening its apprehension of emotional relations with other beings.

The Aims of Education

Its first stage of generalisation is the use of language for a classified and enlarged enjoyment of objects.

This first cycle of intellectual progress from the achievement of perception to the acquirement of language, and from the acquirement of language to classified thought and keener perception, will bear more careful study. It is the only cycle of progress which we can observe in its purely natural state. The later cycles are necessarily tinged by the procedure of the current mode of education. There is a characteristic of it which is often sadly lacking in subsequent education; I mean, that it achieves complete success. At the end of it the child *can* speak, its ideas *are* classified, and its perceptions *are* sharpened. The cycle achieves its object. This is a great deal more than can be said for most systems of education as applied to most pupils. But why should this be so? Certainly, a new-born baby looks a most unpromising subject for intellectual progress when we remember the difficulty of the task before it. I suppose it is because nature, in the form of surrounding circumstances, sets it a task for which the normal development of its brain is exactly fitted. I do not think that there is any particular mystery about the fact of a child learning to speak and in consequence thinking all the better; but it does offer food for reflection.

In the subsequent education we have not sought for cyclic processes which in a finite time run their course and within their own limited sphere achieve a complete success. This completion is one outstanding character in the natural cycle for infants. Later on we start a child on some subject, say Latin, at the age of ten, and hope by a uniform system of formal training to achieve success at the age of twenty. The natural result is failure, both in interest and in acquirement. When I speak of failure, I am comparing our results with the brilliant success of the first natural cycle. I do not think that it is because our tasks are intrinsically too hard, when I remember that the infant's cycle is the hardest of all. It is because our tasks are set in an unnatural way, without rhythm and without the stimulus of intermediate successes and without concentration.

I have not yet spoken of this character of concentration which so conspicuously attaches to the infant's progress. The whole being of the infant is absorbed in the practice of its cycle. It has nothing else to divert its mental development. In this respect there is a striking difference between this natural cycle and the subsequent history of the student's development. It is perfectly obvious that life is very various and that the mind and brain naturally develop so as to adapt themselves to the many-hued world in which their lot is cast. Still, after making allowance for this consideration, we will be wise to preserve some measure of concentration for each of the subsequent cycles. In particular, we should avoid a competition of diverse subjects in the same stage of their cycles. The fault of the older education was unrhythmic concentration on a single undifferentiated subject. Our modern system, with its insistence on a preliminary general education, and with its easy toleration of the analysis of knowledge into distinct subjects, is an equally unrhythmic collection of distracting scraps. I am pleading that we shall endeavour to weave in the learner's mind a harmony of patterns, by co-ordinating the various elements of instruction into subordinate cycles each of intrinsic worth for the immediate apprehension of the pupil. We must garner our crops each in its due season.

The Romance of Adolescence

We will now pass to some concrete applications of the ideas which have been developed in the former part of my address.

The first cycle of infancy is succeeded by the cycle of adolescence, which opens with by far the greatest stage of romance which we ever experience. It is in this stage that the lines of character are graven. How the child emerges from the romantic stage of adolescence is how the subsequent life will be moulded by ideals and coloured by imagination. It rapidly follows on the generalisation of capacity produced by the acquirement of spoken language and of reading. The stage of generalisation belonging to the infantile cycle is comparatively short because the romantic material of infancy is so scanty. The initial knowledge of the world in any developed sense of the word "knowledge" really commences after the achievement of the first cycle, and thus issues in the tremendous age of romance. Ideas, facts, relationships, stories, histories, possibilities, artistry in words, in sounds, in form and in colour, crowd into the child's life, stir his feelings, excite his appreciation, and incite his impulses to kindred activities. It is a saddening thought that on this golden age there falls so often the shadow of the crammer. I am thinking of a period of about four years of the child's life, roughly, in ordinary cases, falling between the ages of eight and twelve or thirteen. It is the first great period of the utilisation of the native language, and of developed powers of observation and of manipulation. The infant cannot manipulate, the child can; the infant cannot observe, the child can; the infant cannot retain thoughts by the recollection of words, the child can. The child thus enters upon a new world.

Of course, the stage of precision prolongs itself as recurring in minor cycles which form eddies in the great romance. The perfecting of writing, of spelling, of the elements of arithmetic, and of lists of simple facts, such as the Kings of England, are all elements of precision, very necessary both as training in concentration and as useful acquirements. However, these are essentially fragmentary in character, whereas the great romance is the flood which bears on the child towards the life of the spirit.

The success of the Montessori system is due to its recognition of the dominance of romance at this period of growth. If this be the explanation, it also points to the limitations in the usefulness of that method. It is the system which in some measure is essential for every romantic stage. Its essence is browsing and the encouragement of vivid freshness. But it lacks the restraint which is necessary for the great stages of precision.

The Mastery of Language

As he nears the end of the great romance the cyclic course of growth is swinging the child over towards an aptitude for exact knowledge. Language is now the natural subject-matter for concentrated attack. It is the mode of expression with which he is thoroughly familiar. He is acquainted with stories, histories, and poems illustrating the lives of other people and of other civilisations. Accordingly, from the age of eleven onwards there is wanted a gradually increasing concentration towards precise knowledge of language. Finally, the three years from twelve to fifteen should be dominated by a mass attack upon language, so planned that a definite result, in itself worth having, is thereby achieved. I should guess that within these limits of time, and given adequate concentration, we might ask that at the end of that period the children should have command of English, should be able to read fluently fairly simple French, and should have completed the elementary stage of Latin; I mean, a precise knowledge of the more straightforward parts of Latin grammar, the knowledge of the construction of Latin sentences, and the reading of some parts of appropriate Latin authors, perhaps simplified and largely supplemented by the aid of the best literary translations so that their reading of the original, plus translation, gives them a grip of the book as a literary whole. I conceive that such a measure of attainment in these three languages is well within the reach of the ordinary child, provided that he has not been distracted by the effort at precision in a multiplicity of other subjects. Also some more gifted children could go further. The Latin would come to them easily, so that it would be possible to start Greek before the end of the period, always provided that their bent is literary and that they mean later to pursue that study at least for some years. Other subjects will occupy a subordinate place in the time-table and will be undertaken in a different spirit. In the first place, it must be remembered that the semi-literary subjects, such as history, will largely have been provided in the study of the languages. It will be hardly possible to read some English, French, and Latin literature without imparting some knowledge of European history. I do not mean that all special history teaching should be abandoned. I do, however, suggest that the subject should be exhibited in what I have termed the romantic spirit, and that the pupils should not be subjected to the test of precise recollection of details on any large systematic scale.

At this period of growth science should be in its stage of romance. The pupils should see for themselves, and experiment for themselves, with only fragmentary precision of thought. The essence of the importance of science, both for interest in theory or for technological purposes, lies in its application to concrete detail, and every such application evokes a novel problem for research. Accordingly, all training in science should begin as well as end in research, and in getting hold of the subject-matter as it occurs in nature. The exact form of guidance suitable to this age and the exact limitations of experiment are matters depending on experience. But I plead that this period is the true age for the romance of science.

Concentration on Science

Towards the age of fifteen the age of precision in language and of romance in science draws to its close, to be succeeded by a period of generalisation in language and of precision in science. This should be a short period, but one of vital importance. I am thinking of about one year's work, and I suggest that it would be well decisively to alter the balance of the preceding curriculum. There should be a concentration on science and a decided diminution of the linguistic work. A year's work on science, coming on the top of the previous romantic study, should make everyone understand the main principles which govern the development of mechanics, physics, chemistry, algebra and geometry. Understand that they are not beginning these subjects, but they are putting together a previous discursive study by an exact formulation of their main ideas. For example, take algebra and geometry, which I single out as being subjects with which I have some slight familiarity. In the previous three years there has been work on the applications of the simplest algebraic formulae and geometrical propositions to problems of surveying, or of some other scientific work involving calculations. In this way arithmetic has been carefully strengthened by the insistence on definite numerical results, and familiarity with the ideas of literal formulae and of geometrical properties has been gained; also some minor methods of manipulation have been inculcated. There is thus no long time to be wasted in getting used to the ideas of the sciences. The pupils

Chapter 2　The Rhythm of Education

are ready for the small body of algebraic and geometrical truths which they ought to know thoroughly. Furthermore, in the previous period some boys will have shown an aptitude for mathematics and will have pushed on a little more, besides in the final year somewhat emphasising their mathematics at the expense of some of the other subjects. I am simply taking mathematics as an illustration.

Meanwhile, the cycle of language is in its stage of generalisation. In this stage the precise study of grammar and composition is discontinued, and the language study is confined to reading the literature with emphasised attention to its ideas and to the general history in which it is embedded; also the time allotted to history will pass into the precise study of a short definite period, chosen to illustrate exactly what does happen at an important epoch and also to show how to pass the simpler types of judgments on men and policies.

I have now sketched in outline the course of education from babyhood to about sixteen and a half, arranged with some attention to the rhythmic pulses of life. In some such way a general education is possible in which the pupil throughout has the advantage of concentration and of freshness. Thus precision will always illustrate subject-matter already apprehended and crying out for drastic treatment. Every pupil will have concentrated in turn on a variety of different subjects, and will know where his strong points lie. Finally — and this of all the objects to be attained is the most dear to my heart — the science students will have obtained both an invaluable literary education and also at the most impressionable age an early initiation into habits of thinking for themselves in the region of science.

After the age of sixteen new problems arise. For literary students science passes into the stage of generalisation, largely in the form of lectures on its main results and general ideas. New cycles of linguistic, literary, and historical study commence. But further detail is now unnecessary. For the scientists the preceding stage of precision maintains itself to the close of the school period with an increasing apprehension of wider general ideas.

However, at this period of education the problem is too individual, or at least breaks up into too many cases, to be susceptible of broad general treatment. I do suggest, nevertheless, that all scientists should now keep up their French, and initiate the study of German if they have not already acquired it.

University Education

I should now like, if you will bear with me, to make some remarks respecting the import of these ideas for a University education.

The whole period of growth from infancy to manhood forms one grand cycle. Its stage of romance stretches across the first dozen years of life, its stage of precision comprises the whole school period of secondary education, and its stage of generalisation is the period of entrance into manhood. For those whose formal education is prolonged beyond the school age, the University course or its equivalent is the great period of generalisation. The spirit of generalisation should dominate a University. The lectures should be addressed to those to whom details and procedure are familiar; that is to say, familiar at least in the sense of being so congruous to pre-existing training as to be easily acquirable. During the school period the student has been mentally bending over his desk; at the University he should stand up and look around. For this reason it is fatal if the first year at the University be frittered away in going over the old work in the old spirit. At school the boy painfully rises from the particular towards glimpses at general ideas; at the University he should start from general ideas and study their applications to concrete cases. A well-planned University course is a study of the wide sweep of generality. I do not mean that it should be abstract in the sense of divorce from concrete fact, but that concrete fact should be studied as illustrating the scope of general ideas.

Cultivation of Mental Power

This is the aspect of University training in which theoretical interest and practical utility coincide. Whatever be the detail with which you cram your student, the chance of his meeting in after-life exactly that detail is almost infinitesimal; and if he does meet it, he will probably have forgotten what you taught him about it. The really useful training yields a comprehension of a few general principles with a thorough grounding in the way they apply to a variety of concrete details. In subsequent practice the men will have forgotten your particular details; but they will remember by an unconscious common sense how to apply principles to immediate circumstances. Your learning is useless to you till you have lost your text-books, burnt your lecture notes, and forgotten the minutiae which you learnt by heart for the examination. What, in the way of detail, you continually require will stick in your memory as obvious facts like the sun and moon; and what you casually require can be looked up in any work of reference. The function of a University is to enable you to shed details in favour of principles. When I speak of principles I am hardly even thinking of verbal formulations. A principle which has thoroughly soaked into you is rather a mental habit than a formal statement. It becomes the way the mind reacts to the appropriate stimulus in the form of illustrative circumstances. Nobody goes about with his knowledge clearly and consciously before him. Mental cultivation is nothing else than the satisfactory way in which the mind will function when it is poked up into activity. Learning is often spoken of as if we are watching the open pages of all the books which we have ever read, and then, when occasion arises, we select the right page to read aloud to the universe.

Luckily, the truth is far otherwise from this crude idea; and for this reason the antagonism between the claims of pure knowledge and professional acquirement should be much less acute than a faulty view of education would lead us to anticipate. I can put my point otherwise by saying that the ideal of a University is not so much knowledge, as power. Its business is to convert the knowledge of a boy into the power of a man.

The Rhythmic Character of Growth

I will conclude with two remarks which I wish to make by way of caution in the interpretation of my meaning. The point of this address is the rhythmic character of growth. The interior spiritual life of man is a web of many strands. They do not all grow together by uniform extension. I have tried to illustrate this truth by considering the normal unfolding of the capacities of a child in somewhat favourable circumstances but otherwise with fair average capacities. Perhaps I have misconstrued the usual phenomena. It is very likely that I have so failed, for the evidence is complex and difficult. But do not let any failure in this respect prejudice the main point which I am here to enforce. It is that the development of mentality exhibits itself as a rhythm involving an interweaving of cycles, the whole process being dominated by a greater cycle of the same general character as its minor eddies. Furthermore, this rhythm exhibits certain ascertainable general laws which are valid for most pupils, and the quality of our teaching should be so adapted as to suit the stage in the rhythm to which our pupils have advanced. The problem of a curriculum is not so much the succession of subjects; for all subjects should in essence be begun with the dawn of mentality. The truly important order is the order of quality which the educational procedure should assume.

My second caution is to ask you not to exaggerate into sharpness the distinction between the three stages of a cycle. I strongly suspect that many of you, when you heard me detail the three stages in each cycle, said to yourselves — How like a mathematician to make such formal divisions! I assure you that it is not mathematics but literary incompetence that may have led me into the error against which I am warning you. Of course, I mean throughout a distinction of emphasis, of pervasive quality — romance, precision, generalisation, are all present throughout. But there is an alternation of dominance, and it is this alternation which constitutes the cycles.

CHAPTER 3

THE RHYTHMIC CLAIMS OF FREEDOM AND DISCIPLINE

The fading of ideals is sad evidence of the defeat of human endeavour. In the schools of antiquity philosophers aspired to impart wisdom, in modern colleges our humbler aim is to teach subjects. The drop from the divine wisdom, which was the goal of the ancients, to text-book knowledge of subjects, which is achieved by the moderns, marks an educational failure, sustained through the ages. I am not maintaining that in the practice of education the ancient were more successful than ourselves. You have only to read Lucian, and to note his satiric dramatizations of the pretentious claims of philosophers, to see that in this respect the ancients can boast over us no superiority. My point is that, at the dawn of our European civilisation, men started with the full ideals which should inspire education, and that gradually our ideals have sunk to square with our practice.

But when ideals have sunk to the level of practice, the result is stagnation. In particular, so long as we conceive intellectual education as merely consisting in the acquirement of mechanical mental aptitudes, and of formulated statements of useful truths, there can be no progress; though there will be much activity, amid aimless re-arrangement of syllabuses, in the fruitless endeavour to dodge the inevitable lack of time. We must take it as an unavoidable fact, that God has so made the world that there are more topics desirable for knowledge than any one person can possibly acquire. It is hopeless to approach the problem by the way of the enumeration of subjects which every one ought to have mastered. There are too many of them, all with excellent title-deeds. Perhaps, after all, this plethora of

The Aims of Education

material is fortunate; for the world is made interesting by a delightful ignorance of important truths. What I am anxious to impress on you is that though knowledge is one chief aim of intellectual education, there is another ingredient, vaguer but greater, and more dominating in its importance. The ancients called it "wisdom." You cannot be wise without some basis of knowledge; but you may easily acquire knowledge and remain bare of wisdom.

Now wisdom is the way in which knowledge is held. It concerns the handling of knowledge, its selection for the determination of relevant issues, its employment to add value to our immediate experience. This mastery of knowledge, which is wisdom, is the most intimate freedom obtainable. The ancients saw clearly — more clearly than we do — the necessity for dominating knowledge by wisdom. But, in the pursuit of wisdom in the region of practical education, they erred sadly. To put the matter simply, their popular practice assumed that wisdom could be imparted to the young by procuring philosophers to spout at them. Hence the crop of shady philosophers in the schools of the ancient world. The only avenue towards wisdom is by freedom in the presence of knowledge. But the only avenue towards knowledge is by discipline in the acquirement of ordered fact. Freedom and discipline are the two essentials of education, and hence the title of my discourse to-day, "The Rhythmic Claims of Freedom and Discipline."

The antithesis in education between freedom and discipline is not so sharp as a logical analysis of the meanings of the terms might lead us to imagine. The pupil's mind is a growing organism. On the one hand, it is not a box to be ruthlessly packed with alien ideas; and, on the other hand, the ordered acquirement of knowledge is the natural food for a developing intelligence. Accordingly, it should be the aim of an ideally constructed education that the discipline should be the voluntary issue of free choice, and that the freedom should gain an enrichment of possibility as the issue of discipline. The two principles, freedom and discipline, are not antagonists, but should be so adjusted in the child's life that they correspond to a

Chapter 3 The Rhythmic Claims of Freedom and Discipline

natural sway, to and fro, of the developing personality. It is this adaptation of freedom and discipline to the natural sway of development that I have elsewhere called The Rhythm of Education. I am convinced that much disappointing failure in the past has been due to neglect of attention to the importance of this rhythm. My main position is that the dominant note of education at its beginning and at its end is freedom, but that there is an intermediate stage of discipline with freedom in subordination. Furthermore, that there is not one unique threefold cycle of freedom, discipline, and freedom; but that all mental development is composed of such cycles, and of cycles of such cycles. Such a cycle is a unit cell, or brick; and the complete stage of growth is an organic structure of such cells. In analysing any one such cell, I call the first period of freedom the "stage of Romance," the intermediate period of discipline I call the "stage of Precision," and the final period of freedom is the "stage of Generalisation."

Let me now explain myself in more detail. There can be no mental development without interest. Interest is the *sine qua non* for attention and apprehension. You may endeavour to excite interest by means of birch rods, or you may coax it by the incitement of pleasurable activity. But without interest there will be no progress. Now the natural mode by which living organisms are excited towards suitable self-development is enjoyment. The infant is lured to adapt itself to its environment by its love of its mother and its nurse; we eat because we like a good dinner; we subdue the forces of nature because we have been lured to discovery by an insatiable curiosity; we enjoy exercise; and we enjoy the unchristian passion of hating our dangerous enemies. Undoubtedly pain is one subordinate means of arousing an organism to action. But it only supervenes on the failure of pleasure. Joy is the normal healthy spur for the *élan vital*. I am not maintaining that we can safely abandon ourselves to the allurement of the greater immediate joys. What I do mean is that we should seek to arrange the development of character along a path of natural activity, in itself pleasurable. The subordinate stiffening of discipline must be directed to secure some long-time good; although an adequate object must not be too far below the horizon, if the necessary interest is to be retained.

The second preliminary point which I wish to make, is the unimportance — indeed the evil — of barren knowledge. The importance of knowledge lies in its use, in our active mastery of it — that is to say, it lies in wisdom. It is a convention to speak of mere knowledge, apart from wisdom, as of itself imparting a peculiar dignity to its possessor. I do not share in this reverence for knowledge as such. It all depends on who has the knowledge and what he does with it. That knowledge which adds greatness to character is knowledge so handled as to transform every phase of immediate experience. It is in respect to the activity of knowledge that an over-vigorous discipline in education is so harmful. The habit of active thought, with freshness, can only be generated by adequate freedom. Undiscriminating discipline defeats its own object by dulling the mind. If you have much to do with the young as they emerge from school and from the university, you soon note the dulled minds of those whose education has consisted in the acquirement of inert knowledge. Also the deplorable tone of English society in respect to learning is a tribute to our educational failure. Furthermore, this overhaste to impart mere knowledge defeats itself. The human mind rejects knowledge imparted in this way. The craving for expansion, for activity, inherent in youth is disgusted by a dry imposition of disciplined knowledge. The discipline, when it comes, should satisfy a natural craving for the wisdom which adds value to bare experience.

But let us now examine more closely the rhythm of these natural cravings of the human intelligence. The first procedure of the mind in a new environment is a somewhat discursive activity amid a welter of ideas and experience. It is a process of discovery, a process of becoming used to curious thoughts, of shaping questions, of seeking for answers, of devising new experiences, of noticing what happens as the result of new ventures. This general process is both natural and of absorbing interest. We must often have noticed children between the ages of eight and thirteen absorbed in its ferment. It is dominated by wonder, and cursed be the dullard who destroys wonder. Now undoubtedly this stage of development requires help, and even discipline.

Chapter 3 The Rhythmic Claims of Freedom and Discipline

The environment within which the mind is working must be carefully selected. It must, of course, be chosen to suit the child's stage of growth, and must be adapted to individual needs. In a sense it is an imposition from without; but in a deeper sense it answers to the call of life within the child. In the teacher's consciousness the child has been sent to his telescope to look at the stars, in the child's consciousness he has been given free access to the glory of the heavens. Unless, working somewhere, however obscurely, even in the dullest child, there is this transfiguration of imposed routine, the child's nature will refuse to assimilate the alien material. It must never be forgotten that education is not a process of packing articles in a trunk. Such a simile is entirely inapplicable. It is, of course, a process completely of its own peculiar genus. Its nearest analogue is the assimilation of food by a living organism; and we all know how necessary to health is palatable food under suitable conditions. When you have put your boots in a trunk, they will stay there till you take them out again; but this is not at all the case if you feed a child with the wrong food.

This initial stage of romance requires guidance in another way. After all the child is the heir to long ages of civilisation, and it is absurd to let him wander in the intellectual maze of men in the Glacial Epoch. Accordingly, a certain pointing out of important facts, and of simplifying ideas, and of usual names, really strengthens the natural impetus of the pupil. In no part of education can you do without discipline or can you do without freedom; but in the stage of romance the emphasis must always be on freedom, to allow the child to see for itself and to act for itself. My point is that a block in the assimilation of ideas inevitably arises when a discipline of precision is imposed before a stage of romance has run its course in the growing mind. There is no comprehension apart from romance. It is my strong belief that the cause of so much failure in the past has been due to the lack of careful study of the due place of romance. Without the adventure of romance, at the best you get inert knowledge without initiative, and at the worst you get contempt of ideas — without knowledge.

But when this stage of romance has been properly guided another craving grows. The freshness of inexperience has worn off; there is general knowledge of the groundwork of fact and theory; and, above all, there has been plenty of independent browsing amid first-hand experiences, involving adventures of thought and of action. The enlightenment which comes from precise knowledge can now be understood. It corresponds to the obvious requirements of common sense, and deals with familiar material. Now is the time for pushing on, for knowing the subject exactly, and for retaining in the memory its salient features. This is the stage of precision. This stage is the sole stage of learning in the traditional scheme of education, either at school or university. You had to learn your subject, and there was nothing more to be said on the topic of education. The result of such an undue extension of a most necessary period of development was the production of a plentiful array of dunces, and of a few scholars whose natural interest had survived the car of Juggernaut. There is, indeed, always the temptation to teach pupils a little more of fact and of precise theory than at that stage they are fitted to assimilate. If only they could, it would be so useful. We — I am talking of schoolmasters and of university dons — are apt to forget that we are only subordinate elements in the education of a grown man; and that, in their own good time, in later life our pupils will learn for themselves. The phenomena of growth cannot be hurried beyond certain very narrow limits. But an unskilful practitioner can easily damage a sensitive organism. Yet, when all has been said in the way of caution, there is such a thing as pushing on, of getting to know the fundamental details and the main exact generalisations, and of acquiring an easy mastery of technique. There is no getting away from the fact that things have been found out, and that to be effective in the modern world you must have a store of definite acquirement of the best practice. To write poetry you must study metre; and to build bridges you must be learned in the strength of material. Even the Hebrew prophets had learned to write, probably in those days requiring no mean effort. The untutored art of genius is — in the words of the Prayer Book — a vain thing, fondly invented.

During the stage of precision, romance is the background. The stage is dominated by the inescapable fact that there are right ways and wrong

Chapter 3　The Rhythmic Claims of Freedom and Discipline

ways, and definite truths to be known. But romance is not dead, and it is the art of teaching to foster it amidst definite application to appointed task. It must be fostered for one reason, because romance is after all a necessary ingredient of that balanced wisdom which is the goal to be attained. But there is another reason: The organism will not absorb the fruits of the task unless its powers of apprehension are kept fresh by romance. The real point is to discover in practice that exact balance between freedom and discipline which will give the greatest rate of progress over the things to be known. I do not believe that there is any abstract formula which will give information applicable to all subjects, to all types of pupils, or to each individual pupil; except indeed the formula of rhythmic sway which I have been insisting on, namely, that in the earlier stage the progress requires that the emphasis be laid on freedom, and that in the later middle stage the emphasis be laid on the definite acquirement of allotted tasks. I freely admit that if the stage of romance has been properly managed, the discipline of the second stage is much less apparent, that the children know how to go about their work, want to make a good job of it, and can be safely trusted with the details. Furthermore, I hold that the only discipline, important for its own sake, is self-discipline, and that this can only be acquired by a wide use of freedom. But yet — so many are the delicate points to be considered in education — it is necessary in life to have acquired the habit of cheerfully undertaking imposed tasks. The conditions can be satisfied if the tasks correspond to the natural cravings of the pupil at his stage of progress, if they keep his powers at full stretch, and if they attain an obviously sensible result, and if reasonable freedom is allowed in the mode of execution.

　　The difficulty of speaking about the way a skilful teacher will keep romance alive in his pupils arises from the fact that what takes a long time to describe, takes a short time to do. The beauty of a passage of Virgil may be rendered by insisting on beauty of verbal enunciation, taking no longer than prosy utterance. The emphasis on the beauty of a mathematical argument, in its marshalling of general considerations to unravel complex fact, is the speediest mode of procedure. The responsibility of the teacher at this stage is immense. To speak the truth, except in the rare case of genius in the teacher, I do not think that it is possible to take a whole class very far along the road of precision without some dulling of the interest. It is the unfortunate dilemma that initiative and training are both necessary, and that training is apt to kill initiative.

But this admission is not to condone a brutal ignorance of methods of mitigating this untoward fact. It is not a theoretical necessity, but arises because perfect tact is unattainable in the treatment of each individual case. In the past the methods employed assassinated interest; we are discussing how to reduce the evil to its smallest dimensions. I merely utter the warning that education is a difficult problem, to be solved by no one simple formula.

In this connection there is, however, one practical consideration which is largely neglected. The territory of romantic interest is large, ill-defined, and not to be controlled by any explicit boundary. It depends on the chance flashes of insight. But the area of precise knowledge, as exacted in any general educational system, can be, and should be, definitely determined. If you make it too wide you will kill interest and defeat your own object; if you make it too narrow your pupils will lack effective grip. Surely, in every subject in each type of curriculum, the precise knowledge required should be determined after the most anxious inquiry. This does not now seem to be the case in any effective way. For example, in the classical studies of boys destined for a scientific career — a class of pupils in whom I am greatly interested — What is the Latin vocabulary which they ought definitely to know? Also what are the grammatical rules and constructions which they ought to have mastered? Why not determine these once and for all, and then bend every exercise to impress just these on the memory, and to understand their derivatives, both in Latin and also in French and English. Then, as to other constructions and words which occur in the reading of texts, supply full information in the easiest manner. A certain ruthless definiteness is essential in education. I am sure that one secret of a successful teacher is that he has formulated quite clearly in his mind what the pupil has got to know in precise fashion. He will then cease from half-hearted attempts to worry his pupils with memorising a lot of irrelevant stuff of inferior importance. The secret of success is pace, and the secret of pace is concentration. But, in respect to precise knowledge, the watchword is pace, pace, pace. Get your knowledge quickly, and then use it. If you can use it, you will retain it.

We have now come to the third stage of the rhythmic cycle, the stage of generalisation. There is here a reaction towards romance. Something definite is now known; aptitudes have been acquired; and general rules and laws are clearly apprehended both in their formulation and their detailed exemplification. The pupil now wants to use his new weapons. He is an effective individual, and it is effects that he wants to produce. He relapses into the discursive adventures of the romantic stage, with the advantage that his mind is now a disciplined regiment instead of a rabble. In this sense, education should begin in research and end in research. After all, the whole affair is merely a preparation for battling with the immediate experiences of life, a preparation by which to qualify each immediate moment with relevant ideas and appropriate actions. An education which does not begin by evoking initiative and end by encouraging it must be wrong. For its whole aim is the production of active wisdom.

In my own work at universities I have been much struck by the paralysis of thought induced in pupils by the aimless accumulation of precise knowledge, inert and unutilised. It should be the chief aim of a university professor to exhibit himself in his own true character — that is, as an ignorant man thinking, actively utilising his small share of knowledge. In a sense, knowledge shrinks as wisdom grows; for details are swallowed up in principles. The details of knowledge which are important will be picked up *ad hoc* in each avocation of life, but the habit of the active utilisation of well-understood principles is the final possession of wisdom. The stage of precision is the stage of growing into the apprehension of principles by the acquisition of a precise knowledge of details. The stage of generalisations is the stage of shedding details in favour of the active application of principles, the details retreating into subconscious habits. We don't go about explicitly retaining in our own minds that two and two make four, though once we had to learn it by heart. We trust to habit for our elementary arithmetic. But the essence of this stage is the emergence from the comparative passivity of being trained into the active freedom of application. Of course, during this stage, precise knowledge will grow, and more actively than ever before, because the mind has experienced the power of definiteness, and responds to the acquisition of general truth, and of richness of illustration. But the growth of knowledge becomes progressively unconscious, as being an incident derived from some active adventure of thought.

So much for the three stages of the rhythmic unit of development. In a general way the whole period of education is dominated by this threefold rhythm. Till the age of thirteen or fourteen there is the romantic stage, from fourteen to eighteen the stage of precision, and from eighteen to two and twenty the stage of generalisation. But these are only average characters, tinging the mode of development as a whole. I do not think that any pupil completes his stages simultaneously in all subjects. For example, I should plead that while language is initiating its stage of precision in the way of acquisition of vocabulary and of grammar, science should be in its full romantic stage. The romantic stage of language begins in infancy with the acquisition of speech, so that it passes early towards a stage of precision; while science is a late comer. Accordingly a precise inculcation of science at an early age wipes out initiative and interest, and destroys any chance of the topic having any richness of content in the child's apprehension. Thus, the romantic stage of science should persist for years after the precise study of language has commenced.

There are minor eddies, each in itself a threefold cycle, running its course in each day, in each week, and in each term. There is the general apprehension of some topic in its vague possibilities, the mastery of the relevant details, and finally the putting of the whole subject together in the light of the relevant knowledge. Unless the pupils are continually sustained by the evocation of interest, the acquirement of technique, and the excitement of success, they can never make progress, and will certainly lose heart. Speaking generally, during the last thirty years the schools of England have been sending up to the universities a disheartened crowd of young folk, inoculated against any outbreak of intellectual zeal. The universities have seconded the efforts of the schools and emphasised the failure. Accordingly, the cheerful gaiety of the young turns to other topics, and thus educated England is not hospitable to ideas. When we can point to some great achievement of our nation — let us hope that it may be something other than a war — which has been won in the class-room of our schools, and not in their playing-fields, then we may feel content with our modes of education.

So far I have been discussing intellectual education, and my argument has been cramped on too narrow a basis. After all, our pupils are alive, and cannot be chopped into separate bits, like the pieces of a jig-saw puzzle. In the production of a mechanism the constructive energy lies outside it, and adds discrete parts to discrete parts. The case is far different for a living organism which grows by its own impulse towards self-development. This impulse can be stimulated and guided from outside the organism, and it can also be killed. But for all your stimulation and guidance the creative impulse towards growth comes from within, and is intensely characteristic of the individual. Education is the guidance of the individual towards a comprehension of the art of life; and by the art of life I mean the most complete achievement of varied activity expressing the potentialities of that living creature in the face of its actual environment. This completeness of achievement involves an artistic sense, subordinating the lower to the higher possibilities of the indivisible personality. Science, art, religion, morality, take their rise from this sense of values within the structure of being. Each individual embodies an adventure of existence. The art of life is the guidance of this adventure. The great religions of civilisation include among their original elements revolts against the inculcation of morals as a set of isolated prohibitions. Morality, in the petty negative sense of the term, is the deadly enemy of religion. Paul denounces the Law, and the Gospels are vehement against the Pharisees. Every outbreak of religion exhibits the same intensity of antagonism — an antagonism diminishing as religion fades. No part of education has more to gain from attention to the rhythmic law of growth than has moral and religious education. Whatever be the right way to formulate religious truths, it is death to religion to insist on a premature stage of precision. The vitality of religion is shown by the way in which the religious spirit has survived the ordeal of religious education.

The problem of religion in education is too large to be discussed at this stage of my address. I have referred to it to guard against the suspicion that the principles here advocated are to be conceived in a narrow sense. We are analysing the general law of rhythmic progress in the higher stages of life, embodying the initial awakening, the discipline, and the fruition on the higher plane. What I am now insisting is that the principle of progress is from within: the discovery is made by ourselves, the discipline is self-discipline, and the fruition is the outcome of our own initiative. The teacher has a double function. It is for him to elicit the enthusiasm by resonance from his own personality, and to create the environment of a larger knowledge and a firmer purpose. He is there to avoid the waste, which in the lower stages of existence is nature's way of evolution. The ultimate motive power, alike in science, in morality, and in religion, is the sense of value, the sense of importance. It takes the various forms of wonder, of curiosity, of reverence, or worship, of tumultuous desire for merging personality in something beyond itself. This sense of value imposes on life incredible labours, and apart from it life sinks back into the passivity of its lower types. The most penetrating exhibition of this force is the sense of beauty, the aesthetic sense of realised perfection. This thought leads me to ask, whether in our modern education we emphasise sufficiently the functions of art.

The typical education of our public schools was devised for boys from well-to-do cultivated homes. They travelled in Italy, in Greece, and in France, and often their own homes were set amid beauty. None of these circumstances hold for modern national education in primary or secondary schools, or even for the majority of boys and girls in our enlarged system of public schools. You cannot, without loss, ignore in the life of the spirit so great a factor as art. Our aesthetic emotions provide us with vivid apprehensions of value. If you maim these, you weaken the force of the whole system of spiritual apprehensions. The claim for freedom in education carries with it the corollary that the development of the whole personality must be attended to. You must not arbitrarily refuse its urgent demands. In these days of economy, we hear much of the futility of our educational efforts and of the possibility of curtailing them. The endeavour to develop a bare intellectuality is bound to issue in a large crop of failure. This is just what we have done in our national schools. We do just enough to excite and not enough to satisfy. History shows us that an efflorescence of art is the first activity of nations on the road to civilisation. Yet, in the face of this plain fact, we practically shut out art from the masses of the population. Can we wonder that such an education, evoking and defeating cravings, leads to failure and discontent? The stupidity of the whole procedure is, that art in simple popular forms is just what we can give to the nation without undue strain on our resources. You may, perhaps, by some great reforms, obviate the worse kind of sweated labour and the insecurity of employment. But you can never greatly increase average incomes. On that side all hope of Utopia is closed to you. It would, however, require no very great effort to use our schools to produce a population with some love of music, some enjoyment of drama, and some joy in beauty of form and colour. We could also provide means for the satisfaction of these emotions in the general life of the population. If you think of the simplest ways, you will see that the strain on material resources would be negligible; and when you have done that, and when your population widely appreciates what art can give — its joys and its terrors — do you not think that your prophets and your clergy and your statesmen will be in a stronger position when they speak to the population of the love of God, of the inexorableness of duty, and of the call of patriotism?

Shakespeare wrote his plays for English people reared in the beauty of the country, amid the pageant of life as the Middle Age merged into the Renaissance, and with a new world across the ocean to make vivid the call of romance. To-day we deal with herded town populations, reared in a scientific age. I have no doubt that unless we can meet the new age with new methods, to sustain for our populations the life of the spirit, sooner or later, amid some savage outbreak of defeated longings, the fate of Russia will be the fate of England. Historians will write as her epitaph that her fall issued from the spiritual blindness of her governing classes, from their dull materialism, and from their Pharisaic attachment to petty formulae of statesmanship.

CHAPTER 4

TECHNICAL EDUCATION AND ITS RELATION TO SCIENCE AND LITERATURE

The subject of this address is Technical Education. I wish to examine its essential nature and also its relation to a liberal education. Such an inquiry may help us to realise the conditions for the successful working of a national system of technical training. It is also a very burning question among mathematical teachers; for mathematics is included in most technological courses.

Now it is unpractical to plunge into such a discussion without framing in our own minds the best ideal towards which we desire to work, however modestly we may frame our hopes as to the result which in the near future is likely to be achieved.

People are shy of ideals; and accordingly we find a formulation of the ideal state of mankind placed by a modern dramatist[1] in the mouth of a mad priest: "In my dreams it is a country where the State is the Church and the Church the people: three in one and one in three. It is a commonwealth in which work is play and play is life: three in one and one in three. It is a temple in which the priest is the worshipper and the worshipper the worshipped: three in one and one in three. It is a godhead in which all life is human and all humanity divine: three in one and one in three. It is, in short, the dream of a madman."

Now the part of this speech to which I would direct attention is embodied in the phrase, "It is a commonwealth in which work is play and play is life."

---

[1] Cf. Bernard Shaw: *John Bull's Other Island*.

The Aims of Education

This is the ideal of technical education. It sounds very mystical when we confront it with the actual facts, the toiling millions, tired, discontented, mentally indifferent, and then the employers — I am not undertaking a social analysis, but I shall carry you with me when I admit that the present facts of society are a long way off this ideal. Furthermore, we are agreed that an employer who conducted his workshop on the principle that "work should be play" would be ruined in a week.

The curse that has been laid on humanity, in fable and in fact, is, that by the sweat of its brow shall it live. But reason and moral intuition have seen in this curse the foundation for advance. The early Benedictine monks rejoiced in their labours because they conceived themselves as thereby made fellow-workers with Christ.

Stripped of its theological trappings, the essential idea remains, that work should be transfused with intellectual and moral vision and thereby turned into a joy, triumphing over its weariness and its pain. Each of us will re-state this abstract formulation in a more concrete shape in accordance with his private outlook. State it how you like, so long as you do not lose the main point in your details. However you phrase it, it remains the sole real hope of toiling humanity; and it is in the hands of technical teachers, and of those who control their spheres of activity, so to mould the nation that daily it may pass to its labours in the spirit of the monks of old.

The immediate need of the nation is a large supply of skilled workmen, of men with inventive genius, and of employers alert in the development of new ideas.

There is one — and only one — way to obtain these admirable results. It is by producing workmen, men of science, and employers who enjoy their work. View the matter practically in the light of our knowledge of average human nature. Is it likely that a tired, bored workman, however skilful his hands, will produce a large output of first-class work? He will limit his production, scamp his work, and be an adept at evading inspection; he will be slow in adapting himself to new methods; he will be a focus of discontent, full of unpractical revolutionary ideas, controlled by no sympathetic apprehension

Chapter 4 Technical Education and Its Relation to Science and Literature

of the real working of trade conditions. If, in the troubled times which may be before us, you wish appreciably to increase the chance of some savage upheaval, introduce widespread technical education and ignore the Benedictine ideal. Society will then get what it deserves.

Again, inventive genius requires pleasurable mental activity as a condition for its vigorous exercise. "Necessity is the mother of invention" is a silly proverb. "Necessity is the mother of futile dodges" is much nearer to the truth. The basis of the growth of modern invention is science, and science is almost wholly the outgrowth of pleasurable intellectual curiosity.

The third class are the employers, who are to be enterprising. Now it is to be observed that it is the successful employers who are the important people to get at, the men with business connections all over the world, men who are already rich. No doubt there will always be a continuous process of rise and fall of businesses. But it is futile to expect flourishing trade, if in the mass the successful houses of business are suffering from atrophy. Now if these men conceive their businesses as merely indifferent means for acquiring other disconnected opportunities of life, they have no spur to alertness. They are already doing very well, the mere momentum of their present business engagements will carry them on for their time. They are not at all likely to bother themselves with the doubtful chances of new methods. Their real soul is in the other side of their life. Desire for money will produce hard-fistedness and not enterprise. There is much more hope for humanity from manufacturers who enjoy their work than from those who continue in irksome business with the object of founding hospitals.

Finally, there can be no prospect of industrial peace so long as masters and men in the mass conceive themselves as engaged in a soulless operation of extracting money from the public. Enlarged views of the work performed, and of the communal service thereby rendered, can be the only basis on which to found sympathetic co-operation.

The conclusion to be drawn from this discussion is, that alike for masters and for men a technical or technological education, which is to have any chance of satisfying the practical needs of the nation, must be conceived in a liberal spirit as a real intellectual enlightenment in regard to principles applied and services rendered. In such an education geometry and poetry are as essential as turning laths.

The mythical figure of Plato may stand for modern liberal education as does that of St. Benedict for technical education. We need not entangle ourselves in the qualifications necessary for a balanced representation of the actual thoughts of the actual men. They are used here as symbolic figures typical of antithetical notions. We consider Plato in the light of the type of culture he now inspires.

In its essence a liberal education is an education for thought and for aesthetic appreciation. It proceeds by imparting a knowledge of the masterpieces of thought, of imaginative literature, and of art. The action which it contemplates is command. It is an aristocratic education implying leisure. This Platonic ideal has rendered imperishable services to European civilisation. It has encouraged art, it has fostered that spirit of disinterested curiosity which is the origin of science, it has maintained the dignity of mind in the face of material force, a dignity which claims freedom of thought. Plato did not, like St. Benedict, bother himself to be a fellow-worker with his slaves; but he must rank among the emancipators of mankind. His type of culture is the peculiar inspiration of the liberal aristocrat, the class from which Europe derives what ordered liberty it now possesses. For centuries, from Pope Nicholas V to the school of the Jesuits, and from the Jesuits to the modern headmasters of English public schools, this educational ideal has had the strenuous support of the clergy.

For certain people it is a very good education. It suits their type of mind and the circumstances amid which their life is passed. But more has been claimed for it than this. All education has been judged adequate or defective according to its approximation to this sole type.

The essence of the type is a large discursive knowledge of the best literature. The ideal product of the type is the man who is acquainted with the best that has been written. He will have acquired the chief languages, he will have considered the histories of the rise and fall of nations, the poetic

Chapter 4 Technical Education and Its Relation to Science and Literature

expression of human feeling, and have read the great dramas and novels. He will also be well grounded in the chief philosophies, and have attentively read those philosophic authors who are distinguished for lucidity of style.

It is obvious that, except at the close of a long life, he will not have much time for anything else if any approximation is to be made to the fulfilment of this programme. One is reminded of the calculation in a dialogue of Lucian that, before a man could be justified in practising any one of the current ethical systems, he should have spent a hundred and fifty years in examining their credentials.

Such ideals are not for human beings. What is meant by a liberal culture is nothing so ambitious as a full acquaintance with the varied literary expression of civilised mankind from Asia to Europe, and from Europe to America. A small selection only is required; but then, as we are told, it is a selection of the very best. I have my doubts of a selection which includes Xenophon and omits Confucius, but then I have read through neither in the original. The ambitious programme of a liberal education really shrinks to a study of some fragments of literature included in a couple of important languages.

But the expression of the human spirit is not confined to literature. There are the other arts, and there are the sciences. Also education must pass beyond the passive reception of the ideas of others. Powers of initiative must be strengthened. Unfortunately initiative does not mean just one acquirement — there is initiative in thought, initiative in action, and the imaginative initiative of art; and these three categories require many subdivisions.

The field of acquirement is large, and the individual so fleeting and so fragmentary: classical scholars, scientists, headmasters are alike ignoramuses.

There is a curious illusion that a more complete culture was possible when there was less to know. Surely the only gain was, that it was more possible to remain unconscious of ignorance. It cannot have been a gain to Plato to have read neither Shakespeare, nor Newton, nor Darwin. The achievements of a liberal education have in recent times not been worsened. The change is that its pretensions have been found out.

My point is, that no course of study can claim any position of ideal completeness. Nor are the omitted factors of subordinate importance. The insistence in the Platonic culture on disinterested intellectual appreciation is a psychological error. Action and our implication in the transition of events amid the inevitable bond of cause to effect are fundamental. An education which strives to divorce intellectual or aesthetic life from these fundamental facts carries with it the decadence of civilisation. Essentially culture should be for action, and its effect should be to divest labour from the associations of aimless toil. Art exists that we may know the deliverances of our senses as good. It heightens the sense-world.

Disinterested scientific curiosity is a passion for an ordered intellectual vision of the connection of events. But the goal of such curiosity is the marriage of action to thought. This essential intervention of action even in abstract science is often overlooked. No man of science wants merely to know. He acquires knowledge to appease his passion for discovery. He does not discover in order to know, he knows in order to discover. The pleasure which art and science can give to toil is the enjoyment which arises from successfully directed intention. Also it is the same pleasure which is yielded to the scientist and to the artist.

The antithesis between a technical and a liberal education is fallacious. There can be no adequate technical education which is not liberal, and no liberal education which is not technical: that is, no education which does not impart both technique and intellectual vision. In simpler language, education should turn out the pupil with something he knows well and something he can do well. This intimate union of practice and theory aids both. The intellect does not work best in a vacuum. The stimulation of creative impulse requires, especially in the case of a child, the quick transition to practice. Geometry and mechanics, followed by workshop practice, gain that reality without which mathematics is verbiage.

There are three main methods which are required in a national system

Chapter 4 Technical Education and Its Relation to Science and Literature

of education, namely, the literary curriculum, the scientific curriculum, the technical curriculum. But each of these curricula should include the other two. What I mean is, that every form of education should give the pupil a technique, a science, an assortment of general ideas, and aesthetic appreciation, and that each of these sides of his training should be illuminated by the others. Lack of time, even for the most favoured pupil, makes it impossible to develop fully each curriculum. Always there must be a dominant emphasis. The most direct aesthetic training naturally falls in the technical curriculum in those cases when the training is that requisite for some art or artistic craft. But it is of high importance in both a literary and a scientific education.

The educational method of the literary curriculum is the study of language, that is, the study of our most habitual method of conveying to others our states of mind. The technique which should be acquired is the technique of verbal expression, the science is the study of the structure of language and the analysis of the relations of language to the states of mind conveyed. Furthermore, the subtle relations of language to feeling, and the high development of the sense organs to which written and spoken words appeal, lead to keen aesthetic appreciations being aroused by the successful employment of language. Finally, the wisdom of the world is preserved in the masterpieces of linguistic composition.

This curriculum has the merit of homogeneity. All its various parts are co-ordinated and play into each other's hands. We can hardly be surprised that such a curriculum, when once broadly established, should have claimed the position of the sole perfect type of education. Its defect is unduly to emphasise the importance of language. Indeed the varied importance of verbal expression is so overwhelming that its sober estimation is difficult. Recent generations have been witnessing the retreat of literature, and of literary forms of expression, from their position of unique importance in intellectual life. In order truly to become a servant and a minister of nature something more is required than literary aptitudes.

A scientific education is primarily a training in the art of observing natural phenomena, and in the knowledge and deduction of laws concerning the sequence of such phenomena. But here, as in the case of a liberal education, we are met by the limitations imposed by shortness of time. There are many types of natural phenomena, and to each type there corresponds a science with its peculiar modes of observation, and its peculiar types of thought employed in the deduction of laws. A study of science in general is impossible in education, all that can be achieved is the study of two or three allied sciences. Hence the charge of narrow specialism urged against any education which is primarily scientific. It is obvious that the charge is apt to be well-founded; and it is worth considering how, within the limits of a scientific education and to the advantage of such an education, the danger can be avoided.

Such a discussion requires the consideration of technical education. A technical education is in the main a training in the art of utilising knowledge for the manufacture of material products. Such a training emphasises manual skill, and the co-ordinated action of hand and eye, and judgment in the control of the process of construction. But judgment necessitates knowledge of those natural processes of which the manufacture is the utilisation. Thus somewhere in technical training an education in scientific knowledge is required. If you minimise the scientific side, you will confine it to the scientific experts; if you maximise it, you will impart it in some measure to the men, and — what is of no less importance — to the directors and managers of the businesses.

Technical education is not necessarily allied exclusively to science on its mental side. It may be an education for an artist or for apprentices to an artistic craft. In that case aesthetic appreciation will have to be cultivated in connection with it.

An evil side of the Platonic culture has been its total neglect of technical education as an ingredient in the complete development of ideal human beings. This neglect has arisen from two disastrous antitheses, namely, that between mind and body, and that between thought and action. I will here interject, solely to avoid criticism, that I am well aware that the Greeks

Chapter 4 Technical Education and Its Relation to Science and Literature

highly valued physical beauty and physical activity. They had, however, that perverted sense of values which is the nemesis of slave-owning.

I lay it down as an educational axiom that in teaching you will come to grief as soon as you forget that your pupils have bodies. This is exactly the mistake of the post-renaissance Platonic curriculum. But nature can be kept at bay by no pitchfork; so in English education, being expelled from the class-room, she returned with a cap and bells in the form of all-conquering athleticism.

The connections between intellectual activity and the body, though diffused in every bodily feeling, are focussed in the eyes, the ears, the voice, and the hands. There is a co-ordination of senses and thought, and also a reciprocal influence between brain activity and material creative activity. In this reaction the hands are peculiarly important. It is a moot point whether the human hand created the human brain, or the brain created the hand. Certainly the connection is intimate and reciprocal. Such deep-seated relations are not widely atrophied by a few hundred years of disuse in exceptional families.

The disuse of hand-craft is a contributory cause to the brainlethargy of aristocracies, which is only mitigated by sport where the concurrent brain-activity is reduced to a minimum and the handcraft lacks subtlety. The necessity for constant writing and vocal exposition is some slight stimulus to the thought-power of the professional classes. Great readers, who exclude other activities, are not distinguished by subtlety of brain. They tend to be timid conventional thinkers. No doubt this is partly due to their excessive knowledge outrunning their powers of thought; but it is partly due to the lack of brain-stimulus from the productive activities of hand or voice.

In estimating the importance of technical education we must rise above the exclusive association of learning with book-learning. First-hand knowledge is the ultimate basis of intellectual life. To a large extent book-learning conveys second-hand information, and as such can never rise to the importance of immediate practice. Our goal is to see the immediate events of our lives as instances of our general ideas. What the learned world tends to offer is one second-hand scrap of information illustrating ideas derived from another second-hand scrap of information. The second-handedness of the learned world is the secret of its mediocrity. It is tame because it has never been scared by facts. The main importance of Francis Bacon's influence does not lie in any peculiar theory of inductive reasoning which he happened to express, but in the revolt against second-hand information of which he was a leader.

The peculiar merit of a scientific education should be, that it bases thought upon first-hand observation; and the corresponding merit of a technical education is, that it follows our deep natural instinct to translate thought into manual skill, and manual activity into thought.

The thought which science evokes is logical thought. Now logic is of two kinds: the logic of discovery and the logic of the discovered.

The logic of discovery consists in the weighing of probabilities, in discarding details deemed to be irrelevant, in divining the general rules according to which events occur, and in testing hypotheses by devising suitable experiments. This is inductive logic.

The logic of the discovered is the deduction of the special events which, under certain circumstances, would happen in obedience to the assumed laws of nature. Thus when the laws are discovered or assumed, their utilisation entirely depends on deductive logic. Without deductive logic science would be entirely useless. It is merely a barren game to ascend from the particular to the general, unless afterwards we can reverse the process and descend from the general to the particular, ascending and descending like the angels on Jacob's ladder. When Newton had divined the law of gravitation he at once proceeded to calculate the earth's attractions on an apple at its surface and on the moon. We may note in passing that inductive logic would be impossible without deductive logic. Thus Newton's calculations were an essential step in his inductive verification of the great law.

Now mathematics is nothing else than the more complicated parts of the art of deductive reasoning, especially where it concerns number, quantity,

Chapter 4 Technical Education and Its Relation to Science and Literature

and space.

In the teaching of science, the art of thought should be taught: namely, the art of forming clear conceptions applying to first-hand experience, the art of divining the general truths which apply, the art of testing divinations, and the art of utilising general truths by reasoning to more particular cases of some peculiar importance. Furthermore, a power of scientific exposition is necessary, so that the relevant issues from a confused mass of ideas can be stated clearly, with due emphasis on important points.

By the time a science, or a small group of sciences, has been taught thus amply, with due regard to the general art of thought, we have gone a long way towards correcting the specialism of science. The worst of a scientific education based, as necessarily must be the case, on one or two particular branches of science, is that the teachers under the influence of the examination system are apt merely to stuff their pupils with the narrow results of these special sciences. It is essential that the generality of the method be continually brought to light and contrasted with the speciality of the particular application. A man who only knows his own science, as a routine peculiar to that science, does not even know that. He has no fertility of thought, no power of quickly seizing the bearing of alien ideas. He will discover nothing, and be stupid in practical applications.

This exhibition of the general in the particular is extremely difficult to effect, especially in the case of younger pupils. The art of education is never easy. To surmount its difficulties, especially those of elementary education, is a task worthy of the highest genius. It is the training of human souls.

Mathematics, well taught, should be the most powerful instrument in gradually implanting this generality of idea. The essence of mathematics is perpetually to be discarding more special ideas in favour of more general ideas, and special methods in favour of general methods. We express the conditions of a special problem in the form of an equation, but that equation will serve for a hundred other problems, scattered through diverse sciences. The general reasoning is always the powerful reasoning, because deductive cogency is the property of abstract form.

The Aims of Education

Here, again, we must be careful. We shall ruin mathematical education if we use it merely to impress general truths. The general ideas are the means of connecting particular results. After all, it is the concrete special cases which are important. Thus in the handling of mathematics in your results you cannot be too concrete, and in your methods you cannot be too general. The essential course of reasoning is to generalise what is particular, and then to particularise what is general. Without generality there is no reasoning, without concreteness there is no importance.

Concreteness is the strength of technical education. I would remind you that truths which lack the highest generality are not necessarily concrete facts. For example, $x + y = y + x$ is an algebraic truth more general than $2 + 2 = 4$. But "two and two make four" is itself a highly general proposition lacking any element of concreteness. To obtain a concrete proposition immediate intuition of a truth concerning particular objects is requisite; for example, "these two apples and those apples together make four apples" is a concrete proposition, if you have direct perception or immediate memory of the apples.

In order to obtain the full realisation of truths as applying, and not as empty formulae, there is no alternative to technical education. Mere passive observation is not sufficient. In creation only is there vivid insight into the properties of the object thereby produced. If you want to understand anything, make it yourself, is a sound rule. Your faculties will be alive, your thoughts gain vividness by an immediate translation into acts. Your ideas gain that reality which comes from seeing the limits of their application.

In elementary education this doctrine has long been put into practice. Young children are taught to familiarise themselves with shapes and colours by simple manual operations of cutting out and of sorting. But good though this is, it is not quite what I mean. That is practical experience before you think, experience antecedent to thought in order to create ideas, a very excellent discipline. But technical education should be much more than that: it is creative experience while you think, experience which realises your thought, experience which teaches you to co-ordinate act and thought,

Chapter 4 Technical Education and Its Relation to Science and Literature

experience leading you to associate thought with foresight and foresight with achievement. Technical education gives theory, and a shrewd insight as to where theory fails.

A technical education is not to be conceived as a maimed alternative to the perfect Platonic culture: namely, as a defective training unfortunately made necessary by cramped conditions of life. No human being can attain to anything but fragmentary knowledge and a fragmentary training of his capacities. There are, however, three main roads along which we can proceed with good hope of advancing towards the best balance of intellect and character: these are the way of literary culture, the way of scientific culture, the way of technical culture. No one of these methods can be exclusively followed without grave loss of intellectual activity and of character. But a mere mechanical mixture of the three curricula will produce bad results in the shape of scraps of information never interconnected or utilised. We have already noted as one of the strong points of the traditional literary culture that all its parts are co-ordinated. The problem of education is to retain the dominant emphasis, whether literary, scientific or technical, and without loss of co-ordination to infuse into each way of education something of the other two.

To make definite the problem of technical education fix attention on two ages: one thirteen, when elementary education ends; and the other seventeen, when technical education ends so far as it is compressed within a school curriculum. I am aware that for artisans in junior technical schools a three-years' course would be more usual. On the other hand, for naval officers, and for directing classes generally, a longer time can be afforded. We want to consider the principles to govern a curriculum which shall land these children at the age of seventeen in the position of having technical skill useful to the community.

Their technical manual training should start at thirteen, bearing a modest proportion to the rest of their work, and should increase in each year finally to attain to a substantial proportion. Above all things it should not be too specialised. Workshop finish and workshop dodges, adapted to one

The Aims of Education

particular job, should be taught in the commercial workshop, and should form no essential part of the school course. A properly trained worker would pick them up in no time. In all education the main cause of failure is staleness. Technical education is doomed if we conceive it as a system for catching children young and for giving them one highly specialised manual aptitude. The nation has need of a fluidity of labour, not merely from place to place, but also within reasonable limits of allied aptitudes, from one special type of work to another special type. I know that here I am on delicate ground, and I am not claiming that men while they are specialising on one sort of work should spasmodically be set to other kinds. That is a question of trade organisation with which educationalists have no concern. I am only asserting the principles that training should be broader than the ultimate specialisation, and that the resulting power of adaptation to varying demands is advantageous to the workers, to the employers, and to the nation.

In considering the intellectual side of the curriculum we must be guided by the principle of the co-ordination of studies. In general, the intellectual studies most immediately related to manual training will be some branches of science. More than one branch will, in fact, be concerned; and even if that be not the case, it is impossible to narrow down scientific study to a single thin line of thought. It is possible, however, provided that we do not press the classification too far, roughly to classify technical pursuits according to the dominant science involved. We thus find a sixfold division, namely, (1) Geometrical techniques, (2) Mechanical techniques, (3) Physical techniques, (4) Chemical techniques, (5) Biological techniques, (6) Techniques of commerce and of social service.

By this division, it is meant that apart from auxiliary sciences some particular science requires emphasis in the training for most occupations. We can, for example, reckon carpentry, ironmongery, and many artistic crafts among geometrical techniques. Similarly agriculture is a biological technique. Probably cookery, if it includes food catering, would fall midway between biological, physical, and chemical sciences, though of this I am not

Chapter 4 Technical Education and Its Relation to Science and Literature

sure.

The sciences associated with commerce and social service would be partly algebra, including arithmetic and statistics, and partly geography and history. But this section is somewhat heterogeneous in its scientific affinities. Anyhow the exact way in which technical pursuits are classified in relation to science is a detail. The essential point is, that with some thought it is possible to find scientific courses which illuminate most occupations. Furthermore, the problem is well understood, and has been brilliantly solved in many of the schools of technology and junior technical schools throughout the country.

In passing from science to literature, in our review of the intellectual elements of technical education, we note that many studies hover between the two: for example, history and geography. They are both of them very essential in education, provided that they are the right history and the right geography. Also books giving descriptive accounts of general results, and trains of thought in various sciences fall in the same category. Such books should be partly historical and partly expository of the main ideas which have finally arisen. Their value in education depends on their quality as mental stimulants. They must not be inflated with gas on the wonders of science, and must be informed with a broad outlook.

It is unfortunate that the literary element in education has rarely been considered apart from grammatical study. The historical reason is, that when the modern Platonic curriculum was being formed Latin and Greek were the sole keys which rendered great literature accessible. But there is no necessary connection between literature and grammar. The great age of Greek literature was already past before the arrival of the grammarians of Alexandria. Of all types of men to-day existing, classical scholars are the most remote from the Greeks of the Periclean times.

Mere literary knowledge is of slight importance. The only thing that matters is, how it is known. The facts related are nothing. Literature only exists to express and develop that imaginative world which is our life, the kingdom which is within us. It follows that the literary side of a technical education should consist in an effort to make the pupils enjoy literature. It does not matter what they know, but the enjoyment is vital. The great English Universities, under whose direct authority school-children are examined in plays of Shakespeare, to the certain destruction of their enjoyment, should be prosecuted for soul murder.

Now there are two kinds of intellectual enjoyment: the enjoyment of creation, and the enjoyment of relaxation. They are not necessarily separated. A change of occupation may give the full tide of happiness which comes from the concurrence of both forms of pleasure. The appreciation of literature is really creation. The written word, its music, and its associations, are only the stimuli. The vision which they evoke is our own doing. No one, no genius other than our own, can make our own life live. But except for those engaged in literary occupations, literature is also a relaxation. It gives exercise to that other side which any occupation must suppress during the working hours. Art also has the same function in life as has literature.

To obtain the pleasure of relaxation requires no help. The pleasure is merely to cease doing. Some such pure relaxation is a necessary condition of health. Its dangers are notorious, and to the greater part of the necessary relaxation nature has affixed, not enjoyment, but the oblivion of sleep. Creative enjoyment is the outcome of successful effort and requires help for its initiation. Such enjoyment is necessary for high-speed work and for original achievement.

To speed up production with unrefreshed workmen is a disastrous economic policy. Temporary success will be at the expense of the nation, which, for long years of their lives, will have to support worn-out artisans-unemployables. Equally disastrous is the alternation of spasms of effort with periods of pure relaxation. Such periods are the seed-times of degeneration, unless rigorously curtailed. The normal recreation should be change of activity, satisfying the cravings of instincts. Games afford such activity. Their disconnection emphasises the relaxation, but their excess leaves us empty.

It is here that literature and art should play an essential part in a healthily organised nation. Their services to economic production would be only second to those of sleep or of food. I am not now talking of the training of an artist, but of the use of art as a condition of healthy life. It is analogous to sunshine in the physical world.

When we have once rid our minds of the idea that knowledge is to be exacted, there is no especial difficulty or expense involved in helping the growth of artistic enjoyment. All school-children could be sent at regular intervals to neighbouring theatres where suitable plays could be subsidised. Similarly for concerts and cinema films. Pictures are more doubtful in their popular attraction; but interesting representations of scenes or ideas which the children have read about would probably appeal. The pupils themselves should be encouraged in artistic efforts. Above all the art of reading aloud should be cultivated. The Roger de Coverley essays of Addison are perfect examples of readable prose.

Art and literature have not merely an indirect effect on the main energies of life. Directly, they give vision. The world spreads wide beyond the deliverances of material sense, with subtleties of reaction and with pulses of emotion. Vision is the necessary antecedent to control and to direction. In the contest of races which in its final issues will be decided in the workshops and not on the battlefield, the victory will belong to those who are masters of stores of trained nervous energy, working under conditions favourable to growth. One such essential condition is Art.

If there had been time, there are other things which I should like to have said: for example, to advocate the inclusion of one foreign language in all education. From direct observation I know this to be possible for artisan children. But enough has been put before you to make plain the principles with which we should undertake national education.

In conclusion, I recur to the thought of the Benedictines, who saved for mankind the vanishing civilisation of the ancient world by linking together knowledge, labour, and moral energy. Our danger is to conceive practical affairs as the kingdom of evil, in which success is only possible by the extrusion of ideal aims. I believe that such a conception is a fallacy directly negatived by practical experience. In education this error takes the form of a mean view of technical training. Our forefathers in the dark ages saved themselves by embodying high ideals in great organisations. It is our task, without servile imitation, boldly to exercise our creative energies.

CHAPTER 5

THE PLACE OF CLASSICS IN EDUCATION

The future of classics in this country is not going mainly to be decided by the joy of classics to a finished scholar, and by the utility of scholarly training for scholarly avocations. The pleasure and the discipline of character to be derived from an education based mainly on classical literature and classical philosophy has been demonstrated by centuries of experience. The danger to classical learning does not arise because classical scholars now love classics less than their predecessors. It arises in this way. In the past classics reigned throughout the whole sphere of higher education. There were no rivals; and accordingly all students were steeped in classics throughout their school life, and its domination at the universities was only challenged by the narrow discipline of mathematics. There were many consequences to this state of things. There was a large demand for classical scholars for the mere purposes of tuition; there was a classical tone in all learned walks of life, so that aptitude for classics was a synonym for ability; and finally every boy who gave the slightest promise in that direction cultivated his natural or acquired interest in classical learning. All this is gone, and gone for ever. Humpty Dumpty was a good egg so long as he was on the top of the wall, but you can never set him up again. There are now other disciplines each involving topics of wide-spread interest, with complex relationships, and exhibiting in their development the noblest feats of genius in its stretch of imagination and its philosophic intuition. Almost every walk of life is now a learned profession, and demands one or more of these disciplines as the substratum for its technical skill. Life is short, and the plastic period when the brain is apt for acquirement is still shorter.

The Aims of Education

Accordingly, even if all children were fitted for it, it is absolutely impossible to maintain a system of education in which a complete training as a classical scholar is the necessary preliminary to the acquirement of other intellectual disciplines. As a member of the Prime Minister's Committee on the Place of Classics in Education it was my misfortune to listen to much ineffectual wailing from witnesses on the mercenary tendencies of modern parents. I do not believe that the modern parent of any class is more mercenary than his predecessors. When classics was the road to advancement, classics was the popular subject for study. Opportunity has now shifted its location, and classics is in danger. Was it not Aristotle who said that a good income was a desirable adjunct to an intellectual life? I wonder how Aristotle, as a parent, would have struck a headmaster of one of our great public schools. From my slight knowledge of Aristotle, I suspect that there would have been an argument, and that Aristotle would have got the best of it. I have been endeavouring to appreciate at its full value the danger which besets classics in the educational curriculum. The conclusion that I draw is that the future classics will be decided during the next few years in the secondary schools of this country. Within a generation the great public schools will have to follow suit, whether they like it or not.

The situation is dominated by the fact that in the future ninety per cent of the pupils who leave school at the age of eighteen will never again read a classical book in the original. In the case of pupils leaving at an earlier age, the estimate of ninety per cent may be changed to one of ninety-nine per cent. I have heard and read many a beautiful exposition of the value of classics to the scholar who reads Plato and Virgil in his armchair. But these people will never read classics either in their armchairs or in any other situation. We have got to produce a defence of classics which applies to this ninety per cent of the pupils. If classics is swept out of the curriculum for this section, the remaining ten per cent will soon vanish. No school will have the staff to teach them. The problem is urgent.

It would, however, be a great mistake to conclude that classics is faced with a hostile opinion either in the learned professions or from leaders of

Chapter 5 The Place of Classics in Education

industry who have devoted attention to the relation between education and efficiency. The last discussion, public or private, on this subject, at which I have been present was a short and vigorous one at one of the leading committees of a great modern university. The three representatives of the Faculty of Science energetically urged the importance of classics on the ground of its value as a preliminary discipline for scientists. I mention this incident because in my experience it is typical.

We must remember that the whole problem of intellectual education is controlled by lack of time. If Methuselah was not a well-educated man, it was his own fault or that of his teachers. But our task is to deal with five years of secondary school-life. Classics can only be defended on the ground that within that period, and sharing that period with other subjects, it can produce a necessary enrichment of intellectual character more quickly than any alternative discipline directed to the same object.

In classics we endeavour by a thorough study of language to develop the mind in the regions of logic, philosophy, history and of aesthetic apprehension of literary beauty. The learning of the languages — Latin or Greek — is a subsidiary means for the furtherance of this ulterior object. When the object has been obtained, the languages can be dropped unless opportunity and choice lead to their further pursuit. There are certain minds, and among them some of the best, for which the analysis of language is not the avenue of approach to the goal of culture. For these a butterfly or a steam-engine has a wider range of significance than a Latin sentence. This is especially the case where there is a touch of genius arising from vivid apprehensions stimulating originality of thought. The assigned verbal sentence almost always says the wrong thing for such people, and confuses them by its trivial irrelevance.

But on the whole the normal avenue is the analysis of language. It represents the greatest common measure for the pupils, and by far the most manageable job for the teachers.

At this point I must cross-question myself. My other self asks me, Why do you not teach the children logic, if you want them to learn that

The Aims of Education

subject? Wouldn't that be the obvious procedure? I answer in the words of a great man who to our infinite loss has recently died, Sanderson, the late headmaster of Oundle. His phrase was, They learn by contact. The meaning to be attached to this saying goes to the root of the true practice of education. It must start from the particular fact, concrete and definite for individual apprehension, and must gradually evolve towards the general idea. The devil to be avoided is the cramming of general statements which have no reference to individual personal experiences.

Now apply this principle to the determination of the best method to help a child towards a philosophical analysis of thought. I will put it in more homely style, What is the best way to make a child clear-headed in its thoughts and its statements? The general statements of a logic book have no reference to anything the child has ever heard of. They belong to the grown-up stage of education at — or not far from — the university. You must begin with the analysis of familiar English sentences. But this grammatical procedure, if prolonged beyond its elementary stages, is horribly dry. Furthermore, it has the disadvantage that it only analyses so far as the English language analyses. It does nothing to throw light upon the complex significance of English phrases, and words, and habits of mental procedure. Your next step is to teach the child a foreign language. Here you gain an enormous advantage. You get away from the nauseating formal drill for the drill's sake. The analysis is now automatic, while the pupil's attention is directed to expressing his wants in the language, or to understanding someone who is speaking to him, or to making out what an author has written. Every language embodies a definite type of mentality, and two languages necessarily display to the pupil some contrast between their two types. Common sense dictates that you start with French as early as possible in the child's life. If you are wealthy, you will provide a French nursery-governess. Less fortunate children will start French in a secondary school about the age of twelve. The direct method is probably used, by which the child is immersed in French throughout the lesson and is taught to think in French without the intervention of English between the French words and their significations. Even an average child will get on well, and soon acquires the power of handling and understanding simple French sentences. As I have said before, the gain is enormous; and, in addition, a useful instrument for after life is acquired. The sense for language grows, a sense which is the subconscious appreciation of language as an instrument of definite structure.

It is exactly now that the initiation of Latin is the best stimulus for mental expansion. The elements of Latin exhibit a peculiarly plain concrete case of language as a structure. Provided that your mind has grown to the level of that idea, the fact stares you in the face. You can miss it over English and French. Good English of a simple kind will go straight into slipshod French, and conversely good French will go into slipshod English. The difference between the slipshod French of the literal translation and the good French, which ought to have been written, is often rather subtle for that stage of mental growth, and is not always easy to explain. Both languages have the same common modernity of expression. But in the case of English and Latin the contrast of structure is obvious, and yet not so wide as to form an insuperable difficulty.

According to the testimony of schoolmasters, Latin is rather a popular subject; I know that as a schoolboy I enjoyed it myself. I believe that this popularity is due to the sense of enlightenment that accompanies its study. You know that you are finding out something. The words somehow stick in the sentences in a different way to what they do either in English or French, with odd queer differences of connotation. Of course in a way Latin is a more barbaric language than English. It is one step nearer to the sentence as the unanalysed unit.

This brings me to my next point. In my catalogue of the gifts of Latin I placed philosophy between logic and history. In this connection, that is its true place. The philosophic instinct which Latin evokes, hovers between the two and enriches both. The analysis of thought involved in translation, English to Latin or Latin to English, imposes that type of experience which is the necessary introduction to philosophic logic. If in after life your job is to think, render thanks to Providence which ordained that, for five years of your youth, you did a Latin prose once a week and daily construed some Latin author. The introduction to any subject is the process of learning by contact. To that majority of people for whom language is the readiest stimulus to thought-activity, the road towards enlightenment of understanding runs from simple English grammar to French, from French to Latin, and also traverses the elements of Geometry and of Algebra. I need not remind my readers that I can claim Plato's authority for the general principle which I am upholding.

From the philosophy of thought we now pass to the philosophy of history. I again recur to Sanderson's great saying, They learn by contact. How on earth is a child to learn history by contact? The original documents, charters and laws and diplomatic correspondence, are double Dutch to it. A game of football is perhaps a faint reflection of the Battle of Marathon. But that is only to say that human life in all ages and circumstances has common qualities. Furthermore, all this diplomatic and political stuff with which we cram children is a very thin view of history. What is really necessary is that we should have an instinctive grasp of the flux of outlook, and of thought, and of aesthetic and racial impulses, which have controlled the troubled history of mankind. Now the Roman Empire is the bottleneck through which the vintage of the past has passed into modern life. So far as European civilisation is concerned the key to history is a comprehension of the mentality of Rome and the work of its Empire.

In the language of Rome, embodying in literary form the outlook of Rome, we possess the simplest material, by contact with which we can gain appreciation of the tides of change in human affairs. The mere obvious relations of the languages, French and English, to Latin are in themselves a philosophy of history. Consider the contrast which English presents to French: the entire break of English with the civilised past of Britain and the slow creeping back of words and phrases of Mediterranean origin with their cargoes of civilised meaning; in French we have continuity of development, amid obvious traces of rude shock. I am not asking for pretentious abstract

Chapter 5　The Place of Classics in Education

lectures on such points. The thing illustrates itself. An elementary knowledge of French and Latin with a mother-tongue of English imparts the requisite atmosphere of reality to the story of the racial wanderings which created our Europe. Language is the incarnation of the mentality of the race which fashioned it. Every phrase and word embodies some habitual idea of men and women as they ploughed their fields, tended their homes, and built their cities. For this reason there are no true synonyms as between words and phrases in different languages. The whole of what I have been saying is merely an embroidery upon this single theme, and our endeavour to emphasise its critical importance. In English, French, and Latin we possess a triangle, such that one pair of vertices, English and French, exhibits a pair of diverse expressions of two chief types of modern mentality, and the relations of these vertices to the third exhibit alternative processes of derivation from the Mediterranean civilisation of the past. This is the essential triangle of literary culture, containing within itself freshness of contrast, embracing both the present and the past. It ranges through space and time. These are the grounds by which we justify the assertion, that in the acquirement of French and Latin is to be found the easiest mode of learning by contact the philosophy of logic and the philosophy of history. Apart from some such intimate experience, your analyses of thought and your histories of actions are mere sounding brasses. I am not claiming, and I do not for a moment believe, that this route of education is more than the simplest, easiest route for the majority of pupils. I am certain that there is a large minority for which the emphasis should be different. But I do believe that it is the route which can give the greatest success for the largest majority. It has also the advantage of having survived the test of experience. I believe that large modifications require to be introduced into existing practice to adapt it for present needs. But on the whole this foundation of literary education involves the best understood tradition and the largest corps of experienced scholarly teachers who can realise it in practice.

　　The reader has perhaps observed that I have as yet said nothing of the glories of Roman literature. Of course the teaching of Latin must proceed by the means of reading Latin literature with the pupils. This literature possesses vigorous authors who have succeeded in putting across the footlights the Roman mentality on a variety of topics, including its appreciation of Greek thought. One of the merits of Roman literature is its comparative lack of outstanding genius. There is very little aloofness about its authors, they express their race and very little which is beyond all differences of race. With the exception of Lucretius, you always feel the limitations under which they are working. Tacitus expressed the views of the Die-hards of the Roman Senate, and, blind to the achievements of Roman provincial administration, could only see that Greek freedmen were replacing Roman aristocrats. The Roman Empire and the mentality which created it absorbed the genius of Romans. Very little of Roman literature will find its way into the kingdom of heaven, when the events of this world will have lost their importance. The languages of heaven will be Chinese, Greek, French, German, Italian, and English, and the blessed Saints will dwell with delight on these golden expressions of eternal life. They will be wearied with the moral fervour of Hebrew literature in its battle with a vanished evil, and with Roman authors who have mistaken the Forum for the footstool of the living God.

We do not teach Latin in the hope that Roman authors, read in the original, may be for our pupils companions through life. English literature is so much greater: it is richer, deeper, and more subtle. If your tastes are philosophic, would you abandon Bacon and Hobbes, Locke, Berkeley, Hume, and Mill for the sake of Cicero? Not unless your taste among the moderns would lead you to Martin Tupper. Perhaps you crave for reflection on the infinite variety of human existence and the reaction of character to circumstance. Would you exchange Shakespeare and the English novelists for Terence, Plautus, and the banquet of Trimalchio? Then there are our humorists, Sheridan, Dickens, and others. Did anyone ever laugh like that as he read a Latin author? Cicero was a great orator, staged amid the pomp of Empire. England also can show statesmen inspired to expound policies with imagination. I will not weary you with an extended catalogue embracing poetry and history. I simply wish to justify my scepticism as to the claim for Latin literature that it expresses with outstanding perfection the universal element in human life. It cannot laugh and it can hardly cry.

You must not tear it from its context. It is not a literature in the sense that Greece and England have produced literatures, expressions of universal human feeling. Latin has one theme and that is Rome — Rome, the mother of Europe, and the great Babylon, the harlot whose doom is described by the writer of the Apocalypse:

"Standing afar off for the fear of her torment, saying, Alas, alas, that great city Babylon, that mighty city! For in one hour is thy judgment come. And the merchants of the earth shall weep and mourn over her; for no man buyeth their merchandise any more;

"The merchandise of gold, and silver, and precious stones, and of pearls, and fine linen, and purple, and silk, and scarlet, and all thyine wood, and all manner vessels of ivory, and all manner vessels of most precious wood, and of brass, and iron, and marble;

"And cinnamon, and odours, and ointments, and frankincense, and wine, and oil, and fine flour, and wheat, and beasts, and sheep, and horses, and chariots, and slaves, and souls of men."

This is the way Roman civilisation appeared to an early Christian. But then Christianity itself is part of the outcrop of the ancient world which Rome passed on to Europe. We inherit the dual aspect of the civilisations of the eastern Mediterranean.

The function of Latin literature is its expression of Rome. When to England and France your imagination can add Rome in the background, you have laid firm the foundations of culture. The understanding of Rome leads back to that Mediterranean civilisation of which Rome was the last phase, and it automatically exhibits the geography of Europe, and the functions of seas and rivers and mountains and plains. The merit of this study in the education of youth is its concreteness, its inspiration to action, and the uniform greatness of persons, in their characters and their staging. Their aims were great, their virtues were great, and their vices were great.

The Aims of Education

They had the saving merit of sinning with cart-ropes. Moral education is impossible apart from the habitual vision of greatness. If we are not great, it does not matter what we do or what is the issue. Now the sense of greatness is an immediate intuition and not the conclusion of an argument. It is permissible for youth in the agonies of religious conversion to entertain the feeling of being a worm and no man, so long as there remains the conviction of greatness sufficient to justify the eternal wrath of God. The sense of greatness is the groundwork of morals. We are at the threshold of a democratic age, and it remains to be determined whether the equality of man is to be realised on a high level or a low level. There was never a time in which it was more essential to hold before the young the vision of Rome: in itself a great drama, and with issues greater than itself. We are now already immersed in the topic of aesthetic appreciation of literary quality. It is here that the tradition of classical teaching requires most vigorous reformation for adaptation to new conditions. It is obsessed with the formation of finished classical scholars. The old tradition was remorselessly to devote the initial stages to the acquirement of the languages and then to trust to the current literary atmosphere to secure enjoyment of the literature. During the latter part of the nineteenth century other subjects encroached on the available time. Too often the result has been merely time wasted in the failure to learn the language. I often think that the ruck of pupils from great English schools show a deplorable lack of intellectual zest, arising from this sense of failure. The school course of classics must be planned so that a definite result is clearly achieved. There has been too great a product of failures on the road to an ambitious ideal of scholarship.

In approaching every work of art we have to comport ourselves suitably in regard to two factors, scale and pace. It is not fair to the architect if you examine St. Peter's at Rome with a microscope, and the Odyssey becomes insipid if you read it at the rate of five lines a day. Now the problem before us is exactly this. We are dealing with pupils who will never know Latin well enough to read it quickly, and the vision to be illumed is of vast scale, set in the history of all time. A careful study of scale and pace, and of the

Chapter 5 The Place of Classics in Education

correlative functions of various parts of our work, should appear to be essential. I have not succeeded in hitting upon any literature which deals with this question with reference to the psychology of the pupils. Is it a masonic secret?

I have often noticed that, if in an assembly of great scholars the topic of translations be introduced, they function as to their emotions and sentiments in exactly the same way as do decent people in the presence of a nasty sex-problem. A mathematician has no scholastic respectability to lose, so I will face the question.

It follows from the whole line of thought which I have been developing, that an exact appreciation of the meanings of Latin words, of the ways in which ideas are connected in grammatical constructions, and of the whole hang of a Latin sentence with its distribution of emphasis, forms the very backbone of the merits which I ascribe to the study of Latin. Accordingly any woolly vagueness of teaching, slurring over the niceties of language defeats the whole ideal which I have set before you. The use of a translation to enable the pupils to get away from the Latin as quickly as possible, or to avoid the stretch of mind in grappling with construction, is erroneous. Exactness, definiteness, and independent power of analysis are among the main prizes of the whole study.

But we are still confronted with the inexorable problem of pace, and with the short four or five years of the whole course. Every poem is meant to be read within certain limits of time. The contrasts, and the images, and the transition of moods must correspond with the sway of rhythms in the human spirit. These have their periods, which refuse to be stretched beyond certain limits. You may take the noblest poetry in the world, and, if you stumble through it at snail's pace, it collapses from a work of art into a rubbish heap. Think of the child's mind as he pores over his work: he reads "as when," then follows a pause with a reference to the dictionary, then he goes on — "an eagle," then another reference to the dictionary, followed by a period of wonderment over the construction, and so on, and so on. Is that going to help him to the vision of Rome? Surely, surely, common sense dictates that you procure the best literary translation you can, the one which best preserves the charm and vigour of the original, and that you read it aloud at the right pace, and append such comments as will elucidate the comprehension. The attack on the Latin will then be fortified by the sense that it enshrines a living work of art.

But someone objects that a translation is woefully inferior to the original. Of course it is, that is why the boy has to master the Latin original. When the original has been mastered, it can be given its proper pace. I plead for an initial sense of the unity of the whole, to be given by a translation at the right pace, and for a final appreciation of the full value of the whole to be given by the original at the right pace. Wordsworth talks of men of science who "murder to dissect." In the past, classical scholars have been veritable assassins compared to them. The sense of beauty is eager and vehement, and should be treated with the reverence which is its due. But I go further. The total bulk of Latin literature necessary to convey the vision of Rome is much greater than the students can possibly accomplish in the original. They should read more Virgil than they can read in Latin, more Lucretius than they can read in Latin, more history than they can read in Latin, more Cicero than they can read in Latin. In the study of an author the selected portions in Latin should illumine a fuller disclosure of his whole mind, although without the force of his own words in his own language. It is, however, a grave evil if no part of an author be read in his own original words.

The difficulty of scale is largely concerned in the presentation of classical history. Everything set before the young must be rooted in the particular and the individual. Yet we want to illustrate the general characters of whole periods. We must make students learn by contact. We can exhibit the modes of life by visual representations. There are photographs of buildings, casts of statues, and pictures from vases or frescoes illustrating religious myths or domestic scenes. In this way we can compare Rome with the preceding civilisation of the eastern Mediterranean, and with the succeeding period of the Middle Ages. It is essential to get into the children's minds how men altered, in their appearance, their dwellings, their technology, their art, and their religious beliefs. We must imitate the procedure of the zoologists who have the whole of animal creation on their hands. They teach by demonstrating typical examples. We must do likewise, to exhibit the position of Rome in history.

The life of man is founded on Technology, Science, Art and Religion. All four are inter-connected and issue from his total mentality. But there are particular intimacies between Science and Technology, and between Art and Religion. No social organisation can be understood without reference to these four underlying factors. A modern steam-engine does the work of a thousand slaves in the ancient world. Slave-raiding was the key to much of the ancient imperialism. A modern printing-press is an essential adjunct to a modern democracy. The key to modern mentality is the continued advance of science with the consequential shift of ideas and progress of technology. In the ancient world Mesopotamia and Egypt were made possible by irrigation. But the Roman Empire existed by virtue of the grandest application of technology that the world had hitherto seen: its roads, its bridges, its aqueducts, its tunnels, its sewers, its vast buildings, its organised merchant navies, its military science, its metallurgy, and its agriculture. This was the secret of the extension and the unity of Roman civilisation. I have often wondered why Roman engineers did not invent the steamengine. They might have done it at any time, and then how different would have been the history of the world. I ascribe it to the fact that they lived in a warm climate and had not introduced tea and coffee. In the eighteenth century thousands of men sat by fires and watched their kettles boil. We all know of course that Hiero of Alexandria invented some slight anticipation. All that was wanted was that the Roman engineers should have been impressed with the motive force of steam by the humble process of watching their kettles.

The history of mankind has yet to be set in its proper relation to the gathering momentum of technological advance. Within the last hundred years, a developed science has wedded itself to a developed technology and a new epoch has opened.

Similarly about a thousand years before Christ the first great literary epoch commenced when the art of writing was finally popularised. In its earlier dim origins the art had been used for traditional hieratic formulae and for the formal purposes of governmental record and chronicle. It is a great mistake to think that in the past the full sweep of a new invention has ever been anticipated at its first introduction. It is not even so at the present day, when we are all trained to meditate on the possibilities of new ideas. But in the past, with its different direction of thought, novelty slowly ate its way into the social system. Accordingly writing, as a stimulus to the preservation of individual novelty of thought, was but slowly grasped on the borders of the eastern Mediterranean. When the realisation of its possibilities was complete, in the hands of the Greeks and the Hebrews, civilisation took a new turn; though the general influence of Hebrew mentality was delayed for a thousand years till the advent of Christianity. But it was now that their prophets were recording their inward thoughts, when Greek civilisation was beginning to take shape.

What I want to illustrate is that in the large scale treatment of history necessary for the background and the foreground of the vision of Rome, the consecutive chronicle of political events on the scale traditional to our histories absolutely vanishes. Even verbal explanations partly go into the background. We must utilise models, and pictures, and diagrams, and charts to exhibit typical examples of the growth of technology and its impact on the current modes of life. In the same way art, in its curious fusion with utility and with religion, both expresses the actual inward life of imagination and changes it by its very expression. The children can see the art of previous epochs in models and pictures, and sometimes the very objects in museums. The treatment of the history of the past must not start with generalised statements, but with concrete examples exhibiting the slow succession of period to period, and of mode of life to mode of life, and of race to race.

The same concreteness of treatment must apply when we come to the literary civilisations of the eastern Mediterranean. When you come to think

Chapter 5　The Place of Classics in Education

of it, the whole claim for the importance of classics rests on the basis that there is no substitute for first-hand knowledge. In so far as Greece and Rome are the founders of European civilisation, a knowledge of history means above all things a first-hand knowledge of the thoughts of Greeks and Romans. Accordingly, to put the vision of Rome into its proper setting, I urge that the pupils should read at first hand some few examples of Greek literature. Of course it must be in translation. But I prefer a translation of what a Greek actually said, to any talk about the Greeks written by an Englishman, however well he has done it. Books about Greece should come after some direct knowledge of Greece.

　　The sort of reading I mean is a verse translation of the Odyssey, some Herodotus, some choruses of plays translated by Gilbert Murray, some lives of Plutarch, especially the part about Archimedes in the life of Marcellus, and the definitions and axioms and one or two propositions from Euclid's Elements in the exact scholarly translation of Heath. In all this, just enough explanation is wanted to give the mental environment of the authors. The marvellous position of Rome in relation to Europe comes from the fact that it has transmitted to us a double inheritance. It received the Hebrew religious thought, and has passed on to Europe its fusion with Greek civilisation. Rome itself stands for the impress of organization and unity upon diverse fermenting elements. Roman Law embodies the secret of Roman greatness in its Stoic respect for intimate rights of human nature within an iron framework of empire. Europe is always flying apart because of the diverse explosive character of its inheritance, and coming together because it can never shake off that impress of unity it has received from Rome. The history of Europe is the history of Rome curbing the Hebrew and the Greek, with their various impulses of religion, and of science, and of art, and of quest for material comfort, and of lust of domination, which are all at daggers drawn with each other. The vision of Rome is the vision of the unity of civilisation.

CHAPTER 6

THE MATHEMATICAL CURRICULUM

The situation in regard to education at the present time cannot find its parallel without going back for some centuries to the breakup of the mediaeval traditions of learning. Then, as now, the traditional intellectual outlook, despite the authority which it had justly acquired from its notable triumphs, had grown to be too narrow for the interests of mankind. The result of this shifting of human interest was a demand for a parallel shifting of the basis of education, so as to fit the pupils for the ideas which later in life would in fact occupy their minds. Any serious fundamental change in the intellectual outlook of human society must necessarily be followed by an educational revolution. It may be delayed for a generation by vested interests or by the passionate attachment of some leaders of thought to the cycle of ideas within which they received their own mental stimulus at an impressionable age. But the law is inexorable that education to be living and effective must be directed to informing pupils with those ideas, and to creating for them those capacities which will enable them to appreciate the current thought of their epoch.

There is no such thing as a successful system of education in a vacuum, that is to say, a system which is divorced from immediate contact with the existing intellectual atmosphere. Education which is not modern shares the fate of all organic things which are kept too long.

But the blessed word "modern" does not really solve our difficulties. What we mean is, relevant to modern thought, either in the ideas imparted or in the aptitudes produced. Something found out only yesterday may not really be modern in this sense. It may belong to some bygone system of thought prevalent in a previous age, or, what is very much more likely, it may be too recondite. When we demand that education should be relevant to modern thought, we are referring to thoughts broadly spread throughout cultivated society. It is this question of the unfitness of recondite subjects for use in general education which I wish to make the keynote of my address this afternoon.

It is in fact rather a delicate subject for mathematicians. Outsiders are apt to accuse our subject of being recondite. Let us grasp the nettle at once and frankly admit that in general opinion it is the very typical example of reconditeness. By this word I do not mean difficulty, but that the ideas involved are of highly special application, and rarely influence thought.

This liability to reconditeness is the characteristic evil which is apt to destroy the utility of mathematics in liberal education. So far as it clings to the educational use of the subject, so far we must acquiesce in a miserably low level of mathematical attainment among cultivated people in general. I yield to no one in my anxiety to increase the educational scope of mathematics. The way to achieve this end is not by a mere blind demand for more mathematics. We must face the real difficulty which obstructs its extended use.

Is the subject recondite? Now, viewed as a whole, I think it is. *Securus judicat orbis terrarum* — the general judgment of mankind is sure.

The subject as it exists in the minds and in the books of students of mathematics *is* recondite. It proceeds by deducing innumerable special results from general ideas, each result more recondite than the preceding. It is not my task this afternoon to defend mathematics as a subject for profound study. It can very well take care of itself. What I want to emphasise is, that the very reasons which make this science a delight to its students are reasons which obstruct its use as an educational instrument — namely, the boundless wealth of deductions from the interplay of general theorems, their complication, their apparent remoteness from the ideas from which the argument started, the variety of methods, and their purely abstract character which brings, as its gift, eternal truth.

Of course, all these characteristics are of priceless value to students; for ages they have fascinated some of the keenest intellects. My only remark is that, except for a highly selected class, they are fatal in education. The pupils are bewildered by a multiplicity of detail, without apparent relevance either to great ideas or to ordinary thoughts. The extension of this sort of training in the direction of acquiring more detail is the last measure to be desired in the interests of education.

The conclusion at which we arrive is, that mathematics, if it is to be used in general education, must be subjected to a rigorous process of selection and adaptation. I do not mean, what is of course obvious, that however much time we devote to the subject the average pupil will not get very far. But that, however limited the progress, certain characteristics of the subject, natural at any stage, must be rigorously excluded. The science as presented to young pupils must lose its aspect of reconditeness. It must, on the face of it, deal directly and simply with a few general ideas of farreaching importance.

Now, in this matter of the reform of mathematical instruction, the present generation of teachers may take a very legitimate pride in its achievements. It has shown immense energy in reform, and has accomplished more than would have been thought possible in so short a time. It is not always recognised how difficult is the task of changing a well-established curriculum entrenched behind public examinations.

But for all that, great progress has been made, and, to put the matter at its lowest, the old dead tradition has been broken up. I want to indicate this afternoon the guiding idea which should direct our efforts at reconstruction. I have already summed it up in a phrase, namely, we must aim at the elimination of reconditeness from the educational use of the subject.

Our courses of instruction should be planned to illustrate simply a succession of ideas of obvious importance. All pretty divagations should be rigorously excluded. The goal to be aimed at is that the pupil should acquire familiarity with abstract thought, should realise how it applies to particular concrete circumstances, and should know how to apply general methods to its logical investigation. With this educational ideal nothing can be worse than the aimless accretion of theorems in our text-books, which acquire their position merely because the children can be made to learn them and examiners can set neat questions on them. The bookwork to be learnt should all be very important as illustrating ideas. The examples set — and let there be as many examples as teachers find necessary — should be direct illustrations of the theorems, either by way of abstract particular cases or by way of application to concrete phenomena. Here it is worth remarking that it is quite useless to simplify the bookwork, if the examples set in examinations in fact require an extended knowledge of recondite details. There is a mistaken idea that problems test ability and genius, and that bookwork tests cram. This is not my experience. Only boys who have been specially crammed for scholarships can ever do a problem paper successfully. Bookwork properly set, not in mere snippets according to the usual bad plan, is a far better test of ability, provided that it is supplemented by direct examples. But this is a digression on the bad influence of examinations on teaching.

The main ideas which lie at the base of mathematics are not at all recondite. They are abstract. But one of the main objects of the inclusion of mathematics in a liberal education is to train the pupils to handle abstract ideas. The science constitutes the first large group of abstract ideas which naturally occur to the mind in any precise form. For the purposes of education, mathematics consists of the relations of number, the relations of quantity, and the relations of space. This is not a general definition of mathematics, which, in my opinion, is a much more general science. But we are now discussing the use of mathematics in education. These three groups of relations, concerning number, quantity, and space, are interconnected.

Now, in education we proceed from the particular to the general. Accordingly, children should be taught the use of these ideas by practice among simple examples. My point is this: The goal should be, not an aimless accumulation of special mathematical theorems, but the final recognition that the preceding years of work have illustrated those relations of number, and of quantity, and of space, which are of fundamental importance. Such a training should lie at the base of all philosophical thought. In fact elementary mathematics rightly conceived would give just that philosophical discipline of which the ordinary mind is capable. But what at all costs we ought to avoid, is the pointless accumulation of details. As many examples as you like; let the children work at them for terms, or for years. But these examples should be direct illustrations of the main ideas. In this way, and this only, can the fatal reconditeness be avoided.

I am not now speaking in particular of those who are to be professional mathematicians, o or of those who for professional reasons require a knowledge of certain mathematical details. We are considering the liberal education of all students, including these two classes. This general use of mathematics should be the simple study of a few general truths, well illustrated by practical examples. This study should be conceived by itself, and completely separated in idea from the professional study mentioned above, for which it would make a most excellent preparation. Its final stage should be the recognition of the general truths which the work done has illustrated. As far as I can make out, at present the final stage is the proof of some property of circles connected with triangles. Such properties are immensely interesting to mathematicians. But are they not rather recondite, and what is the precise relation of such theorems to the ideal of a liberal education? The end of all the grammatical studies of the student in classics is to read Virgil and Horace — the greatest thoughts of the greatest men. Are we content, when pleading for the adequate representation in education of our own science, to say that the end of a mathematical training is that the student should know the properties of the nine-point circle? I ask you frankly, is it not rather a "come down"?

This generation of mathematical teachers has done so much strenuous work in the way of reorganising mathematical instruction that there is no need to despair of its being able to elaborate a curriculum which shall leave in the minds of the pupils something even nobler than "the ambiguous case."

Let us think how this final review, closing the elementary course, might be conducted for the more intelligent pupils. Partly no doubt it requires a general oversight of the whole work done, considered without undue detail so as to emphasise the general ideas used, and their possibilities of importance when subjected to further study. Also the analytical and geometrical ideas find immediate application in the physical laboratory where a course of simple experimental mechanics should have been worked through. Here the point of view is twofold, the physical ideas and the mathematical ideas illustrate each other.

The mathematical ideas are essential to the precise formulation of the mechanical laws. The idea of a precise law of nature, the extent to which such laws are in fact verified in our experience, and the role of abstract thought in their formulation, then become practically apparent to the pupil. The whole topic of course requires detailed development with full particular illustration, and is not suggested as requiring merely a few bare abstract statements.

It would, however, be a grave error to put too much emphasis on the mere process of direct explanation of the previous work by way of final review. My point is, that the latter end of the course should be so selected that in fact the general ideas underlying all the previous mathematical work should be brought into prominence. This may well be done by apparently entering on a new subject. For example, the ideas of quantity and the ideas of number are fundamental to all precise thought. In the previous stages they will not have been sharply separated; and children are, rightly enough, pushed on to algebra without too much bother and quantity. But the more intelligent among them at the end of their curriculum would gain immensely by a careful consideration of those fundamental properties of quantity in general which lead to the introduction of numerical measurement. This is a topic which also has the advantage that the necessary books are actually to hand. Euclid's fifth book is regarded by those qualified to judge as one of the triumphs of Greek mathematics. It deals with this very point. Nothing can be more characteristic of the hopelessly illiberal character of the traditional mathematical education than the fact that this book has always been omitted. It deals with ideas, and therefore was ostracised. Of course a careful selection of the more important propositions and a careful revision of the argument are required. The whole book would not be wanted, but just the few propositions which embody the fundamental ideas. The subject is not fit for backward pupils; but certainly it could be made interesting to the more advanced class. There would be great scope for interesting discussion as to the nature of quantity, and the tests which we should apply to ascertain when we are dealing with quantities. The work would not be at all in the air, but would be illustrated at every stage by reference to actual examples of cases where the quantitative character is absent, or obscure, or doubtful, or evident. Temperature, heat, electricity, pleasure and pain, mass and distance could all be considered.

Another idea which requires illustration is that of functionality. A function in analysis is the counterpart of a law in the physical universe, and of a curve in geometry. Children have studied the relations of functions to curves from the first beginning of their study of algebra, namely in drawing graphs. Of recent years there has been a great reform in respect to graphs. But at its present stage it has either gone too far or not far enough. It is not enough merely to draw a graph. The idea behind the graph — like the man behind the gun — is essential in order to make it effective. At present there is some tendency merely to set the children to draw curves, and there to leave the whole question.

In the study of simple algebraic functions and of trigonometrical functions we are initiating the study of the precise expression of physical laws. Curves are another way of representing these laws. The simple fundamental laws — such as the inverse square and the direct distance — should be passed under review, and the applications of the simple functions to express important concrete cases of physical laws considered. I cannot help thinking that the final review of this topic might well take the form of a study of some of the main ideas of the differential calculus applied to simple curves. There is nothing particularly difficult about the conception of a rate of change;

and the differentiation of a few powers of x, such as x^2, x^3, etc., could easily be effected; perhaps by the aid of geometry even $\sin x$ and $\cos x$ could be differentiated. If we once abandon our fatal habit of cramming the children with theorems which they do not understand, and will never use, there will be plenty of time to concentrate their attention on really important topics. We can give them familiarity with conceptions which really influence thought.

Before leaving this topic of physical laws and mathematical functions, there are other points to be noticed. The fact that the precise law is never really verified by observation in its full precision is capable of easy illustration and of affording excellent examples. Again, statistical laws, namely laws which are only satisfied on the average by large numbers, can easily be studied and illustrated. In fact a slight study of statistical methods and their application to social phenomena affords one of the simplest examples of the application of algebraic ideas.

Another way in which the students' ideas can be generalised is by the use of the History of Mathematics, conceived not as a mere assemblage of the dates and names of men, but as an exposition of the general current of thought which occasioned the subjects to be objects of interest at the time of their first elaboration. I merely draw attention to it now, to point out that perhaps it is the very subject which may best obtain the results for which I am pleading.

We have indicated two main topics, namely general ideas of quantity and of laws of nature, which should be an object of study in the mathematical curriculum of a liberal education. But there is another side to mathematics which must not be overlooked. It is the chief instrument for discipline in logical method.

Now, what is logical method, and how can any one be trained in it?

Logical method is more than the mere knowledge of valid types of reasoning and practice in the concentration of mind necessary to follow them. If it were only this, it would still be very important; for the human mind was not evolved in the bygone ages for the sake of reasoning, but merely to enable mankind with more art to hunt between meals for fresh food supplies. Accordingly few people can follow close reasoning without considerable practice.

More than this is wanted to make a good reasoner, or even to enlighten ordinary people with knowledge of what constitutes the essence of the art. The art of reasoning consists in getting hold of the subject at the right end, of seizing on the few general ideas which illuminate the whole, and of persistently marshalling all subsidiary facts round them. Nobody can be a good reasoner unless by constant practice he has realised the importance of getting hold of the big ideas and of hanging on to them like grim death. For this sort of training geometry is, I think, better than algebra. The field of thought of algebra is rather obscure, whereas space is an obvious insistent thing evident to all. Then the process of simplification, or abstraction, by which all irrelevant properties of matter, such as colour, taste, and weight, are put aside is an education in itself. Again, the definitions, and the propositions assumed without proof, illustrate the necessity of forming clear notions of the fundamental facts of the subject-matter and of the relations between them. All this belongs to the mere prolegomena of the subject. When we come to its development, its excellence increases. The learner is not initially confronted with any symbolism which bothers the memory by its rules, however simple they may be. Also, from the very beginning the reasoning, if properly conducted, is dominated by well-marked ideas which guide each stage of development. Accordingly the essence of logical method receives immediate exemplification.

Let us now put aside for the moment the limitations introduced by the dullness of average pupils and the pressure on time due to other subjects, and consider what geometry has to offer in the way of a liberal education. I will indicate some stages in the subject, without meaning that necessarily they are to be studied in this exclusive order. The first stage is the study of *congruence*. Our perception of congruence is in practice dependent on our judgments of the invariability of the intrinsic properties of bodies when their external circumstances are varying. But however it arises, congruence is in essence the correlation of two regions of space, point by point, so that all homologous distances and all homologous angles are equal. It is to be noticed that the definition of the equality of lengths and angles is their congruence, and all tests of equality, such as the use of the yard measure, are merely devices for making immediate judgments of congruence easy. I make these remarks to suggest that apart from the reasoning connected with it, congruence, both as an example of a larger and very far-reaching idea and also for its own sake, is well worthy of attentive consideration. The propositions concerning it elucidate the elementary properties of the triangle, the parallelogram, and the circle, and of the relations of two planes to each other. It is very desirable to restrict the proved propositions of this part within the narrowest bounds, partly by assuming redundant axiomatic propositions, and partly by introducing only those propositions of absolutely fundamental importance.

The second stage is the study of similarity. This can be reduced to three or four fundamental propositions. Similarity is an enlargement of the idea of congruence, and, like that idea, is another example of a one-to-one correlation of points of spaces. Any extension of study of this subject might well be in the direction of the investigation of one or two simple properties of similar and similarly situated rectilinear figures. The whole subject receives its immediate applications in plans and maps. It is important, however, to remember that trigonometry is really the method by which the main theorems are made available for use.

The third stage is the study of the elements of trigonometry. This is the study of the periodicity introduced by rotation and of properties preserved in a correlation of similar figures. Here for the first time we introduce a slight use of the algebraic analysis founded on the study of number and quantity. The importance of the periodic character of the functions requires full illustration. The simplest properties of the functions are the only ones required for the solution of triangles, and the consequent applications to surveying. The wealth of formulae, often important in themselves, but entirely useless for this type of study, which crowd our books should be rigorously excluded, except so far as they are capable of being proved by the pupils as direct examples of the bookwork.

This question of the exclusion of formulae is best illustrated by considering this example of Trigonometry, though of course I may well have hit on an unfortunate case in which my judgment is at fault. A great part of the educational advantage of the subject can be obtained by confining study to Trigonometry of one angle and by exclusion of the addition formulae for the sine and cosine and the sum of two angles. The functions can be graphed, and the solution of triangles effected. Thus the aspects of the science as (1) embodying analytically the immediate results of some of the theorems deduced from congruence and similarity, (2) as a solution of the main problem of surveying, (3) as a study of the fundamental functions required to express periodicity and wave motion, will all be impressed on the pupils' minds both by bookwork and example.

If it be desired to extend this course, the addition formulae should be added. But great care should be taken to exclude specialising the pupils in the wealth of formulae which comes in their train. By "exclude" is meant that the pupils should not have spent time or energy in acquiring any facility in their deduction. The teacher may find it interesting to work a few such examples before a class. But such results are not among those which learners need retain. Also, I would exclude the whole subject of circumscribed and inscribed circles both from Trigonometry and from the previous geometrical courses. It is all very pretty, but I do not understand what its function is in an elementary non-professional curriculum.

Accordingly, the actual bookwork of the subject is reduced to very manageable proportions. I was told the other day of an American college where the students are expected to know by heart ninety formulae or results in Trigonometry alone. We are not quite so bad as that. In fact, in Trigonometry we have nearly approached the ideal here sketched out as far as our elementary courses are concerned.

The fourth stage introduces Analytical Geometry. The study of graphs in algebra has already employed the fundamental notions, and all that is now required is a rigorously pruned course on the straight line, the circle, and the three types of conic sections, defined by the forms of their equations. At this point there are two remarks to be made. It is often desirable to give our pupils mathematical information which we do not prove. For example, in co-ordinate geometry, the reduction of the general equation of the second degree is probably beyond the capacities of most of the type of students whom we are considering. But that need not prevent us from explaining the fundamental position of conics, as exhausting the possible types of such curves.

The second remark is to advocate the entire sweeping away of "geometrical conics" as a separate subject. Naturally, on suitable occasions the analysis of analytical geometry will be lightened by the use of direct deduction from some simple figure. But geometrical conics, as developed from the definition of a conic section by the focus and directrix property, suffers from glaring defects. It is hopelessly recondite. The fundamental definition of a conic, $SP=e.PM$, usual in this subject at this stage, is thoroughly bad. It is very recondite, and has no obvious importance. Why should such curves be studied at all, any more than those defined by an indefinite number of other formulae? But when we have commenced the study of the Cartesian methods, the equations of the first and second degrees are naturally the first things to think about.

In this ideal course of Geometry, the fifth stage is occupied with the elements of Projective Geometry. The general ideas of cross ratio and of projection are here fundamental. Projection is yet a more general instance of that one-to-one correlation which we have already considered under congruence and similarity. Here again we must avoid the danger of being led into a bewildering wealth of detail.

The intellectual idea which projective geometry is to illustrate is the importance in reasoning of the correlation of all cases which can be proved to possess in common certain identical properties. The preservation of the projective properties in projection is the one important educational idea of the subject. Cross ratio only enters as the fundamental metrical property which is preserved. The few propositions considered are selected to illustrate the two allied processes which are made possible by this procedure. One is proof by simplification. Here the simplification is psychological and not logical — for the general case is logically the simplest. What is meant is: Proof by considering the case which is in fact the most familiar to us, or the easiest to think about. The other procedure is the deduction of particular cases from known general truths, as soon as we have a means of discovering such cases or a criterion for testing them.

The projective definition of conic sections and the identity of the results obtained with the curves derived from the general equation of the second degree are capable of simple exposition, but lie on the border-line of the subject. It is the sort of topic on which information can be given, and the proofs suppressed.

The course of geometry as here conceived in its complete ideal — and ideals can never be realised — is not a long one. The actual amount of mathematical deduction at each stage in the form of bookwork is very slight. But much more explanation would be given, the importance of each proposition being illustrated by examples, either worked out or for students to work, so selected as to indicate the fields of thought to which it applies. By such a course the student would gain an analysis of the leading properties of space, and of the chief methods by which they are investigated.

The study of the elements of mathematics, conceived in this spirit, would constitute a training in logical method together with an acquisition of the precise ideas which lie at the base of the scientific and philosophical investigations of the universe. Would it be easy to continue the excellent reforms in mathematical instruction which this generation has already achieved, so as to include in the curriculum this wider and more philosophic spirit? Frankly, I think that this result would be very hard to achieve as the result of single individual efforts. For reasons which I have already briefly indicated, all reforms in education are very difficult to effect. But the continued pressure of combined effort, provided that the ideal is really present in the minds of the mass of teachers, can do much, and effects in the end surprising modification. Gradually the requisite books get written, still more gradually the examinations are reformed so as to give weight to the less technical aspects of the subject, and then all recent experience has shown that the majority of teachers are only too ready to welcome any practicable means of rescuing the subject from the reproach of being a mechanical discipline.

CHAPTER 7

UNIVERSITIES AND THEIR FUNCTION

I

The expansion of universities is one marked feature of the social life in the present age. All countries have shared in this movement, but more especially America, which thereby occupies a position of honour. It is, however, possible to be overwhelmed even by the gifts of good fortune; and this growth of universities, in number of institutions, in size, and in internal complexity of organization, discloses some danger of destroying the very sources of their usefulness, in the absence of a widespread understanding of the primary functions which universities should perform in the service of a nation. These remarks, as to the necessity for reconsideration of the function of universities, apply to all the more developed countries. They are only more especially applicable to America, because this country has taken the lead in a development which, under wise guidance, may prove to be one of the most fortunate forward steps which civilisation has yet taken.

This article will only deal with the most general principles, though the special problems of the various departments in any university are, of course, innumerable. But generalities require illustration, and for this purpose I choose the business school of a university. This choice is dictated by the fact that business schools represent one of the newer developments of university activity. They are also more particularly relevant to the dominant social activities of modern nations, and for that reason are good examples of the way in which the national life should be affected by the activities of its universities. Also at Harvard, where I have the honour to hold office, the new foundation of a business school on a scale amounting to magnificence has just reached its completion.

There is a certain novelty in the provision of such a school of training, on this scale of magnitude, in one of the few leading universities of the world. It marks the culmination of a movement which for many years past has introduced analogous departments throughout American universities. This is a new fact in the university world; and it alone would justify some general reflections upon the purpose of a university education, and upon the proved importance of that purpose for the welfare of the social organism.

The novelty of business schools must not be exaggerated. At no time have universities been restricted to pure abstract learning. The University of Salerno in Italy, the earliest of European universities, was devoted to medicine. In England, at Cambridge, in the year 1316, a college was founded for the special purpose of providing "clerks for the King's service." Universities have trained clergy, medical men, lawyers, engineers. Business is now a highly intellectualized vocation, so it well fits into the series. There is, however, this novelty: the curriculum suitable for a business school, and the various modes of activity of such a school, are still in the experimental stage. Hence the peculiar importance of recurrence to general principles in connection with the moulding of these schools. It would, however, be an act of presumption on my part if I were to enter upon any consideration of details, or even upon types of policy affecting the balance of the whole training. Upon such questions I have no special knowledge, and therefore have no word of advice.

II

The universities are schools of education, and schools of research. But the primary reason for their existence is not to be found either in the mere knowledge conveyed to the students or in the mere opportunities for research afforded to the members of the faculty.

Both these functions could be performed at a cheaper rate, apart from these very expensive institutions. Books are cheap, and the system of apprenticeship is well understood. So far as the mere imparting of information is concerned, no university has had any justification for existence since the popularisation of printing in the fifteenth century. Yet the chief impetus to the foundation of universities came after that date, and in more recent times has even increased.

The justification for a university is that it preserves the connection between knowledge and the zest of life, by uniting the young and the old in the imaginative consideration of learning. The university imparts information, but it imparts it imaginatively. At least, this is the function which it should perform for society. A university which fails in this respect has no reason for existence. This atmosphere of excitement, arising from imaginative consideration, transforms knowledge. A fact is no longer a bare fact: it is invested with all its possibilities. It is no longer a burden on the memory: it is energising as the poet of our dreams, and as the architect of our purposes.

Imagination is not to be divorced from the facts: it is a way of illuminating the facts. It works by eliciting the general principles which apply to the facts, as they exist, and then by an intellectual survey of alternative possibilities which are consistent with those principles. It enables men to construct an intellectual vision of a new world, and it preserves the zest of life by the suggestion of satisfying purposes.

Youth is imaginative, and if the imagination be strengthened by discipline this energy of imagination can in great measure be preserved through life. The tragedy of the world is that those who are imaginative have but slight experience, and those who are experienced have feeble imaginations. Fools act on imagination without knowledge; pedants act on knowledge without imagination. The task of a university is to weld together imagination and experience.

The initial discipline of imagination in its period of youthful vigour requires that there be no responsibility for immediate action. The habit of unbiased thought, whereby the ideal variety of exemplification is discerned in its derivation from general principles, cannot be acquired when there is the daily task of preserving a concrete organisation. You must be free to think rightly and wrongly, and free to appreciate the variousness of the universe undisturbed by its perils.

These reflections upon the general functions of a university can be at once translated in terms of the particular functions of a business school. We need not flinch from the assertion that the main function of such a school is to produce men with a greater zest for business. It is a libel upon human nature to conceive that zest for life is the product of pedestrian purposes directed toward the narrow routine of material comforts. Mankind by its pioneering instinct, and in a hundred other ways, proclaims the falsehood of that lie.

In the modern complex social organism, the adventure of life cannot be disjoined from intellectual adventure. Amid simpler circumstances, the pioneer can follow the urge of his instinct, directed toward the scene of his vision from the mountain top. But in the complex organisations of modern business the intellectual adventure of analysis, and of imaginative reconstruction, must precede any successful reorganisation. In a simpler world, business relations were simpler, being based on the immediate contact of man with man and on immediate confrontation with all relevant material circumstances. Today business organisation requires an imaginative grasp of the psychologies of populations engaged in differing modes of occupation; of populations scattered through cities, through mountains, through plains; of populations on the ocean, and of populations in mines, and of populations in forests. It requires an imaginative grasp of conditions in the tropics, and of conditions in temperate zones. It requires an imaginative grasp of the interlocking interests of great organisations, and of the reactions of the whole complex to any change in one of its elements. It requires an imaginative understanding of laws of political economy, not merely in the abstract, but also with the power to construe them in terms of the particular circumstances of a concrete business. It requires some knowledge of the habits of government, and of the variations of those habits under diverse conditions. It requires an imaginative vision of the binding forces of any human organisation, a sympathetic vision of the limits of human nature and of the conditions which evoke loyalty of service. It requires some knowledge of the laws of health, and of the laws of fatigue, and of the conditions for sustained reliability. It requires an imaginative understanding of the social effects of the conditions of factories. It requires a sufficient conception of the role of applied science in modern society. It requires that discipline of character which can say "yes" and "no" to other men, not by reason of blind obstinacy, but with firmness derived from a conscious evaluation of relevant alternatives.

The universities have trained the intellectual pioneers of our civilisation — the priests, the lawyers, the statesmen, the doctors, the men of science, and the men of letters. They have been the home of those ideals which lead men to confront the confusion of their present times. The Pilgrim Fathers left England to found a state of society according to the ideals of their religious faith; and one of their earlier acts was the foundation of Harvard University in Cambridge, named after that ancient mother of ideals in England, to which so many of them owed their training. The conduct of business now requires intellectual imagination of the same type as that which in former times has mainly passed into those other occupations; and the universities are the organisations which have supplied this type of mentality for the service of the progress of the European races.

In early mediaeval history the origin of universities was obscure and almost unnoticed. They were a gradual and natural growth. But their existence is the reason for the sustained, rapid progressiveness of European life in so many fields of activity. By their agency the adventure of action met the adventure of thought. It would not have been possible antecedently to have divined that such organisations would have been successful. Even now, amid the imperfections of all things human, it is sometimes difficult to understand how they succeed in their work. Of course there is much failure in the work of universities. But, if we take a broad view of history, their success has been remarkable and almost uniform. The cultural histories of Italy, of France, of Germany, of Holland, of Scotland, of England, of the United

The Aims of Education

States, bear witness to the influence of universities. By "cultural history" I am not chiefly thinking of the lives of scholars; I mean the energising of the lives of those men who gave to France, to Germany, and to other countries that impress of types of human achievement which, by their addition to the zest of life, form the foundation of our patriotism. We love to be members of a society which can do those things.

There is one great difficulty which hampers all the higher types of human endeavour. In modern times this difficulty has even increased in its possibilities for evil. In any large organisation the younger men, who are novices, must be set to jobs which consist in carrying out fixed duties in obedience to orders. No president of a large corporation meets his youngest employee at his office door with the offer of the most responsible job which the work of that corporation includes. The young men are set to work at a fixed routine, and only occasionally even see the president as he passes in and out of the building. Such work is a great discipline. It imparts knowledge, and it produces reliability of character; also it is the only work for which the young men, in that novice stage, are fit, and it is the work for which they are hired. There can be no criticism of the custom, but there may be an unfortunate effect — prolonged routine work dulls the imagination.

The result is that qualities essential at a later stage of a career are apt to be stamped out in an earlier stage. This is only an instance of the more general fact, that necessary technical excellence can only be acquired by a training which is apt to damage those energies of mind which should direct the technical skill. This is the key fact in education, and the reason for most of its difficulties.

The way in which a university should function in the preparation for an intellectual career, such as modern business or one of the older professions, is by promoting the imaginative consideration of the various general principles underlying that career. Its students thus pass into their period of technical apprenticeship with their imaginations already practised in connecting details with general principles. The routine then receives its meaning, and also illuminates the principles which give it that meaning.

Hence, instead of a drudgery issuing in a blind rule of thumb, the properly trained man has some hope of obtaining an imagination disciplined by detailed facts and by necessary habits.

Thus the proper function of a university is the imaginative acquisition of knowledge. Apart from this importance of the imagination, there is no reason why business men, and other professional men, should not pick up their facts bit by bit as they want them for particular occasions. A university is imaginative or it is nothing — at least nothing useful.

III

Imagination is a contagious disease. It cannot be measured by the yard, or weighed by the pound, and then delivered to the students by members of the faculty. It can only be communicated by a faculty whose members themselves wear their learning with imagination. In saying this, I am only repeating one of the oldest of observations. More than two thousand years ago the ancients symbolised learning by a torch passing from hand to hand down the generations. That lighted torch is the imagination of which I speak. The whole art in the organisation of a university is the provision of a faculty whose learning is lighted up with imagination. This is the problem of problems in university education; and unless we are careful the recent vast extension of universities in number of students and in variety of activities — of which we are so justly proud — will fail in producing its proper results, by the mishandling of this problem.

The combination of imagination and learning normally requires some leisure, freedom from restraint, freedom from harassing worry, some variety of experiences, and the stimulation of other minds diverse in opinion and diverse in equipment. Also there is required the excitement of curiosity, and the self-confidence derived from pride in the achievements of the surrounding society in procuring the advance of knowledge. Imagination cannot be acquired once and for all, and then kept indefinitely in an ice box to be produced periodically in stated quantities. The learned and imaginative life is a way of living, and is not an article of commerce.

It is in respect to the provision and utilisation of these conditions for an efficient faculty that the two functions of education and research meet together in a university. Do you want your teachers to be imaginative? Then encourage them to research. Do you want your researchers to be imaginative? Then bring them into intellectual sympathy with the young at the most eager, imaginative period of life, when intellects are just entering upon their mature discipline. Make your researchers explain themselves to active minds, plastic and with the world before them; make your young students crown their period of intellectual acquisition by some contact with minds gifted with experience of intellectual adventure. Education is discipline for the adventure of life; research is intellectual adventure; and the universities should be homes of adventure shared in common by young and old. For successful education there must always be a certain freshness in the knowledge dealt with. It must either be new in itself or it must be invested with some novelty of application to the new world of new times. Knowledge does not keep any better than fish. You may be dealing with knowledge of the old species, with some old truth; but somehow or other it must come to the students, as it were, just drawn out of the sea and with the freshness of its immediate importance.

It is the function of the scholar to evoke into life wisdom and beauty which, apart from his magic, would remain lost in the past. A progressive society depends upon its inclusion of three groups — scholars, discoverers, inventors. Its progress also depends upon the fact that its educated masses are composed of members each with a tinge of scholarship, a tinge of discovery, and a tinge of invention. I am here using the term "discovery" to mean the progress of knowledge in respect to truths of some high generality, and the term "invention" to mean the progress of knowledge in respect to the application of general truths in particular ways subservient to present needs. It is evident that these three groups merge into each other, and also that men engaged in practical affairs are properly to be called inventors so far as they contribute to the progress of society. But any one individual has his own limitation of function, and his own peculiar needs. What is important for a nation is that there shall be a very close relation between all types of its progressive elements, so that the study may influence the market place, and the market place the study. Universities are the chief agencies for this fusion of progressive activities into an effective instrument of progress. Of course they are not the only agencies, but it is a fact that today the progressive nations are those in which universities flourish.

It must not be supposed that the output of a university in the form of original ideas is solely to be measured by printed papers and books labeled with the names of their authors. Mankind is as individual in its mode of output as in the substance of its thoughts. For some of the most fertile minds composition in writing, or in a form reducible to writing, seems to be an impossibility. In every faculty you will find that some of the more brilliant teachers are not among those who publish. Their originality requires for its expression direct intercourse with their pupils in the form of lectures, or of personal discussion. Such men exercise an immense influence; and yet, after the generation of their pupils has passed away, they sleep among the innumerable unthanked benefactors of humanity. Fortunately, one of them is immortal — Socrates.

Thus it would be the greatest mistake to estimate the value of each member of a faculty by the printed work signed with his name. There is at the present day some tendency to fall into this error; and an emphatic protest is necessary against an attitude on the part of authorities which is damaging to efficiency and unjust to unselfish zeal.

But, when all such allowances have been made, one good test for the general efficiency of a faculty is that as a whole it shall be producing in published form its quota of contributions of thought. Such a quota is to be estimated in weight of thought, and not in number of words.

This survey shows that the management of a university faculty has no analogy to that of a business organisation. The public opinion of the faculty, and a common zeal for the purposes of the university, form the only effective safeguards for the high level of university work. The faculty should be a band of scholars, stimulating each other, and freely determining their various activities. You can secure certain formal requirements, that lectures are given at stated times and that instructors and students are in attendance. But the heart of the matter lies beyond all regulation.

The question of justice to the teachers has very little to do with the case. It is perfectly just to hire a man to perform any legal services under any legal conditions as to times and salary. No one need accept the post unless he so desires.

The sole question is, what sort of conditions will produce the type of faculty which will run a successful university? The danger is that it is quite easy to produce a faculty entirely unfit — a faculty of very efficient pedants and dullards. The general public will only detect the difference after the university has stunted the promise of youth for scores of years.

The modern university system in the great democratic countries will only be successful if the ultimate authorities exercise singular restraint, so as to remember that universities cannot be dealt with according to the rules and policies which apply to the familiar business corporations. Business schools are no exception to this law of university life. There is really nothing to add to what the presidents of many American universities have recently said in public on this topic. But whether the effective portion of the general public, in America or other countries, will follow their advice appears to be doubtful. The whole point of a university, on its educational side, is to bring the young under the intellectual influence of a band of imaginative scholars. There can be no escape from proper attention to the conditions which — as experience has shown — will produce such a band.

IV

The two premier universities of Europe, in age and in dignity, are the University of Paris and the University of Oxford. I will speak of my own country because I know it best. The University of Oxford may have sinned in many ways. But, for all her deficiencies, she has throughout the ages preserved one supreme merit, beside which all failures in detail are as dust in the balance: for century after century, throughout the long course of her existence, she has produced bands of scholars who treated learning imaginatively. For that service alone, no one who loves culture can think of her without emotion.

But it is quite unnecessary for me to cross the ocean for my examples. The author of the Declaration of Independence, Mr. Jefferson, has some claim to be the greatest American. The perfection of his various achievements certainly places him among the few great men of all ages. He founded a university, and devoted one side of his complex genius to placing that university amid every circumstance which could stimulate the imagination — beauty of buildings, of situation, and every other stimulation of equipment and organisation.

There are many other universities in America which can point my moral, but my final example shall be Harvard — the representative university of the Puritan movement. The New England Puritans of the seventeenth and eighteenth centuries were the most intensely imaginative people, restrained in their outward expression, and fearful of symbolism by physical beauty, but, as it were, racked with the intensity of spiritual truths intellectually imagined. The Puritan faculties of those centuries must have been imaginative indeed, and they produced great men whose names have gone round the world. In later times Puritanism softened, and, in the golden age of literary New England, Emerson, Lowell, and Longfellow set their mark upon Harvard. The modern scientific age then gradually supervenes, and again in William James we find the typical imaginative scholar.

To-day business comes to Harvard; and the gift which the University has to offer is the old one of imagination, the lighted torch which passes from hand to hand. It is a dangerous gift, which has started many a conflagration. If we are timid as to that danger, the proper course is to shut down our universities. Imagination is a gift which has often been associated with great commercial peoples — with Greece, with Florence, with Venice, with the learning of Holland, and with the poetry of England. Commerce and imagination thrive together. It is a gift which all must pray for their country who desire for it that abiding greatness achieved by Athens: —

Her citizens, imperial spirits,
Rule the present from the past.

For American education no smaller ideal can suffice.

世界教育经典名著丛书

★ 遴选了十四位世界著名的教育家、哲学家、心理学家的教育代表作
★ 国内多所高校的十余位权威专家领衔精心译校，翻译皆历时一年以上
★ 多部图书采用了汉英双语的出版形式，可满足读者阅读原著的需求
★ 大量的译者注和精彩的"译者导读"，有助于读者领略名著的思想精髓

《课程与教学的基本原理》（汉英双语版）
【美】拉尔夫·泰勒 著
罗康 等 译
定价：42.00元

美国教育家泰勒的代表作，被誉为"现代课程理论的'圣经'"。学习课程与教学理论的必读经典。

《去学校化社会》（汉英双语版）
【美】伊万·伊利奇 著
吴康宁 译
定价：58.00元

当代著名教育思想家伊万·伊利奇在书中炮轰美国教育、现代学校和社会，并绘制了"去学校化社会"的美好图景。著名教育社会学者吴康宁教授倾情翻译并解读这一思想巨著。

《教育的目的》（汉英双语版）
【英】阿尔弗雷德·诺斯·怀特海 著
靳玉乐 等 译
定价：48.00元

英国哲学家、教育家和数学家怀特海的教育代表作。著名教育学者靳玉乐教授等翻译，译者注释丰富，十分有助于品味经典。

《民主主义与教育》（中文版）
【美】约翰·杜威 著
陶志琼 译
定价：42.00元

《民主主义与教育》（英文版）
【美】约翰·杜威 著
定价：68.00元

美国教育家杜威最有影响力的教育著作。译者历时两年译成，数易其稿，字斟句酌，译文流畅。

《我们如何思维》（汉英双语版）
【美】约翰·杜威 著
杨韶刚 等 译
定价：78.00元

思维训练领域的奠基之作，美国教育哲学家和心理学家杜威的重要代表作。该书曾于1925年被胡适、潘家洵等海内外名流学者列为"青年必读书十部"之一。

《经验与教育》（汉英双语版）
【美】约翰·杜威 著
盛群力 译
定价：38.00元

美国教育家杜威在书中深刻地诠释了"教育即生活""教育即生长""教育即经验的改造"等实用主义教育思想。评论者认为，该书"也许是杜威作品中最简明扼要、最通俗易懂且意义最深刻的一部"。

《童年的秘密》（汉英双语版）
【意】玛利亚·蒙台梭利 著
郑福明 译
定价：78.00元

意大利儿童教育家蒙台梭利所有作品中最有影响力的一部，为我们破解了儿童成长过程中的诸多密码。

《论教育学·系科之争》
【德】伊曼努埃尔·康德 著
杨云飞 邓晓芒 译
邓晓芒 校
定价：58.00元

全面地反映了德国伟大的哲学家和教育家康德的教育思想。我国著名哲学家邓晓芒教授和其弟子杨云飞博士根据德文原著历时一年多精心翻译，并撰写了大量的译者注和精彩的"译者导读"。

《理想国》
【古希腊】柏拉图 著
陶志琼 译
定价：62.00元

古希腊哲学家、教育家柏拉图的代表作，它既是一部"哲学大全"、政治学名篇，也是一部经典的教育著作。译者历时一年多，参考国内外二十余种译本翻译此书，并在书中增加了大量注释。

《爱弥儿》（精选本）
【法】让-雅克·卢梭 著
檀传宝 等 译
定价：48.00元

法国启蒙思想家和教育家卢梭的代表作，一本小说体教育名著。著名教育学者檀传宝教授领衔选译《爱弥儿》全书的精华部分。

《儿童教育心理学》
【奥】阿尔弗雷德·阿德勒 著
杨韶刚 译
定价：35.00元

又名《儿童的人格教育》，与弗洛伊德、荣格齐名的心理学大师阿德勒的代表作，帮助教师、家长捕捉儿童的心理敏感期，培养儿童健全的人格。

《童年的王国：听斯坦纳讲华德福教育》
【奥】鲁道夫·斯坦纳 著
霍力岩 等 译
定价：38.00元

奥地利哲学家、教育家，华德福教育创始人斯坦纳博士在本书中全面呈现了华德福教育的理念和做法。我国著名幼儿教育专家霍力岩教授领衔翻译。

《教育漫话·理解能力指导散论》
【英】约翰·洛克 著
郭元祥 等 译校
定价：48.00元

英国教育家、哲学家洛克的两部教育名著的合集，绅士教育理论的集大成之作。著名教育学者郭元祥教授精心组织翻译。

《大教学论》（评注版）
【捷】约翰·阿莫斯·夸美纽斯 著
刘富利 等 译
定价：48.00元

被誉为"现代教育之父"的捷克教育家、哲学家、神学家夸美纽斯的代表作，标志着教学论的诞生。牛津大学教育学者莫里斯·沃尔特·基廷在书中做出了精彩的评论，中文版译者撰写了大量译者注。

《教育论：智育、德育和体育》（评注版）
【英】赫伯特·斯宾塞 著
王占魁 译
定价：42.00元

英国教育学家、哲学家和社会学家斯宾塞的代表作，英国和法国的四位教育学家在书中对斯宾塞的教育观点做了独到的点评。

《教育学讲授纲要》（评注版）
【德】约翰·弗里德里希·赫尔巴特 著
盛群力 赵卫平 译
定价：50.00元

德国著名教育学家、心理学家和哲学家赫尔巴特的教育代表作，被誉为"真正的教书经"。美国康奈尔大学教授查尔斯·德加谟在书中针对赫尔巴特许多观点的社会现实意义做出了精彩的评注。

¥42.00

¥58.00

《课程与教学的基本原理》（汉英双语版）
【美】拉尔夫·泰勒 著
罗康 等 译

"现代课程理论之父"泰勒的代表作，被誉为"现代课程理论的'圣经'"。高等院校教育专业师生和中小学教师的必读经典。

《去学校化社会》（汉英双语版）
【美】伊万·伊利奇 著
吴康宁 译

当代著名教育思想家伊万·伊利奇的代表作。著名教育社会学者吴康宁教授倾情翻译并解读这一思想巨著。

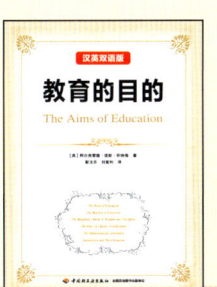

¥48.00

¥58.00

《教育的目的》（汉英双语版）
【英】阿尔弗雷德·诺斯·怀特海 著
靳玉乐 等 译

英国哲学家、教育家和数学家怀特海的教育代表作。著名教育学者靳玉乐教授等翻译，译者注释丰富，汉英双语对照，十分有助于品味经典。

《论教育学·系科之争》
【德】伊曼努埃尔·康德 著
杨云飞 邓晓芒 译／邓晓芒 校

全面地反映了德国哲学家和教育家康德的教育思想。我国著名哲学家邓晓芒教授和其弟子杨云飞博士根据德文原著历时一年多精心翻译。

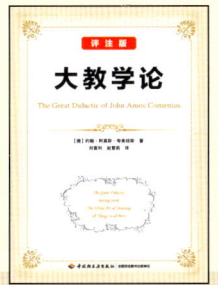

¥48.00

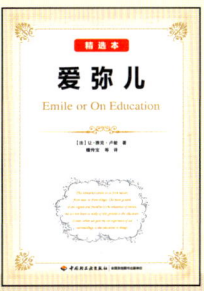

¥48.00

《大教学论》（评注版）
【捷】约翰·阿莫斯·夸美纽斯 著
刘富利 等 译

捷克教育家夸美纽斯的代表作，标志着教学论的诞生。牛津大学教育学者莫里斯·沃尔特·基廷在书中做出了精彩的评论。

《爱弥儿》（精选本）
【法】让-雅克·卢梭 著
檀传宝 等 译

法国启蒙思想家和教育家卢梭的代表作，一本小说体教育名著。著名教育学者檀传宝教授领衔选译《爱弥儿》全书的精华部分。

"世界教育经典名著丛书"阅读推广计划

尊敬的老师：

您好！感谢您对"万千教育"的关注与支持！

近年来，我们策划出版了"世界教育经典名著丛书"。该丛书包括16部世界著名的教育家、哲学家和心理学家的教育代表作，由国内十余位权威专家精心译校。大量的译者注和精彩的"译者导读"有助于读者领略名著的思想精髓。用纸考究、印刷清晰和软精装使丛书可读宜藏。我们有幸取得了数部著作在中国大陆的独家中文版权和英文版权。

其中《课程与教学的基本原理》《民主主义与教育》《教育的目的》《去学校化社会》《经验与教育》等7种名著采用了**汉英双语**的出版形式，可满足读者阅读原汁原味的经典之需。这些图书也适合作为高校师生专业外语教学文本。

为了让更多的人走近经典，值此"万千教育"编辑部成立20周年之际，我们制订了"世界教育经典名著丛书"阅读推广计划。

如果您对我们出版的经典名著感兴趣，我们将特别为您提供下列服务：

1. **免费样书**。如果您选用上述名著作为教学文本或为了便于您推荐给学生阅读，我们可以免费向您提供教师样书。

2. **优惠折扣**。若您所在院校的学生欲团购上述名著，我们将给予特定的优惠折扣。

欲了解"世界教育经典名著丛书"及阅读推广计划的详情，请扫描右边的二维码。此计划长期有效。

欢迎您与我们联系！

万千教育编辑部

咨询电话：010-65181109
读者邮箱：1012305542@qq.com
万千教育客服微信号：wqjy1998